ALL AGES

Reflections on Straight Edge

by Beth Lahickey

ISBN 1-889703-00-1

Library of Congress 96-070567

Published by Revelation Books
P.O. Box 5232, Huntington Beach, CA 92615-5232

Printed in the United States of America

First printing, 1997

This book is dedicated to the kids.

Contents

Acknowledgments

Luke Abbey, Dan Adair, Jonathan Anastas, Greg Anderson, Norm Arenas, Chad Barnes, Greg Bennick, Richie Birkenhead, Justin Borucki, Alex Brown, Ray Cappo, Civ, Justine DeMetrick, Jade Devitt, Mike Down, Don Fury, Ron Guardipee, Derek Harn, Mike Hartsfield, Mercia Howard, Glynis Hull-Rochelle, Gary Hustwit, Mike Judge, Allison Kelly, Chris Kelly, Eric Kinder, Joan Elizabeth Knight, Hilly Kristal, Chris Ludwig, Ian MacKaye, Dave Mandel, Diona Mavis, John Mockus, Paul Norris of Hendricks & Lewis, John Nutcher, Dan O'Mahony, Stephen O'Malley, Tim Owen, Gus Pena, Porcell, Raybeez, Neil Robinson, Duane Rossignol, Mark Ryan, Dave Schlanbusch, Walter Schreifels, Kevin Seconds, Sam Seigler, Brian Sheridan, Sean Sheridan, Dave Sine, Tim Singer, Arthur Smilios, Kelsey Smith, Joshua Lane Stanton, Dave Stein, Adam Tanner, Drew Thomas, Chris Toliver, Becky Tupper, Pete Verbal Assault, Tony Victory, Matt Warnke, Sterling Wilson, and Jason Woodland

Special thanks to Rich Jacobs and Laura Porto for lending their editing skills, to Rhonda Pelikan for lending her graphic design skills and to Susan Martinez. Extra special thanks and love to Jordan Cooper, for believing in me over the years.

Foreword

by Ray Cappo

A 15-year-old skater in a confrontational and sparring spirit approached an older punk one night outside a hardcore show in Connecticut. The skater had a bleached Marine cut, a worn gray hooded Champion Sweatshirt and long plaid skate shorts. His vans had silver duct tape wrapped around the toe and sole probably to repair a hole in them. The tops of his hands had two oversized X's scrawled on them with a black marker. The punk guy he approached was a little older, maybe in his twenties and wearing jeans and combat boots. His Damned shirt was old and worn and covered by his leather biker jacket which advertised hand painted Siouxsie Sioux and The Residents logos.

The younger one spoke, apparently meeting this guy for the first time in a scrutinizing manner with a twist of an East Coast surfer dialect, "Are you or aren't you?" The dude with the Damned shirt looked puzzled. So did I, propped up against my mom's Ford Festiva drinking a Cherry Coke, thumbing through fanzines but now noticing the exchange.

"Am I or am not what?" the older punk said, sort of smugly but puzzled.

"S.E.?" spoke the skater, equally amazed that the punk was baffled.

"What is S...E?" said the elder, pronouncing each letter distinctly, now a little annoyed and twiddling his fingers nervously.

"Straight edge!" he answered in a matter-of-fact way.

"Well," said the punk, "I don't drink, and I really don't smoke or smoke pot or anything, but I don't know ... I really don't label myself as 'straight edge'," he said a little righteously and maturely.

"That's way lame!" said the skater, abruptly ending the inquisition and laughing at himself while walking off. The punk guy looked a little frustrated and still a little puzzled. I laughed at the skater's audacity, his off-color humor and how I watched this scene change so drastically.

"This," I thought, "is what killed straight edge, and at the same time, this is what made it grow into an enormous subculture worldwide—a punk attitude with conservative principles."

For all its great points, "punk rock liberalism" had its bad points, too. It became too broad. Some kids in the scene did follow straight principles, like the older punk, while others were heroin addicts, glue huffers and gang members. To this new generation the entire spectrum seemed too wishy-washy. In 1983, a common punk slogan to paint on your jacket was "No One Rules." I laughed to myself in 1986 when I saw a similar motto on the back of a sweatshirt.

It read, "Rules!" The pendulum of liberalism swung from "No Rules" to "Rules are good." The fashion pendulum swung from mohawks, leather and Doc Martens to a clean cut collegiate Beaver Cleaver-meets-Tony Hawk look. Indulgence swung to self control. "Free form" slam dancing turned to very stylized moshing and stage diving. For better or for worse, straight edge took off stronger than I could ever imagine, choking out punk rock, or a least ignoring it and creating a veritable scene within a scene.

I could really see both sides. I was punk. I mean I was reared on punk rock, ska, and Oi! from Sham 69 to X Ray Spex to The Business; never seeing a live punk gig but living vicariously through movies like *Decline of Western Civilization* and *The Great Rock and Roll Swindle.*

I got up some courage one weekend to go into the city to CBGB's. This was (and still is) an underground and punk club especially noted for giving bands like The Police, Patti Smith and the Ramones their start. I was flipping through the Village Voice and saw that the UK Subs were playing Saturday night, so I thought, "Yeah! Punk rock show! I got to go!" Little did I know that this one show was going to change my life. It was a show that served as a spring board for me to dive head first into American Hardcore.

Opening the show was a band called The Young and the Useless. This actually turned out to be Adam from the Beastie Boys' first band. They were all my age, about 15, and going nuts on stage while the crowd was moshing (moshing was not a universal word at that time—only New Yorkers knew what it meant) and diving off the three-foot stage. I was impressed. No, impressed isn't the word. I was in love. I fell in love with hardcore. I went home and started a band and went back every weekend for CBGB's hardcore matinees. For $3 every Sunday you could see three bands, bands that were unbelievable, bands that have never been matched since, bands whose lyric became scripture, bands that we would lay our life on the line for: Minor Threat (years ahead of their time), Void (so loose that it sounded like the entire song would fall apart, but so forceful), Agnostic Front (hometown favorites), SS Decontrol (forerunners and heroes of the straight edge scene who made cigarette smoking seem like a criminal offense). All of these bands played CB's matinees, leaving kids like myself bruised from the pit, blown away by the music and with ears still buzzing Monday morning in algebra class, realizing their entire suburban high school had no idea what they had been through the previous afternoon.

American Hardcore was a more down-to-earth part of the punk scene. It was less of a costume show. The biggest bands often looked like guys you might know in high school who wore T-shirts, jeans, tennis sneakers and normal haircuts. Every now and then they'd shave their heads. That was the look, but the scene still embraced a lot of the punk ethics. A ground breaking band from Reno, Nevada changed all that. They were called 7 Seconds, and they became the most powerful force in the hardcore scene in 1985. Their lyrics were about trust, love, friendship, positive living—things that were considered too "soft" to be said in such a "hard" scene. They made it cool not to be a tough ass. They made it cool to be sensitive and not to be a drunk punk. Their album *The Crew* was the preeminent hardcore record of the time. Although never dubbing themselves a "straight edge" band, they directly had a hand in molding the principles of what became a straight edge explosion in the later 80s.

So back to our original story of the punk dude versus the 15-year-old straight kid in the parking lot. I could see where they were both coming from. My story? I had the mohawk and some engineer boots in junior high. I was ridiculed in my anal retentive Connecticut high school where it was unheard of for a 15-year-old male to ride a skateboard around the halls. Skateboarding was reserved for eight year olds on those little plastic boards you'd get at Caldor (East Coast department store). At the same time some punk ethics didn't impress me. I was athletic. That wasn't punk. I always despised lethargy, violence and intoxication. I was vexed and confused how these things were such a dominating force in my alternative scene. That shit was happening in the regular scenes of the suburbs. I wanted an alternative.

I wasn't alone. When straight edge hit big in '87, it was unbelievable how it took over the club scene, record sales, fanzines and punk culture. Moving to downtown Manhattan in '88, and touring across the nation for the next few years, I watched it blossom firsthand with its stronghold in NYC, Connecticut, New Jersey, L.A. and Florida. This incarnation of straight edge was different than Minor Threat who had broken up in '83 and had officially coined the term "straight edge" on their monumental debut single and further supported it on their second single with songs like "Out of Step" where Ian MacKaye howled verses like, "I don't drink, I don't smoke, I don't fuck…at least I can fucking think!" But there wasn't much of a scene to support that philosophy in those days, so this newer generation took the ball and ran with it, and since then it has existed, leaving the Minor Threat singles as the straight edge version of the Dead Sea Scrolls.

Straight edge bands of this era were criticized for being hackneyed, macho and often redundant. Often the accusations were true, but most kids didn't care because some bands were just so damn awesome. Coming into Los Angeles with a real New York attitude, Porcell and I were blown away the first time we saw Uniform Choice. They single handedly whipped Southern California into a straight edge frenzy. Straight Ahead from New York City were incredible, the fastest and the hardest band at the time. Bold were junior high school heroes being only 13 and 14 when they started, but preaching like sagacious grown men between songs. The entire melange was clean cut straight laced power jock rock with a snobby "better than you" attitude. Even the old school punkers had to admit its potency.

New trends started. Kids would jam the stage to sing along with the anthemic choruses (a necessary ingredient in straight edge song writing). Although it was done before, Mike Judge made construction gloves famous. Porcell made the "dive off stage with your guitar" famous, and Jules from Side by Side made famous pointing a finger straight out and screaming "Go!"

Revelation Records sprung up, specializing in colored wax limited edition 7"s of everyone's favorite bands, cornering the market initially and making record collecting the scenester's new favorite pastime. Schism Records followed, releasing fanzines and singles and debuting with a free Project X record in the first 200 copies.

Now as I type this nearly 10 years later, I was unaware of the whirlpool I was caught up in—a whirlpool that still has an affect on the music scene internationally. But I feel these days were foundation building, especially within my own life. The straight edge scene gave me a society of like-minded individuals (not a contradiction in terms) who appreciated punk energy, but didn't want to end up in the gutter. And most didn't. Since I still live in New York City, I still see people from the scene back in the day. Some aren't straight edge and some are. Some are really still into music and some are not. Some have changed costumes, politics and principles. With all these differences, whenever one of them makes eye contact with me, I always have flash backs to what we were and what we did, and I smile inwardly or publicly. It definitely was a time we'll remember.

Preface

This book is a documentation of a certain place at a certain time. It is not intended to be a complete discourse on the intricacies of straight edge. I do not claim to be an expert on or an advocate of the straight edge movement. My goal with this book is to pay tribute through words and pictures to a small part of the whole story of underground music which I had the good fortune to witness firsthand.

It is apparent that straight edge means different things to different people. While some may simply appreciate the "substance free" philosophy that it embodies, others may take it to the extreme. Regardless of personal interpretations, the straight edge philosophy is expounded through powerful music. Music is its vehicle.

My involvement with straight edge was based purely on its musical merits. Like many people I know, I grew up with a fairly diverse musical background. Billie Holiday's rudimentary recordings were sandwiched between the local band, Lost Generation and Jimi Hendrix in my record collection. Mostly I listened to local hardcore bands, but I liked a few of the more nationally known bands as well. Black Flag, Minor Threat, X and the Descendents were high school favorites, and later on, Negative Approach, Urban Waste, Youth Brigade, Fang and one of the greatest bands of the time, Bad Brains.

My initial contact with straight edge came in 1985, while I was a junior at South Windsor High School in suburban Connecticut. The quintessential club in Connecticut to see all ages shows at that time was the Anthrax. The Anthrax was run by two brothers, Brian and Sean Sheridan, and originally opened in Stamford, Connecticut. By day, it was a storefront art gallery. In the back of the gallery was a small room with a couple of couches. The entrance was through the back door in the parking lot. The walls were painted inside and out with graffiti. Shows were held in the basement, which wasn't much bigger than 600 square feet. The ceiling was low, and the stage was basically on the floor in the back.

Although Stamford was a long way from South Windsor, it wasn't long before I was finding my way down to the Anthrax almost every weekend. As a result, I eventually became friends with people from all over the Tri-state area and managed to see most of the bands that toured through Connecticut between 1986 and 1989. A big part of what was going on in the scene was the emergence of the second generation of straight edge. Even if I appreciated the music more than the message, the banner that these bands waved defined a part of hardcore history that affected my life, and continues nearly a decade later, to affect the lives of kids all over the world.

At the time, I wasn't fully aware of the magnitude that straight edge would reach. It was just something that I did, going to shows, hanging out. I never thought that anyone was famous. I never went on tour, so I never saw the reaction of crowds all over the United States and abroad. I was aware that our scene loved straight edge. I even knew there was a big straight edge scene on the West Coast.

Coming back to work at Revelation Records in 1993, I was surprised to see how new straight edge kids loved these bands. As I filled mail orders, I read numerous letters from kids all over the world filled with questions about the bands featured here. People wanted to know when Gorilla Biscuits, or some other defunct band, was going on tour in their area. Many kids wanted to know what became of specific band members. I found myself responding to their letters on such a regular basis that I decided to put it all down in this book. Having witnessed the New York straight edge movement firsthand, and having personally known most of the people directly involved, I felt that I would be a likely candidate to undertake such a project as this. I've been fortunate to have had the cooperation of so many people, and for this I am grateful.

I have interviewed former members of Youth of Today, Gorilla Biscuits, Bold, Judge, No For an Answer and several other bands from both coasts, as well as people who were involved peripherally in this wave of straight edge and people involved in other waves of it. I decided to compile these interviews to create a space where people can speak today about what happened almost 10 years ago. I have really been surprised at the consistency of the reactions to my questions among my interviewees. There seems to be some very strong, common feelings about straight edge that transcend all of the different directions that people have gone.

During the interview process, I chose not to focus on a series of specific questions. Given only vague outlines, each individual filled them in however she or he saw fit. Primarily, I wanted to know how each person became involved with hardcore, and secondarily, specifically with straight edge. I also wanted to find out how each person related to straight edge then, versus how they relate to it today. My line of questioning was indirect. I encouraged everyone to ramble on a bit, for I find that this meandering is often where the jewels of character are found.

There are many discrepancies between things that different people say in their interviews. Once again, I am not concerned with presenting the official historical and factual documentation of this era. My interest lies in feelings rather than facts. And while the subject of this book is straight edge, it is not a glorification of the straight edge movement.

Introduction

Beth and Susan

South Windsor is a suburb outside of Hartford, Connecticut, making the two-hour trek down to the Anthrax an activity in itself. I would pack clothes for the weekend on Friday morning and leave straight from school. The school bus would drop me off at the city bus stop, where a bus ran to Hartford. From Hartford, I could take either the train or another bus to New Haven, where I would board the train to Stamford. From the Stamford train station the Anthrax was a ten minute walk. In New Haven, I would usually meet up with my friends Susan, Becky, Glynis and Aura. We would evade the fare by running on board and immediately feigning sleep, with our heads on each other's shoulders. Sometimes we would steal toilet paper along the way for the Anthrax's bathroom. By the time we arrived, the shows would usually be starting.

The Anthrax booked innumerable memorable shows. It was there that I saw so many bands that became a part of my fabric. Many of those bands were local: Vatican Commandos, Violent Children, Lost Generation, 76% Uncertain, No Milk on Tuesday, CIA, and Reflex from Pain.

One night Black Flag was scheduled to play. By the time we got to the show, everyone was standing out in the parking lot. The show, and the entire Anthrax had been shut down. I was standing in the parking lot with everyone else and somehow sensed this was going to be the end of the Anthrax.

On the way home that night, there was a problem with the trains, and we were detained in a waiting room while we waited for the next train to New Haven. Susan had come with her friend Jordan that night. While we waited, he entertained us by sticking one arm inside his leather jacket, grabbing the empty sleeve with his other arm, and punching outward with the inside arm to make it look like his chest cavity was bulging with an alien. That was how I met Jordan Cooper.

Jordan and I hit it off immediately. He grew up in Mahopac, New York and finished

JUSTIN BORUCKI

Richie and Ray—Youth of Today at CBGB's.

public high school in Danbury, Connecticut after being thrown out of a private school. By the time we met, I was a senior in high school, and he was attending Southern Connecticut State University in New Haven. I graduated in June of 1986 and moved to New Haven. I worked at a health food restaurant, attended SCSU part-time and went to shows on the weekends.

JOSHUA LANE STANTON

Arthur and Alex of Gorilla Biscuits

Being from Danbury, Jordan had become friends with Ray Cappo. At the time Jordan and I were living in New Haven, Ray had recently formed Youth of Today. We'd go see his band play at the Anthrax, which had since re-opened in Norwalk. Soon there were other bands coming along that shared Youth of Today's straight edge stance, most notably, Crippled Youth. Eventually there were more and more of these bands playing out until there were straight edge bands playing almost every weekend in Connecticut, Boston, New York or Albany. CBGB's was holding hardcore matinees on Sunday afternoons, the Pyramid booked shows, every time you turned around, there was something new going on. In the midst of all of this, Jordan and Ray decided to put out the WarZone 7".

Like any musical movement, straight edge has its pros and cons. I have never seen any live bands that can match the level of physical energy put forth at straight edge shows. The lyrical suggestions of a positive outlook, unity, and basic clean living are admirable, though not necessarily heeded. There was often a striking similarity of terminology among straight edge anthems, but at the same time, I found them to be pretty darned catchy. I definitely tout the motivation behind the straight edge scene, but in the same breath denounce its male-based egocentricity. At any rate, I chose to stand at its sidelines and support its players. And more importantly, I find the subject worthy of documentation.

My primary attraction to the underground music scene was its reverence for individuality. As I began going to shows and listening to hardcore lyrics, I felt an overwhelming sense of relief. Here was a place where I did not feel the traditional adolescent feelings of inadequacy, ostracism and general malaise. I felt connected to the mu-

JOSHUA LANE STANTON

Alex of Gorilla Biscuits

sic. The intimacy of the live shows and the accessibility of the bands were tremendous aspects of my attraction to the scene. I felt that I was a part of what was going on and that I was being accepted for who I was as a person.

Unfortunately as the straight edge scene progressed, it became hauntingly reminiscent of all of the narrow-mindedness that hardcore had given me refuge from. Preaching took over friendliness. All of the negative issues brought to light by the positive scene detracted from the power of the music. It all began to make me feel uncomfortable. I was sad to see these shortcomings. I fell in love with hardcore for the freedom I felt from others' expectations. Straight edge became just a different set of rules.

Luke of Gorilla Biscuits

JOSHUA LANE STANTON

One of the issues that I have been dealing with in doing this book was figuring out why straight edge has such wide appeal. Many of the people that I have interviewed, both formally and informally, have said that during their youth, straight edge brought them a sense of relief from peer pressure to experiment with drinking and drug use. For them, straight edge provided an untraditional form of rebellion—rebelling against the traditional forms of rebellion.

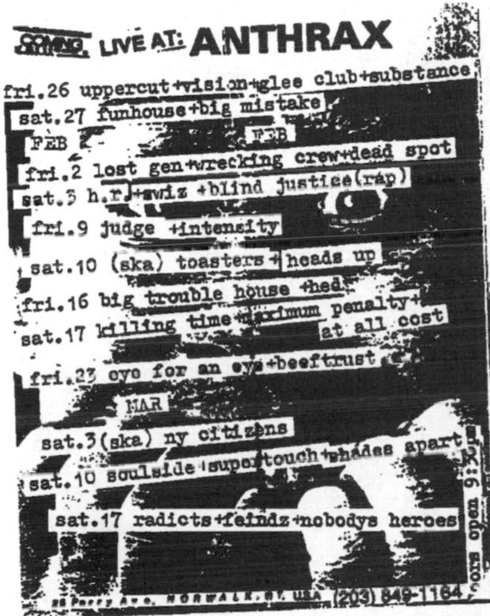
COMING LIVE AT: ANTHRAX
fri.26 uppercut+vision+glee club+substance
sat.27 funhouse+big mistake
FEB
fri.2 lost gen+wrecking crew+dead spot
sat.3 h.r.+swiz +blind justice(rap)
fri.9 judge +intensity
sat.10 (ska) toasters+heads up
fri.16 big trouble house +hed
sat.17 killing time+maximum penalty+
at all cost
fri.23 eye for an eye+beeftrust
MAR
sat.3(ska) ny citizens
sat.10 soulside+supertouch+shades apart
sat.17 radicts+feindz+nobodys heroes
doors open 9:30
28 Perry Ave. NORWALK, CT. USA (203) 849-1164

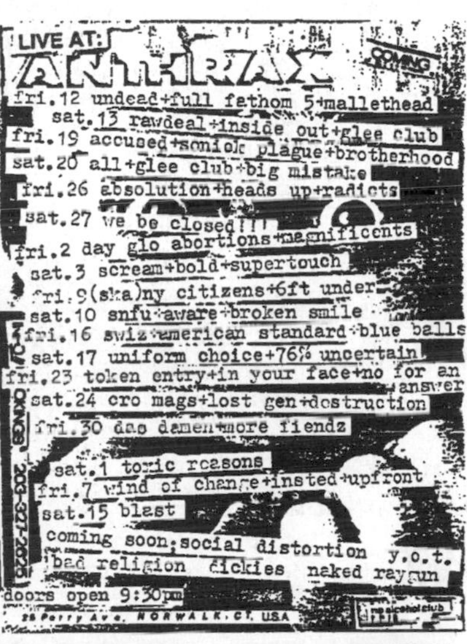
LIVE AT: ANTHRAX
COMING
fri.12 undead+full fathom 5+mallethead
sat.13 rawdeal+inside out+glee club
fri.19 accused+sonick plague+brotherhood
sat.20 all+glee club+big mistake
fri.26 absolution+heads up+radicts
sat.27 we be closed!!!
fri.2 day glo abortions+magnificents
sat.3 scream+bold+supertouch
fri.9(ska)ny citizens+6ft under
sat.10 snfu+aware+broken smile
fri.16 swiz+american standard+blue balls
sat.17 uniform choice+76% uncertain
fri.23 token entry+in your face+no for an answer
sat.24 cro mags+lost gen+destruction
fri.30 das damen+more fiendz
sat.1 toxic reasons
fri.7 wind of change+insted+upfront
sat.15 blast
coming soon: social distortion y.o.t.
bad religion dickies naked raygun
doors open 9:30pm
28 Perry Ave. NORWALK, CT. USA
INFO/BOOKINGS 203-327-2625
no alcohol club

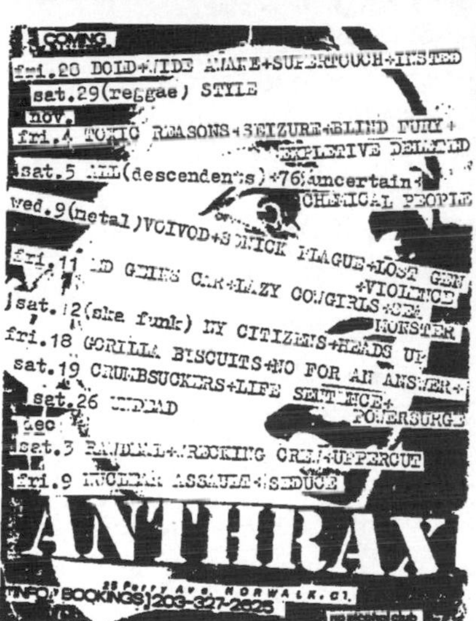
COMING
fri.28 BOLD+WIDE AWAKE+SUPERTOUCH+INSTED
sat.29(reggae) STYLE
nov.
fri.4 TOXIC REASONS+SEIZURE+BLIND FURY+
EXPLETIVE DELETED
sat.5 ALL(descendents)+76% uncertain+
CHEMICAL PEOPLE
wed.9(metal)VOIVOD+SONICK PLAGUE+LOST GEN
+VIOLENCE
sat.12(ska funk) NY CITIZENS+HEADS UP
fri.18 GORILLA BISCUITS+NO FOR AN ANSWER+
sat.19 CRUMBSUCKERS+LIFE SENTENCE+
POWERSURGE
sat.26 UNDEAD
dec
sat.3 RAWDEAL+WRECKING CREW+UPPERCUT
fri.9 NUCLEAR ASSAULT+SEDUCE
ANTHRAX
28 Perry Ave. NORWALK, CT.
INFO/BOOKINGS 203-327-2625
no alcohol club

COMING
fri.17 sonick plague+disaster
sat.18(benefit 3) powersurge+killing time
+crossface+warbucks
fri.24 (ska) ny citizens+the now
sat.25 7seconds+heads up+smile
DEC
fri.1 gbh+c.o.c.+wrecking crew
sat.2 supertouch+american standard+
situated chaos
fri.8 closed!!!
sat.9 judge+react+slipknot
fri.15 gang green+ skeletal ambitions
sat.16 radicts+the wussies
lots more coming:
bad religion token entry
nuclear assault
LIVE AT: ANTHRAX
28 Perry Ave. NORWALK, CT. USA
doors open 9:30pm
INFO/(203) 849-1164

JORDAN COOPER

John Zulu of Bold

I also have noticed that the parameters of straight edge give people the opportunity to make daily decisions about diet and chemical intake, which continually reaffirm the tenets of the straight edge lifestyle. Unfortunately, I have noticed that for many people, adhering to strict guidelines of a "healthy, positive, open-minded life" also leads to feelings of superiority. The fact that it is also a social scene provides a built-in support system. It is this support system that fuels such fierce dedication to the straight edge movement. It is for these reasons that straight edge undeniably provides a sense of identity, and thus has a definite appeal to its typically young audience.

As I mentioned previously, I view this particular era to be second wave of straight edge. DYS, SSD and Minor Threat, whether deliberately or not, provided the initial inspiration of the straight edge scene on the East Coast. These bands were influences of Youth of Today, Bold, Judge and so on. Today, there is a new batch of straight edge bands and record labels, and I am certain that this is not the end of it.

Without a doubt, the New York straight edge scene became immensely popular. It emerged on the Lower East Side of Manhattan at

JORDAN COOPER

Bold at Anthrax

a time when the notion of a straight edge lifestyle was entirely foreign to New York. Within walking distance were all of the major spots that hosted this scene.

CBGB's booked hardcore Sunday matinees often with straight edge bands on the bill. Shows were also often held at the Pyramid or at the Ritz. Some Records was the hub of the scene following CB's matinees, much more intimate than Bleeker Bob's or Venus Records. Don Fury's recording studio was nearby.

Although much of the activity of the time centered in the Lower East Side of New York, the Anthrax was an integral part of the scene. The popularity of these bands repeatedly drew packed shows there. As Revelation Records began releasing records, shows at the Anthrax were a major outlet for the bands to play. I would set up a table in the back of the club to sell merchandise. Once in a while, I would leave the table to someone else to watch the show and climb up on the platform where Bill Knapp did sound.

The intensity of the live shows was unparalleled. The bands were stomping about the stage, jumping into the crowd and screaming into the microphone or at the crowd without it whenever it went out. It got so hot inside that the air hung damp with sweat, which condensed and ran down the walls. And always after the show, anyone who has

been there will tell you, you always had black boogers.

One of the great aspects of the straight edge scene was its fanzines. "Boiling Point" and "Schism" were probably the best known, but not the only zines coming out at the time. Unfortunately, all too often most zines enjoyed only a fleeting existence. Chris Kelly's radio show, On the Edge, out of New York, later highlighted the straight edge scene.

Though it was an exciting time, not all of the excitement was fun. The problem of clubs booking over 21 shows hindered bands whose members were often underage. The fear of a lawsuit caused club owners to discourage "aggressive dancing." And soon enough, as people got a little older, the once united scene began to unravel, and people began going their separate ways in life.

One of the most disappointing things I see in the straight edge scene today is the denouncement of musicians who have either chosen to continue playing music in a non-straight edge, non-DIY vein or have otherwise departed from the straight edge lifestyle. It is not only unrealistic, but also unfair to hold a person accountable for a lifetime to ideas they professed during youth.

This wave of straight edge—which I would consider to be the second wave—is long over. The scene has grown and evolved into something completely different. Just as the scene has changed, so have the people involved in it, and so will the people who are involved in straight edge today. My hope is that these interviews will reflect some of the great things that people are now doing.

"On The Edge" radio show by Chris Kelly.

CONNECTICUT FUN

Another Friday night
And the boys are out tonight
We got our equipment together
Wearing shit clothes and leather
This Punk Rock in Connecticut
We sure do hope it will last
It's the music we love to play and hear
So C'mon let's have a blast

CHORUS:
Hey! Ho! Hey! Ho! Hey! Ho! Hey! Ho!

REPEAT 1st VERSE:
REPEAT CHORUS:

We're having fun in Connecticut
Nobody can put us down
If you want to fight or fuck us up
We don't want you around

REPEAT 2nd VERSE:
We don't want you'round, We don't wan't you'round
We don't want youuuu...

AROUND !!!

INTERVIEWS

Jon Anastas

I met Jon Anastas online last year. He is a former member of perennial Boston straight edge bands DYS and Slapshot. He is currently living in Southern California.

How did you start to get involved with hardcore?

I had an afternoon job at Newbury Comics in Boston which was also Modern Method Records, who put out *This is Boston Not L.A.* and who put out the Boston Rock Magazine. I kind of bounced around. I would work in the store sometimes, and I would work at the record label sometimes and for the magazine other times. I was getting into Dischord stuff making the transition from punk rock to hardcore as the records came out. I remember when all of the first Dischord 7"s came out. I was absorbing through the spore of records. Boston had a big punk rock scene but not a big hardcore scene. Basically getting into SSD sort of got me into hardcore.

SSD were Boston's first hardcore band. Probably every single one of the influential bands grew out of their road crew and their friends, the real straight edge bands. I remember I was really upset because I missed their first show. They used to come around and flyer Newbury Street. They had a show in May or June in this collective space, and I had to go off to summer camp—I had already committed to being a junior counselor. When I went away to camp there wasn't a hardcore scene, and when I came back SSD had played their first two shows, and there it was.

I wanted to form a band after that, so I put up an ad in Newbury Comics, "Bass Player with Guitar Player Seeks Singer and Drummer." Dave Smalley answered the ad. The big joke was that his drummer couldn't play drums and my guitar player wanted to be Eddie Van Halen. After a couple of practices—we used to actually rehearse at the same collective media workshop where the hardcore shows were—it ended up being just Dave and I. We went through a number of other people before the various DYS line-ups that recorded came together. Through Dave I met the guys in SSD, and they became the center of the scene in every way imaginable.

In Boston, we were all fans of Rock with a capital "R." We loved Aerosmith and AC/DC. My first influence to be in a band was Cheap Trick, not the Sex Pistols. I think we all wanted to be rock stars as opposed to punk rock stars. Punk rock was the kind of music we could play. We really believed in all the stuff we were saying, but if you look at the way that DYS and SSD sort of metamorphosized into rock bands, it was a natural progression. When you take hardcore and slow it down and add a little more skill, it becomes hard rock.

Al Barille, the guitar player of SSD, had a black van, and the world revolved around that van. We would load into that van and just drive around every Friday night and Saturday night around the city and harass the old punk rockers. There was a big schism between the punk rock people and the hardcore people. We all had shaved heads, but it was way before the English skinhead thing came in here, so no one even put that association together.

We got our final guitar player from SSD because Al Barille told him that he should play with us. Negative FX and Last Rites were all SSD crew guys. They were the nucleus of the scene. There was the straight edge scene and other groups of bands that grew around it, like The F.U.'s and Jerry's Kids and Gang Green and The Freeze. The Freeze were from Cape Cod, and they weren't hard, and nobody really liked them because they were melodic. Gang Green and Jerry's Kids were from the South Shore, which is the beach community south of Boston, and we were all from the North Shore. It was a very, very different scene. If you look at the bands that have lasted and influenced, I think it is all the bands that sprung up around SSD.

SSD were sort of the first hardcore band from Boston to gain national prominence. We used to road trip with them everywhere. It would be about 19 guys plus equipment in the van. I remember my first trips to New York with them when DYS used to play A7 and CBGB's. I remember driving across the Cross Bronx Expressway for the first time. I was a 16-year-old kid shivering in a van, seeing the burnt out cars and the trash on the streets. It was just unbelievable compared to what we were used to back in Boston. Boston is a very small, sort of patrician city.

We had met all the kids from DC at that point, and there was a bond between Boston and DC. We saw ourselves the same way, we were all straight edge. When hardcore started in New York, it was adamantly "no edge." The New York straight edge thing sprung up much, much later. When I first started going down there, it was almost anti-straight edge. Right about the time the Bad Brains moved to New York, we played a show at A7. Darryl, from the Bad Brains, stood in front of me and my amplifier for the whole set, and I was so intimidated because he was such a musician.

Every city had uniforms. The Boston uniform was a baggy

hooded sweatshirt, some T-shirt underneath and maybe some boots. Then we got into boots, but we thought Doc Martins were really lame, so we all bought motorcycle police boots that zipped up the side. These were the boots you were suppose to have if you were from Boston. Looking back on it, it is really funny because it is no different than the movie *Clueless*, or being a jock, something where everyone had a uniform. There were so many ridiculous rites of passage. The Boston thing wasn't about sleeveless T-shirts, you know with the arms cut off on a 45 degree angle, but we used to take the extra arm off the sleeve and wear it around our heads as a head band, or over our ears to keep our ears warm. When someone first came into the scene and asked about a "sleeve hat," we would reply, "You just can't have a sleeve hat. Every sleeve hat is earned. You have to go into the pit and get yourself a sleeve hat." That was the big laugh. Someone would come to a show for the first time and introduce themselves, and we would tell them the story about the sleeve hat, and they would go off and do it.

I never felt comfortable drinking. I just went along with it for peer pressure. I used to dump my beer when no one was looking. If we were drinking vodka and orange juice, mine would be all orange juice. Becoming involved in hardcore was the first time that I was around people that made me feel comfortable for feeling that way instead of uncomfortable. It gave me a support system because it wasn't saying, "You are weird. You are 15 years old and you don't want to drink." It felt like family, we were definitely family.

The other thing about the Boston scene was that we were really anti-vegetarian. We were really into eating red meat and lifting weights. Al from SSD was a really big guy. It was weird when we would go to New York City and there would be kids begging and Krishnas feeding everybody weird vegetarian food in front of CBGB's. Life for us was to eat food, lift weights, band practice, drive around and hang out on Newbury Street.

How do you feel about the influence that SSD and DYS had on the New York straight edge bands that came along a little later?

There was a lot of strife and acrimony because we felt that they had sort of co-opted our images and our scene without ever being there. Youth of Today was a big prop. This sort of sprung up later when I was in Slapshot.

If you look at Bold and you look at the first DYS record, you'd think they were the same people stuck in a time warp. There was all the same rhetoric: "I'm hanging with my crew" and "old school—we were there back in the day." We thought, "We were there, and you weren't." That is sort of where the animosity came from. I don't think that at the time anybody in Boston stepped back far enough to see that this it was really cool that they were paying homage. It was more like,"Hey, you're appropriating our thing. Do your own thing."

I remember going to New York and playing with SSD, and the two bands were probably tighter than any other bands that played together. We did a lot of things at the same time, just by accident. We both added second guitar players at around the same time, going from four pieces to five pieces. We both started experimenting with rock. We went towards Metallica, and they sort of went 70s, buying expensive guitars and Marshall amplifiers, the whole thing.

We played the first Rock Hotel with SSD. It was a big club, about 1,000 people, which for hardcore back then was huge. We decided that we were going to go down there and pool our equipment. We brought all of our equipment, every Marshall head and cabinet we had. There was six or seven Marshall stacks on stage. A lot of people wore wireless. People were not playing thrift store guitars anymore, but were playing guitars that were custom made or custom ordered. It was as though we were metamorphosizing into a whole different thing. When people started coming in, there were cat calls like,"It looks like Madison Square Garden up there!" It was very uncool to do all those sort of things.

There had been a show earlier that afternoon at CBGB's with Jerry's Kids and The F.U.'s and a band called The Fucking Assholes, which was a fake band put together of one member of all these other bands. They used to put ski masks over their heads. They were a joke band, but every one of their songs—they had about 10 songs—was about how much New York sucked. Of course there were fights. My friend Pat got cut with a knife. All this animosity spilled over into the night show, and everyone was just looking for an excuse for things to happen. SSD and DYS had about $20,000 worth of equipment, and we didn't want kids on the stage. We were writing songs with six or seven different parts and tempo changes, and all of the sudden there are kids bumping into you, and you couldn't play your instrument. We brought our own bouncers, and we were throwing people off the stage during SSD, and they were throwing people off the stage when DYS played. I don't think it was what New York wanted, and I don't think it was what New York expected. The whole show was chaos. It was to the point where I was swinging my guitar at people's heads. When SSD played, we were out in the pit. Boston was a really loyal, support-your-brothers, kind of thing.

"The training that I got from the D.I.Y. of the 80s has sort of been renamed "entrepreneurialism" to me in the 90s."

So we were ripping it up when all of the sudden over at the side, Dave Smalley was in trouble with two guys who were going to pound him. I thought,"I'm going to save my brother's ass." So I go over there, and I just get pounded. Some New York kid hit me with a handful of rings, and I couldn't see. My eyebrows were cut, and there was blood in my eyes. I think that all I have to do is get to the stage, and I'll be OK. So I get to the stage, and Jamie sees that I am bleeding, and everything stops. We ended up hiding in the dressing room until 4:30 a.m. until the people that were waiting to pound us left. I guess you could say that it had been led up to that for a long time.

There was always fights when Boston bands played New York or when Boston kids went down to New York to see DC bands or bands like Black Flag. Al's van would pull up and 17 kids would get out. We used to draw X's on our foreheads before we'd go into the pit because when you were grabbing people to punch them, and they had an X on their forehead, you knew not to punch them because they were from Boston. All sorts of weird things happened. Choke, from Negative FX , and later Slapshot, got the cartilage torn out of his knee at one show. Some kid landed on his leg, and he had to have an operation. He was on crutches for nine months. It was just a whole weird scene.

Other bands came up. SSD had broken up, and then I was in Slapshot.

There was no straight edge scene in New York in 1981. I'm not saying there weren't any kids, but it wasn't organized. Slapshot got into an open war with Youth of Today to the point where it was in our lyrics. Choke was pretty much calling those guys out. Slapshot would play up in Albany, and the Youth of Today guys would be there, and it would just be weird. There was a lot of tension. It was never close. If Boston ever had a sister city, it was DC. The two big bands were Black Flag and the Bad Brains, and we would pretty much road trip anywhere on the East Coast to see those bands. There was one band in New York that we had good relationships with, Reagan Youth. Those guys were really, really cool. I think they were different than all the other bands. We used to stay at their house when we would go to New York and play.

The Boston scene was very different than the New York scene in terms of that it was a suburban, upper-middle-class movement. As opposed to New York, it seemed like a Lower East Side, working class, tough-kid kind of thing. We were a lot like DC—senator's kids and admiral's kids and professor's kids. Dave Smalley's father is an ambassador. LA was kind of like an Orange County rich-kids thing, which was different, too. New York stood out to me in being different in that way, too.

The other thing I remember about the New York thing was the Beastie Boys. We were really down with them. We used to play with the Young and the Useless and the Beastie Boys. They would stay with us when they came up to Boston. Those guys were really cool. They were sort of down with us from back then too.

What about Agnostic Front, Cro Mags, Murphy's Law?

They all kind of fell on the other side of the straight edge/no edge thing. We were publicly friendly with those people for the most part. Everyone remembers Harley and Jimmy Gestapo from way back and CBGB's, but we didn't play together a lot. They were all coming up as we were coming down, in 1985 or so. That was the Slapshot era for me. The golden age of Boston was over. SSD and DYS broke up in 1985. SSD broke up first, and we ended up with their drummer for our last few shows. There was a while when nothing was happening, and then Slapshot got together with the goal to bring back old school Boston punk rock. The name of our first record was *Back on the Map,* which was supposed to be a whole statement. That was about the time the Cro Mags were coming up. We were all into the Cro Mags' music. It was sort of metal, and it was heavy. Murphy's Law went another way. They were funny punk, songs about drinking and stuff. So Slapshot tried to play with bands like Bold.

Why did they try to play with those bands if there was so much animosity between them?

There was no animosity with Bold. To us, and this is going to sound really terrible, Bold was just a bunch of 14-year-old kids, and they were cool and into the right thing. They seemed sincere, but generic. Their hearts were in the right place. With Youth of Today, there was this whole plan to appropriate someone else's thing. It was contrived. There was always someone threatening to kick someone else's ass or a verbal war. It was just a very different time, but it was sort of a carry over of what started in '81.

I wonder if that goes on today.

I don't know. As far as I understand, Boston does not have much of a scene today. The New York thing just regurgitates the same six people again over and over again at this point.

The other thing that was big in Boston, back in the day, was that everyone was into dancing really hard. It was supposed to be a fight, it wasn't supposed to be dancing at all. None of that "going in a circle" thing. It was called "Boston-punch-thrash." If there was a circle, you'd go against it.

What do you think about straight edge today?

I am the firmest believer in it. I am totally horrified when I get on America Online and see all these things attached to it, like veganism or whatever. To me that is not about straight edge at all. I guess you can make a loose connection of being aware of your environment. I am not a drinker today. I'm not going to name names, but there are a lot of people from back then who aren't still. I feel healthier, I feel up. The Boston straight edge thing sprung from this sort of Nietzchean, social Darwinism, and I still sort of feel that today. I was always "Do It Yourself," very entrepreneurial. The training that I got from the D.I.Y. of the 80s has sort of been renamed "entrepreneurialism" to me in the 90s. I really believe in the whole ethic of putting out your own albums, booking your own tours, doing your own posters, and doing it well. That taught me what I need today. That hyper-entrepreneurialism—this ferocious workout—I learned that there. I didn't learn that in high school or college or from my parents. I learned that from having a band. It was a business, and I had to keep it going. If I wanted to go out on tour for a month, I had to make sure I had 28 shows. I had to make sure that I had hotels or floors to crash on, so I didn't lose money every day. I had to figure out how to live on my per diem.

What do you do now?

I am an executive at an advertising agency. To me those are the most important lessons I learned in my life. Those were the best friends I made in my entire life, and they are still my friends today. Twelve years ago, I spent every day with Dave Smalley, Jamie Sherappa from SSD and Christine McCarthy who was Springa's girlfriend and Jamie's best friend. Here it is, 15 years later, and we don't have everyday to spend together, but if we have social time, we spend it with each other.

Did you think back then that you would be this way for a long time?

Yeah. If we had come out five years later, it would have been different. A lot of our contemporaries are doing really well. I look at the Beastie Boys, the Red Hot Chili Peppers, Soundgarden, those people who stuck it out have been rewarded. I knew those were good solid people (Dave, Jamie and Christine) in my life. When you are 18 or 19, you don't think about what you are going to do when you are 30.

A lot of kids say "true till death."

We said that stuff, and it is turning out to be somewhat true. Hardcore is such a weird thing that you go through when you are so young. I probably played my first live show when I was 16 and played my last live show when I was 21. I was a kid when I was done.

How old are you know?

I just turned 30 this year. I don't think I was emotionally or intellectually equipped when I was younger to deal with it. Sort of in the same way when you get to the end of college and you're figuring out what you should have done in high school. It's kind of like that—to be a 17-year-old kid and have to deal with things like groupies and the right code of behavior, to think of signing record contracts. Back then they were not for millions, they were not even for thousands.

Do you play music now?

Not organized with other musicians. I have guitars. I actually sold all my guitars and amplifiers over the years. When I started making money again, when I was done with college, I started collecting again. I have a few collectible Gibson's kicking around. I sit on my couch and play the guitar a couple times a week. I keep saying that I am going to make one more record before my miserable life is over. I am involved in music. As a marketer, I apply what I have learned to my friends' musical careers. I listen to friends' rough cuts and visit them in the studio and go over their video boards. I shoot commercials, stuff like that.

It was wild, Stiff Little Fingers played the other night, and we all went to go see them. It was funny, after two years of ragging on people who paid $125 to sit in the front row to see The Eagles, we basically went to go see The Eagles of our generation. I guess it is not any different.

How much were the tickets?

They were comps. We are still young enough that we know people who work at clubs. Because of being a musician I have become a horrible snob. I won't pay to see anything. If I can't go for free, I won't go at all. If a club holds more than 250 people and I don't have a back stage pass, I don't go. I just get this visual experience from small clubs—who wants to see a band from 100 yards away?

Greg Anderson

A Seattle native, Greg is a former member of False Liberty, Brotherhood and Engine Kid. I met Greg while working at Revelation. After I moved to Seattle, he ended up moving into my basement. This interview was conducted over our kitchen table on 21 June 1995, shortly before Engine Kid broke up.

How did you start listening to hardcore?

I was into metal, like a lot of people. My favorite bands were Motorhead, Raven and Metallica. Since those bands were being influenced by punk, I had this inner curiosity about punk rock. Somebody that I met in high school asked, "Oh you like Metallica? You should listen to DRI because it's faster." I thought faster was better, so I got way into fast bands. The faster the better. That's how I got into hardcore music.

I became friends with the guitar player for False Liberty. After school, every single day, I would follow them to their practice. They would let me watch them. They would tell me which records to buy; they told me to buy 7 Seconds and Septic Death and stuff like that. I would hang on every word that they said as far as what bands were cool. I'd go to Fallout Records and spend all of my money on whatever they said was good. From there, it just kind of dominoed. When you find out about one or two hardcore bands, they're usually associated with one or two more and then your record collection gets built up. So I started out listening to stuff like that, and Adrenalin O. D. and Corrosion of Conformity...

The singer for False Liberty was getting really involved in skiing and he decided to go away for a couple of months and teach skiing classes up at a big mountain resort. The future of False Liberty was hanging in the wings. They knew that I had been to all of their practices and knew all of their songs and had promoted their name more than anyone ever could because I was so into them.

How old were you during all that?

I was fifteen. They asked me to sing and I said, "yes." I got one of my friends to join the band, Justin who was into speed metal—I turned him on to hardcore and he turned me on to speed metal. I had kind of got out of metal when I got into hardcore. So he turned me on to all of these new bands that were coming up that I had kind of missed out on because I was so involved in hardcore. I got him in the band. We got pretty big. We played a lot of shows with bigger bands like Dr. Know, the Accused, Poison Idea, and the Melvins. We played a lot of shows with the Melvins before they were anything. We got to put out a 7" and then we went on a West Coast tour. I was totally wrapped up in the hardcore scene. I would write letters every day and trade tapes with people. I probably got four or five letters with tapes in them every day. I would come home from school and it was like Christmas. My mailbox would be just packed with stuff. I was obsessed with hardcore, I didn't care about anything else. I wasn't involved with anything at school. All I cared about was hardcore. I did fanzines here and there.

When did you start playing guitar?

My mom had bought me a guitar when I was in sixth grade that I just kept in my closet. I started tooling with the guitar and didn't think much of it. I took a guitar class during my senior year in high school, 1988, and got really into it. I thought, "Man, I can play any of these riffs on the Youth of Today record, this is easy. Hardcore is easy to play!" So, I decided to start a band playing guitar.

I was always interested in straight edge. I thought drugs were silly. All of the people who did drugs at my school were kind of losers. They were into Motley Crüe, crappy bands, so I figured that if they're into that kind of music ... I didn't fit into the whole partying thing. I smoked pot once, and I always thought that the taste of alcohol was gross.

I thought speed metal was cool, but I was way more interested in hardcore—true hardcore bands. That's kind of how I got into straight edge. All of the bands that I liked the most that were playing true hardcore were the positive, drug free bands, like Uniform Choice and Youth of Today.

When the Youth of Today 7" came out, that's how I got really into straight edge. It was so raw and really heavy for hardcore. I thought that it was the best thing happening for hardcore then, that and Uniform Choice's first album and Blast!, but they weren't really a straight edge band.

As far as the philosophy of straight edge goes, apart from the music, it was a time in my life when my mom was an alcoholic and this girl that I was seeing was getting really into drugs. She got into some really hard drugs, and so me being kind of gung ho about straight edge was a reaction to the closest people in my life in their involvement with drugs.

Was False Liberty still around?

False Liberty was just about breaking up. Near the end of False Liberty, I was getting more and more into straight edge. It was when the Youth of Today 7" came out. Immediately I started a new band called Inner Strength. We were kind of like early 7 Seconds.

Then I met some people who were into straight edge, and I decided that's what I needed to be doing, a full on straight edge band. So I dropped that band and started Brotherhood with Vic, the drummer for False Liberty and this guy, John White, whom I'd met.

One day I was in Fallout and there was a straight edge fanzine there. I freaked out! Somebody else here is into this kind of stuff?! Seattle was all about rock. Any band around here was a rock band, kind of like the early Sub Pop bands. So when I saw this straight edge fanzine, I called the guy, John, and asked him to sing in Brotherhood. So we started and we were terrible, we were awful, but we kept going. We got Ron to sing (when John left). Ron was this guy that I had known forever. He was in speed metal bands when I was in False Liberty and we had played with them over in Spokane. When Ron moved over here, we'd go to shows all the time. He got really into Youth of Today and Uniform Choice and Crippled Youth.

Brotherhood did one recording session ever. That recording session spawned the demo and it spawned a 7" that Rich Jacobs put out on Skate Edge Records. Rich was a big False Liberty fan whom I'd written to and corresponded with forever and he called me up and asked us to do a 7". The Brotherhood album that came out on Crucial Response in Germany was put out in 1990, way after the fact. It was about two years after the recording had taken place and after the band had broken up even. We did one recording and one tour. We had been asked to go on tour with the Accused across the United States, which was kind of a dream come true for me. The Accused were, besides False Liberty, the first band that I had ever gotten into.

Do you think that it's possible to be "true till death"?

I guess that would have to be a question answered by each individual and what being true meant to them. For me, I guess it's possible to be true to yourself, and what it means for me is that it's possible to be true to yourself and true to an inner quest, an inner growth. That's truth, a search for truth and how it pertains to your life, answering questions and solving problems in your life. A lot of people took it as "true to not doing drugs" or "true to my friends." I never really took it that way personally. The statement for me meant "true to yourself, true to your inner quest and discovering knowledge."

Do you think it's possible to be straight edge forever?

Sure, but then you're going to run into what everyone's different interpretations of straight edge are. That is an argument and discussion that I have no interest in anymore. I gave up on it four or five years ago because everyone had a different interpretation and I realized that defining it at all became worthless. To me, it works better as a personal statement, rather than a movement or a blanket statement, even though I was involved in that type of defining before—but not anymore.

Why did that change for you?

I came to terms with some of the questions and anger that I had in my mind about drugs and alcohol and straight edge as a movement and philosophy. It became irrelevant to where my life was heading. It sort of became stale and old for me.

Now that you look back, how do you feel about it?

It's kind of like a chapter in a book. There are things that I look back at and kind of cringe, that are kind of embarrassing. But I'm glad that it happened for me and that I did it. I learned a lot from it, gained a lot of insight and knowledge.

When you look around and you see a lot of people that you used to be involved in straight edge with, do you think that they feel the same way?

Yeah, not to say that straight edge was a fad or a trend, but I think that a lot of people—including myself—get really into something.

And as time grows, you grow out of it or you progress past its confines and it's no longer relevant to where you're at.

What about people who consider themselves "grown up"?
I think that growing up is a process that doesn't end until you die. I think that I'm always growing, learning different things.

Any last comments to the kids out there?
I just hope that people realize that everyone changes and grows and develops at a different rate and at different levels and for different reasons. To try to hold somebody to what your idea of where they should be at is unrealistic. I would hope that people wouldn't do that.

Richie Birkenhead

Richie was the singer for the original New York band Underdog and was also in Youth of Today for a short period of time. This interview was conducted in Seattle on 26 February 1995. I met with Richie at London Bridge Studios while his current band, Into Another, was recording their third full-length album, Seemless.

JOSHUA LANE STANTION

Richie with Underdog

I got into punk before I was into hardcore. I listened to the Clash, Stiff Little Fingers and the Buzzcocks. Those were some of my favorite bands. I liked the more intelligent brand of punk rock. In fact, when hardcore first got going in New York, I didn't really like most of it, to be honest. It had to grow on me. Actually, I went see the Bad Brains really early on. I was in a rockabilly/ psychobilly kind of band at the time in 1980 or 1981. I went to see the Bad Brains at one of their early New York shows at Max's Kansas City. That, I liked. That was the first really fast punk rock that I liked.

A few New York bands started to grow on me when I first started going to hardcore shows, just kind of as an outsider. There was something really infectious about the incredibly underground, dangerous feel. It felt more punk than punk rock. It was a feeling that doesn't exist at all today. It wasn't parents dropping their kids off at shows, and it wasn't the trendy thing to do in high school. In my high school, there were maybe three or four kids who were into any kind of underground music at all. The rest were either jocks or burnouts. Now punk is just completely trendy, and it's obviously very big business. The biggest bands in the world right now are punk bands. I think a long time ago that really dangerous, special feeling kind of left the hardcore scene, but a lot of really shitty elements were kind of phased out. A lot of really great, really positive—if you'll excuse the hackneyed word—elements came into it. I have to say that just from having toured for many years in a few bands, that hardcore kids—and I'll even say particularly straight edge kids (although I have a lot of problems with a lot of the so-called straight edge kids out there)—make up one of the most intelligent, open-minded factions of the underground music scene.

The first hardcore bands that really knocked me dead, other than the Bad Brains, were: Minor Threat, who I really dug; on the other end of the spectrum, just as far as fun went, I dug The Misfits. I really got into Minor Threat. The thing that really appealed to me about their whole straight edge thing was it really seemed like total rebellion against the typical high school kid, the typical teenager, who would just walk around stoned and drunk with his concert jersey on, Timberland boots, going from keg party to keg party, date raping girls. I initially saw the straight edge thing as a very punk thing—it was total rebellion. It wasn't at all like the jock-like, elitist, exclusionary movement that it turned into in a lot of places. I was really into SSD just because they were so over the top and so insane. You couldn't understand what Springa was saying in any of the songs unless you looked at the lyric sheet. I was also into a lot of the West Coast bands. I got really into Black Flag and the Germs and later on the Adolescents and the Descendants.

I still have a lot of those feelings. I'm still put off by drunken frat guys and people abusing drugs and stuff. I think that has more to do with the fact that I come from a family where there was alcohol abuse, and I really have a strong aversion to it.

At the same time, I'm also put off by people who are so self-righteously straight edge and have such an air of arrogance about them and are so elitist when their knowledge of the world and what goes on in it is so limited. Most of the kids I've met who are like that come from affluent upper-middle-class white families in all-white neighborhoods in the suburbs. They have not experienced the world one bit, except maybe in their high school or college courses. I can identify with those people as little as I can identify with drunken jocks or burnouts.

My whole participation in the straight edge scene was kind of like…I was a fence rider, to be honest. I was never the totally militant straight edger…although I abstained from drinking and doing drugs, and I still do, I always felt kind of uncomfortable putting the X's on my hands. I did that on stage with Youth of Today, and that's the only time I ever did it. Youth of Today kind of had a sense of humor about it…not kind of…absolutely! I was never a bona fide member. I played on *Break Down the Walls* and I toured with them a couple of times, but I was also in Underdog. I was in two bands. I left Underdog for eight months and then went back. My heart was really in Underdog because I felt as if we were doing something a little unique and not just trying to revive the 1982, '83 hardcore thing. So my participation in the straight edge scene was less than the "diehard, get X's tattooed on my fists" kind of guy.

I felt really uncomfortable most of the time that I was in Youth of Today. Sometimes it was really, really fun. I was really close with John Porcelly—he was my roommate for a while in New York. Some of the shows were really amazing. They were incredible. That was really fun, but again, my heart was more in Underdog, just because

JUSTIN BORUCKI

Into Another at CBGB's 9/95

we were like this weird band that didn't really fit in. And I kind of liked being there and being this weird guy that really didn't fit in.

Another reason why I left Youth of Today, aside from the fact that I just didn't feel like it was my thing, my band, was again the straight edge scene started to become something that it wasn't initially. When the straight edge revival thing started up again with Youth of Today—I definitely give them credit, 100 percent credit with starting it, the second wave of straight edge, without a doubt—there was no one else doing that. The first time I went to see them,

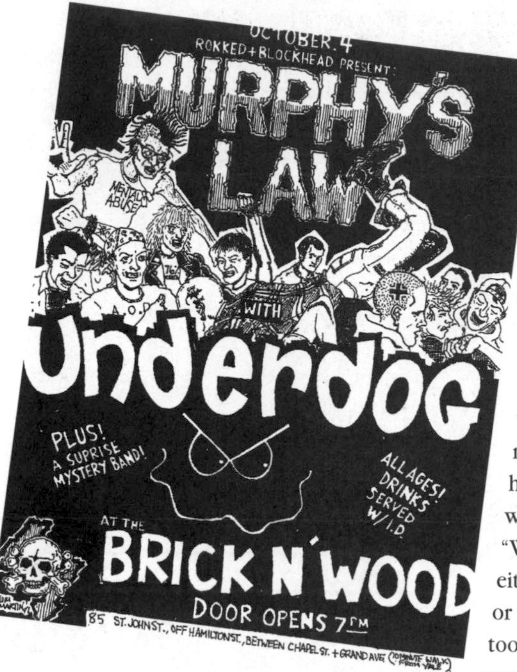

I think it was their first show, at some pizza place or something in Connecticut, it was Youth of Today and Agnostic Front. I hadn't seen anyone saying the things Ray was saying on stage or playing that kind of music since I saw Minor Threat or SSD. They were doing that at the same time a lot of hardcore bands were turning metal or just not really doing the hardcore thing anymore, so I thought it was really cool. They were like these hardcore fundamentalists, and Ray was really charismatic. I was like, "Wow this thing could take off. It's either going to totally fall on its face or it's going to take off," and it really took off. I honestly believe that if it weren't for Ray and Porcell doing that band, whether this is a good or bad thing, that this whole straight edge monster would not have risen from the dead. I really don't think it would have. Maybe someone else would have tried to bring it back. But all these kids who are into it today, for the fact that they are so young, there is no way they ever could have seen Minor Threat or DYS or SSD. I saw all those bands several times, and I thought Youth of Today was really pretty genuine. In a way, they were more over-the-top than any of those bands.

By the time I quit Youth of Today, the straight edge scene had really started to turn into a really ugly jock-like scene. It had become exactly what I thought it had started out as the antithesis of, which was this elitist exclusionary movement full of stupid little soap operas between the guys and the girls. It was very male-dominated and sexist, although I don't think it is now. I think things have really changed a lot and have gotten a lot better, but at that time, it was kind of peaking in all the negative respects. I was really turned off, I just wasn't into

JUSTIN BORUCKI

Into Another at CBGB's 9/95

it. There is still that element to a degree.

When we go on tour, I meet, or see some straight edge kids that just really give me the creeps. They're like Hitler Youth or something, but then for the most part, most of the kids who are into it are just the nicest guys and gals. Boys and girls we meet in straight edge bands are for the most part really cool. They're intelligent, aware, open-minded people. I'd say that it's the minority now that is hating everyone who isn't like them. Although I'm not really a part of that scene anymore, we do tour the country on that level and play with hardcore bands. We play all ages shows and benefits, so we're around it a lot, and I'd say it's better now than it's ever been. I really wish that it had been like this when I was in Youth of Today.

Like I said, the vast majority of hardcore and straight edge kids now are really cool, really open-minded and really open to other kinds of music. It's amazing. We meet kids, straight edge kids, who love all kinds of music. It was never like that before. You listened to hardcore, and that was it. They're well-read and have good taste in movies and other forms of pop culture and have a great sense of humor. It's absolutely better now than it's ever been, and here we are, just cock-rock sell-outs on a major label

JORDAN COOPER

Youth of Today at the Anthrax

and we could be part of that cool hardcore scene... just kidding.

I have to say... I don't really listen to any of the hardcore bands of the day. I don't know why. We play with them, but musically hardcore is just not my thing anymore. Although I do occasionally still listen to Negative Approach or Minor Threat, that's about it...The other day, Drew and I were rocking out to the Adolescents. I definitely still listen to old punk, old British punk, which has nothing at all to do with American straight edge, but I still listen to the Clash, the Buzzcocks. I don't really listen to hardcore anymore. I'm definitely not in a hardcore band. Into Another is absolutely not a hardcore band, even though we've been described as a hardcore band many, many times. At the same time, we have absolutely no contempt for the hardcore scene. We very willingly and actively ally ourselves with the hardcore scene and play in the hardcore scene all of the time. At the same time, we're not a metal band, either. I don't know what we are. I guess we're some mutation of rock or something but, we're just not a "type" of band. We absolutely don't classify ourselves as a hardcore band. So I'm just an old geezer who was once a part of the hardcore scene.

The way kids dance these days...is kind of cool sometimes, but it just used to be very different. It doesn't look scary anymore. They do all that Kung Fu stuff in the pit. It doesn't look scary because you don't have guys like Bloodclot and Harley and you don't have guys like Russ Underdog in the pit anymore. Those guys were scary. That's what made hardcore cool. You used to have to be brave to get into the pit. There was a total different feeling. It used to be this really cool, dark, scary feeling, and now it's just like "funcore," which isn't necessarily bad. That, to me, is the main element that was lost...that it used to really feel like you were a total outcast and a total misfit if you were into hardcore. It was completely underground. Now it doesn't feel that way at all. It's funny, in middle America, the kids who are most respected or feared are the most trendy, cliquey, gossipy kids in their school are the hardcore kids. Not that that's necessarily bad, but it used to be that in schools there was one or two freaks that were into hardcore, and they were totally nuts, like the kid who shaved his head and wore Ronald McDonald shoes.

Maybe for them, it's scary and they get that cool "fear" element.

Yeah, but they've got many more numbers now to feel safe with. Hardcore shows used to be 50 to 200 kids, tops. Now you go see hardcore shows with thousands of kids. There are still those bands that tour in their vans and play to 50 kids, and that's cool, but it just isn't at all what it used to be. Particularly in New York, that whole scene was there. I don't consider myself a real old school New York hardcore guy because even though I was going to hardcore shows at A7 and CB's and the Mud Club and Max's and all those places, I was totally not one of the hardcore guys like Jimmy (Murphy's Law) and Harley (the Cro Mags) and Roger and Vinnie from Agnostic Front. Those guys were really hardcore. I was

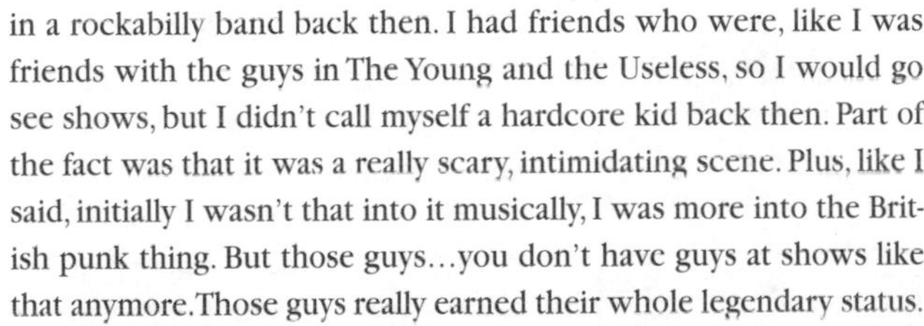

in a rockabilly band back then. I had friends who were, like I was friends with the guys in The Young and the Useless, so I would go see shows, but I didn't call myself a hardcore kid back then. Part of the fact was that it was a really scary, intimidating scene. Plus, like I said, initially I wasn't that into it musically, I was more into the British punk thing. But those guys…you don't have guys at shows like that anymore. Those guys really earned their whole legendary status.

One band that I did love right from the start, just because they

JOSHUA LANE STANTON

Underdog

had the most intense energy, was the Cro Mags, and they kind of came a little bit later, 1984 or '83 or something. I forgot to mention, they were definitely one of the bands that initially started to turn me on to it because they had the most fearsome music. Harley was one of the most charismatic people I ever saw on stage in my life, and also Jimmy. Jimmy from Murphy's Law was really incredibly charismatic. It's really a shame, those guys have more star quality and charisma than any of these guys that I see in any of these punk bands that have made it huge now—I mean much more. Those guys were great showmen and entertainers. Aside from being the real deal, they were exactly what they said they were. As hard as the Cro Mags music was, Harley and Bloodclot were at least as hard. Those guys were the real deal. You don't see that in any of these bands today. You see these like nerdy kids who just got out of their astrophysics class get up on stage and jump around with all these facial contortions and all this angst and pain, and they go home and watch their satellite TV and their Mom is cooking dinner. Those guys weren't going home to lives like that at all. The hardness that you heard in the Cro Mags music, and the vibe you felt at their shows, that was totally real. That was real anger, real pain, from guys who lived lives that produced those feelings.

JOSHUA LANE STANTON

Underdog

That's another thing that kind of bothers me about these bands with all this anger and all this emotion. Where the hell does it come from? All of the extremely judgmental kids that were around at the time I started really getting sick of the straight edge thing, around '88, before it started to get much better again, that's what really bummed me out. Some of these kids who were being so judgmental had no idea what they were talking about. To speak about people who you can not relate to in any way is completely wrong. It's wrong to judge people anyway, but to judge people based on the fact that they live a different lifestyle than you do when you don't know the first thing about their lives, or what they feel, or what they've gone through, is completely wrong. That really turned me off. To automatically exclude and hate an entire group of people because they weren't straight edge I thought was just absolutely disgusting.

Ray Cappo

Watching Ray on stage, one would have to agree that he is a master showman. After drumming for Violent Children, he formed the immensely popular band, Youth of Today. He is now a Krishna devotee and is performing with his band, Shelter. He is also known by his Krishna name, Raghunath Das. This interview was conducted on 11 October 1994.

ADAM TANNER

Youth of Today at CBGB's

In your own words, briefly go through the history of Youth of Today.

The absolute very beginning is: Me and Porcell were in a band called Violent Children. At the time in 1985, the hardcore scene was completely dead. Our last hope was Agnostic Front, and they started playing more metal-influenced songs. Actually, they put out that *Cause for Alarm* record, which was their very beginning of doing crossover music. So we didn't know what to do because we loved hardcore. There was actually one band, 7 Seconds, they were the only last remaining hardcore band that we loved. We always loved them, and they always inspired us. Me and Porcell were straight edge, whereas, it completely was not cool to be straight edge. We were part of the Connecticut scene.

In New York there definitely was not a straight edge scene. I remember Johnny Stiff (NYC personality who booked shows) saying to us, "If you think you're going to start a straight edge scene in New York, you're a joke. There was never a straight edge scene in New York, even when Minor Threat was around. There never will be. There's too many drugs in the scene." So anyway, me and Porcell, we liked the idea of a positive band like 7 Seconds, but at the same time, we liked music that was harder like Negative Approach. We wanted to combine. We thought

hardcore was getting too complicated, so we wanted to bring it back to real simplicity, real hard music, sort of like in the vein of the first Agnostic Front single and the album. So that's how Youth of Today started basically.

From there, we were doing it. We played our first show with Agnostic Front in Connecticut. We always had good shows. Our influences at the time were Agnostic Front, Negative Approach, SS Decontrol, 7 Seconds.

Where did the name come from?

Youth of Today, because we wanted to make it such a generic band. We were into being generic because everything else was getting so complicated. We wanted to just bring it back to real simple hardcore, so we picked the most simple hardcore name—"Youth of Today."

Wasn't that also the name of an Abused song?

It was an Abused song. It was also mentioned in an Avengers lyric. Cause for Alarm also mentioned it in their lyrics, (singing) "Youth of today can be the tool." That was our inspiration for the name.

Since we were friends with 7 Seconds, just from writing them letters, when they came to New York, we played a bunch of shows with them. I remember the time we couldn't get a show in Connecticut, the Anthrax wouldn't let us play. We were really upset.

Youth of Today reunion

CHRIS TOLIVER

CHRIS TOLIVER

Why wouldn't they let you play?

I don't know. Everyone loved 7 Seconds, but we especially loved them because we associated them with the straight edge scene. I think just to spite us, they wouldn't let us play the show, although we were playing Rhode Island with them and Albany with them. I was really bummed, so we complained to 7 Seconds. They tried to get us on the show and they couldn't get us on. Right before they started their set, the Anthrax was so packed—it was the old Anthrax in Stamford. Kevin said, "We're 7 Seconds and we're going to play a song, it's called 'Youth Crew.'" Back then, we didn't have a single out, but everyone knew that song. Me and Kevin staged this whole thing.

So I came on stage and said, "'Youth Crew'? That's a Youth of Today song, you can't play that!"

He said, "Okay, then *you guys* play the song." They gave us all their instruments and we played three songs, "Youth Crew," "Youth of Today," and "Crucial Times," or something like that.

Then they asked us to be on Positive Force, so we were the first band to be on 7 Seconds' label. Those guys went back to school, we were in college at the time. I went back to school too, in New Haven. We all flew out over Christmas break—they'd asked us to go on tour with them on the west coast when they put out our single. We were really psyched to go to the Positive Force House. Our first show we played in Reno on New Year's Eve. The next show we played in front of 800 people with Social Distortion and the Vandals.

Was that your first official Youth of Today tour?

Yeah, we just played some shows before that. The next show after that was at Fenders with Uniform Choice, 7 Seconds and DI. It was like, 3000 people, and it was so awesome. They gave us so much exposure. Then the record came out. I immediately quit college and moved to New York City. Porcell went back to college. It was funny because the day before we left, we played a show at CBGB's with Agnostic Front. It was the release of their *Cause for Alarm* album, and we were an opening band. I was preaching really heavy about straight edge to a crowd back then that was completely not into it. We were scared that we were going to be hated, but when I got back to New York, there was actually a straight edge scene that had started there.

All these bands had come up, like that band Straight Ahead and stuff like that. The guys from Straight Ahead ended up playing for us—Craig, who's now in Sick of it All, and Tommy, who was the singer for Straight Ahead. So there was a huge scene started and from this, so many hardcore bands came because as I said, there was actually nothing. Youth of Today became established in New York and it was great because so many other bands came from that straight edge scene. It started with just a few people, and there were some other kids from Albany, Steve Reddy who now runs Equal Vision Records, and Dave Stein and some kids up in Albany. Then the whole youth crew happened. Crippled Youth became a band, they started playing shows with us at CB's. Slapshot was a band up in Boston. They were straight edge, sort of from a different stock. Uniform Choice was from the West Coast. We gave Gorilla Biscuits and Side by Side their first show. It started snowballing from then. Underdog, Sick of it All came.

"For forty minutes you're on stage and everyone is going nuts, and then you have to go and deal with yourself, who are you really?"

I remember when all these demos came out. When I heard the Sick of it All demo, that's when I decided to put that out on Revelation. It was a good demo, even though they weren't a straight edge band, but they were just good, and that's when Revelation already started getting kicking into gear. Actually, Revelation started because WarZone were breaking up and Jordan and I wanted to put out a WarZone record. I asked them to go back into the studio before they broke up, and they said they weren't going to. So I said, "Just give me whatever tapes you have, practices, and Revelation will put that out." That's how Revelation started.

How many times did you go over to Europe?

We went over to Europe once. That was after I already joined the Krishna temple.

Youth of Today in Boulder, CO

How many times did you go across the country?

We went to California before we had any records out. When *Break Down the Walls* came out, we went on a U.S. tour, and when *We're Not in this Alone* came out, we went on a U.S. tour. We also did half the country with 7 Seconds. Our first *Can't Close My Eyes* tour, we went down to the South and up to Canada. That was *Can't Close My Eyes*—it was three times touring the U.S. and once in Europe. Europe was really ground breaking because no bands had ever gone over there except for big bands like the Dead Kennedys, so we really did a lot of frontier work. Now it's really easy to tour in Europe, the places are all set up. Back then, it was really hard. We ended up playing literally 60 shows, or maybe even more. I think we played two or three months solid, sometimes twice a night, with hardly any days off. We all got ripped off because back then, the tour manager was making the money. He paid your expenses to get over, and the bands didn't make any money. They gave us $500, but there were thousands and thousands of dollars being made. We were really cheated, but it was a really good tour.

Didn't Youth of Today break up, and then get back together, at one point?

We broke up right before *We're Not in this Alone*, and then got back together, hence the song, "We're back!!!"

Why did you break up the first time?

Just being frustrated with the whole straight edge scene. The straight edge scene got so big, but it seemed to be more like a fashion statement, rather than anyone seriously trying to improve themselves. That's when I started getting into spirituality more, and we put out *We're Not in this Alone*, which I think is a little more spiritually oriented. Then I went on tour, but I was really getting seriously into spirituality. Then I went on tour in America and I thought the whole scene was getting misguided. I didn't know if I misguided it, or if people in general misguided it, but they were getting into straight edge for the wrong reasons. It wasn't for a self-purification, it was more ego trips and fashion. It was being blamed on me, but I really didn't want a part of it, so I was very frustrated. I was ready to renounce the whole music scene. I got back, and I moved to India.

How long did you spend there?

Three months. I had an open-ended flight. I didn't really plan on coming back. But I came back and I recorded the Shelter album (*Perfection of Desire*), which was meant to be my last record ever done, that first Shelter album on Revelation. Then, Youth of Today were asked to go on a European tour, that's when we went on our European tour. I was really frustrated on that tour. I was really miserable because I just went to India and had a completely spiritual experience, and then I felt tempted, "Come on, go to Europe, you've never been to Europe before, it'll be great!" I was living in the ashram, so I thought, "All right, I'm going to leave the ashram and go to Europe," but I was still celibate and chanting and stuff like that. Tour became so miserable, I realized how silly it is, and I just said forget it. After that tour, I moved to a farm and lived there for eight months. That was the end of Youth of Today. I think we played one final show in LA. Jordan came and picked me up at the farm and we drove across the country in less than two days.

JORDAN COOPER

Ray on stage with Agnostic Front at Sal D's

In studying Krishna philosophy, the Krishna philosophy isn't to renounce anything falsely, but if you're good at something, you should use it in the service of Krishna, not just neglect it. So I tried to renounce music, but it's part of my nature to do music, to write music. So you use the same music, but you do it spiritually. That's what I think Shelter is, that's how I ended up here. It's the same

BETH LAHICKEY

Youth of Today at the Anthrax

exact thing, but with more of a spiritual twist. At the same time, we follow certain spiritual principles; we're celibate, we're vegetarians, we're straight.

Being on stage in front of a zillion people, how did that make you feel in your head, seeing people react like that, the way they did?

Of course it was fun. It was a full-contact sport, that's what I liked about hardcore. I remember once they put up a barrier. We played with Blast! and the Exploited at Fenders. We drove two days from Texas just to get to play the show. We played that no pay, but it was just an awesome show. We drove for a day and a half, 35 hours or something, from Texas, and we played the show. But Fenders wasn't the same because they put this huge barrier in between and there was all these bouncers in between the barrier, so kids trying to get on stage, they'd kill them. They'd climb over the barrier and then they'd get beat up really bad. We opened with "Break Down the Walls." I jumped right over the barrier into the crowd and the kids just started ripping down the barrier. It was so awesome. It gives you a real power charge.

I remember once Satyaraj, the devotee I did the book (*In Defense of Reality,* Equal Vision Records, 1993) with, told me that he played guitar. I said, "Really? why don't you play guitar for Krishna?"

He answered, "No, because I don't think it's good for my spiritual life."

I asked, "What are you talking about? I thought Krishna consciousness meant doing what you do naturally, but doing it for Krishna."

To which he replied, "Yeah, but I don't think it was good for me."

I said, "I'm doing Youth of Today, but I'm doing it with a spiritual conscience."

He said, "Do it for you, but I can't do it for me because I do it for the wrong reason."

I asked, "What do you mean?"

And he said, "Check for yourself. The next time you're on stage, see if you're being the *servant of* God, or you're trying to *be* God."

Sure enough, we played a show in New Haven and everyone was going nuts. I was thinking, "Wow, I'm on a real God trip." Even subtly, you get on a God trip, if you really think about it. You

JORDAN COOPER

Youth of Today

want to be the most magnanimous. You want to be the most powerful. I realized that unless you do it in a proper consciousness, everything is just an ego trip. Even if you're trying to spread the message of straight edge, or spread a positive message, there can be people who are great altruists or great philanthropists, but if they're doing it for their own ego, then it defeats the purpose.

Realizing that in yourself would be a nauseating feeling, I would imagine.

Realizing it is, but *not realizing it* is very intoxicating. It's actually very disillusioning. That's how that Ray and Porcell single came, because that's when we wrote that song, "Fame." It's really disillusioning because in one sense everyone is saying that, "You're the best, you're great." For forty minutes you're on stage and everyone is going nuts, and then you have to go and deal with yourself, who are you really? What you really are is this tiny little spirit soul bouncing around. Once you leave that environment of all fans, and you're back in the world, you're a nobody again. It freaks you out, because you don't know if you're big or small. So people who are famous, they're very insecure often because they get a false identity of being big, but the fact is, in this world, we're actually very small. That's why a lot of people who are famous either get into some sort of spiritual thing, or they take a lot of drugs, intoxins, or they commit suicide—a lot of them, a lot of the time, you'll see. Someone might argue and say that, "They're an artist, and artists have this type of depression that goes with their creativity." The fact is, they also lose a piece of who they are and why they're doing it, and they go through an identity trip, like that song "Fame" we wrote. That was my realization about getting popular and the feeling on stage. A lot of times, that feeling is just an ego trip. Although there is something nice there, too. There's definitely positive energy there.

Shelter is really popular too, now.

Yeah, now it's a really delicate thing. When I'm on stage I'm very, very conscience of why I'm doing it. So it doesn't matter if you're popular or not, it's your consciousness behind it. I'm not saying that I'm doing it in a completely pure consciousness, either, because when you're conscious of something, you're a little bit more aware of it.

When you know how the machinery works, the whole material world is actually just a very subtle machine, if you know how an ego works and how pride works and how to escape pride. It's almost like knowing a car. If you've never seen a car before, and you open up a hood, it looks very foreign. You wonder, "What the hell are all these wires?" But if you're a mechanic, and you open a car, it's something different; "Here's the carburetor, here's the master cylinder, here's the fuel line." So when you start learning different things in spirituality: how the false ego works, how pride works, why we act the way we do, where this pleasure is coming from, why we are feeling misery right now and why are we feeling pleasure right now, then you can see it for what it is. It is just like mechanics.

CHRIS TOLIVER

Shelter

Lyrics to "Fame":

I've had the itch and scratched it, but it was never cured. Although the desire still arises I realize it's absurd. It fools us into thinking that we're really something great making us so proud of what was handed to us by fate. Well that's fame. Stop lying to me. Why can't I see? Fame, it's just lying to me. I see it making me bigger than I deserve to be. And I know I'll never live up to what they expect from me. A drug we're searching for and when we get it we just want more. It comes as it pleases, then walks right out the door. Well that's fame...When they get the high they'll wonder why we're all mad after fame. It's not you, you've just fooled a few, and when you get it you're just the same. I've had the itch and scratched it but was never satisfied. I heard them say they love me, I know that's a lie. Forget about quenching my thirst, all this is just too dry. But we've heard it before, life's a bore, so we give it one more try. Mad after profit, distinction, adoration, cash never bought me anything I wanted. It only served as false protection. Fight for fame and material gain so our name is etched in stone. Then there's a devastation of our mind's creation when our position's overthrown.

CHRIS TOLIVER

Ray and Porcell

Civ

***22 October 1994**—As the singer for Gorilla Biscuits, Civ demonstrated an endless supply of charisma. After the band broke up, he opened up his own tattoo shop in New York. He is back on stage with most of his former bandmates in a band called "Civ." This interview was conducted on 22 October 1994, the evening before the video shoot for "Can't Wait One Minute More."*

DIONA MAY'S

Civ at the SUP Hall, Seattle, WA 1/13/96

When I was a sophomore in high school, friends in the neighborhood started getting into new wave, but it was kind of a dud. One of the first records that really made us turn the corner was DRI. The Circle Jerks, the Sex Pistols and the Clash were big influences when we first got into it, more like punk stuff. Then, a friend of mine got his hands on Agnostic Front's *Victim in Pain* That was just like "Holy shit!" We opened up the gatefold and saw the live photos of those guys playing and millions of skinheads going sick and we thought, "We gotta get into this" and that's how we got into hardcore. We started going to CB's shows and standing across the street at first and slowly venturing over... It was one of the most frightening things I've ever done, walking across the street from the deli to CB's. This was in 1985.

Where did you grow up?

I grew up in Queens, New York. I was born in Jackson Heights and lived there until I was 18. I thought it was the coolest thing to go out to summer matinees at CB's in 1985 and 1986 when there was a million people hanging out outside. After finally getting across the street, I finally went in and got killed at a Murphy's Law show or something. It was just the best thing ever. After we were into it for a little while, I met Arthur in high school, and he introduced me to Anthony and Ernie from Gilligan's Revenge and then Token Entry. I started hanging out with them in Astoria, Queens, just skating around, being punk rockers. Then Walter moved from Ohio to Astoria and I met him. Walter, Arthur and I started hanging out more and more with people from around the neighborhood.

Walter wanted to start a band and he asked me to sing. I had no ambition at all of being in a band whatsoever. I didn't even really think about it. Walter said, "Why don't you sing? It's hardcore, it doesn't matter, just sing." I was totally not into it. The first times I

All photos: JOSH LANE STANTON

Gorilla Biscuits

tried to sing, I always had to face the wall or look down.

We were practicing in garages and we got this kid to play drums. He wasn't even into anything that we were into, he was into starting a cover band. Arthur started playing with us—that was a big help. Ernie from Token Entry started playing drums and we finally got some songs down. After putting out demo tapes and having them at Some Records and Duane pushing them, we got to play a show with Token Entry, JFA, and the New York Hoods. That was our first show.

Were you called Gorilla Biscuits?

Yeah, actually we were forced to come up with a name. Ernie called us from out on the road with Token Entry and said, "You guys have to give me a name because I have to call up Connie and give her our name for the bill." When we were younger, the drug of choice in the neighborhood was lemon 7-14's, which were these big ludes. They were called "Gorilla Biscuits" because they were so big. We thought it was a stupid, funny name that people would remember.

Were you a straight edge band back then?

Yeah, when we first started, but we got the inspiration for the name from when I wasn't straight edge at all. We figured we could change it, but it stuck and that was it. Once in a while we'd think that we had the stupidest name, but then it was like, "Oh fuck it, it's cool," and it didn't matter.

For our first T-shirts, we bought a dozen shocking blue T-shirts and with a magic marker, I drew a gorilla riding a skateboard on all of them.

You were "manufacturing ..."

Yeah, on my desk at home, I took the ink blotter and pulled the shirt through it. I thought that was an engineering skill. I drew on that. Every one of them was just a gorilla riding on a skateboard.

But then when people sweated, their skin must have turned black ...

We didn't think about anything except that we had shirts to sell. When we first made demo tapes, I didn't even think about getting tapes with cases. I went to the dollar store and bought a pack of crappy 30

JOSHUA LANE STANTON

Gorilla Biscuits

minute tapes, five or six for a dollar. They didn't even come with cases, so we were selling demo tapes like that. We sold them with a handmade lyric sheet; photocopied, cut in pieces. Everything was done at the stationary store, but nobody cared. It was cool.

For one of the last shows we played, I made Gorilla Biscuits pizza shirts. We wanted to do something Roman or Italian. We were eating pizza and I took the pizza box and redrew it. We wrote "Gorilla Biscuits Oven Fresh Pizza" and nobody got it. Everybody said, "These shirts suck!" Now all these kids are wearing every industrial shirt, Reeses Peanut Butter...or any shirt. It's grunge. We didn't know then. We thought we were being funny. Now they'd be begging for those shirts.

How did you end up hooking up with all of those other straight edge kids?

Just from hanging out. We were in the band and were leaning towards the straight edge thing. Anthony from Token Entry used to bring me down to the Lower East Side, Avenue A. We'd hang out on Friday and Saturday nights. He introduced me to Richie from Underdog, Raybeez, Ray Cappo, Todd Youth, Tommy Carroll and all those

JOSHUA LANE STANTON

Civ and Walter

guys. We used to go skateboard Tompkins Square Park every once in a while. It was a time when you didn't even want to look at people, you know, like Harley (Flannagan) and Jimmy (Gestapo) and those guys. (Whispering) "Oh my god, it's Harley!"—You'd say it in a hush. I still kind of say it in a hush. It was people who you wind up knowing and totally being friends with, but at that point it was all new.

The Lower East Side was totally cool. Ray and those guys were all like, "Oh cool, you want to do a straight edge band? We'll try to hook you up with shows." Youth of Today was getting big and straight edge was getting big in New York.

I think the fact that Revelation Records was putting records out for New York totally revitalized everybody into being psyched to play music again and to start bands. At that time—boom, boom, boom: Rest in Pieces, Sick of it All, Gorilla Biscuits, Youth of Today, Bold—all those bands were all right there. Everybody was just like, "Jordan will do it, he doesn't care, he'll put out anything." It just wound up that he put out a bunch of good records.

JOSHUA LANE STANTON

Arthur, Civ and Walter

Just from being on the *Together* compilation, we got a lot of good feedback. So Jordan wasn't too hesitant about putting out the 7". After that, we played shows outside of New York for a while. We

ADAM TANNER

Gorilla Biscuits at CBGB's

were supposed to have the record *Start Today* out in stores by the time we went out on a U.S. tour, but it wasn't out until we played our second to last show in Chicago. It hit the stores the day before we got to Chicago and all the hardcore kids got it. We went there, and it was totally packed, and everybody knew all the lyrics, and I thought, "This is just the *best thing* ever!" Of course, it was our second to last show. Buffalo the next night was awesome.

Did you get to tour after that?

Not in the States, we played shows here and there in the states. We flew out to California and played a couple of shows and went to Chicago. We did little road trips because we were concentrating on going to Europe. We went to Europe with these total squatter people that we didn't know. It was hellish, it was awesome. We kind of did a lot of good for ourselves, going that way, but it also was hellish some nights. The second time we went back, that was total a rock-and-roll tour. Everybody was psyched up, and it was a really well done tour.

Was that before Youth of Today went?

No, right after Youth of Today went. They came back, and a few months later, we went. We were still trying to break down these fucking barriers. At first, we got a lot of shit. A lot of beer bottles thrown at us, we were spit on a bunch of times. The second time we went, there were so many straight edge kids there. It was really nice.

Where did you go both times?

Both times, we played probably about 15 different countries. We drove into Yugoslavia and the show was canceled. When we asked, "What's going on?" they replied, "Oh, the Revolution is coming." So we had to leave. We drove to Italy and hung out. Italy, France, Germany, the Netherlands, England, Spain, everywhere basically we could play, we were there. When the wall came down, we were in Europe. It was cool. We had a lot of fun stuff happen in Europe. But the states are nice.

ADAM TANNER

Gorilla Biscuits final show at the Marquee

What songs were on the demo tape? Anything that became the 7"?

Yeah, "No Reason Why," this song called "Slut," which came out before hardcore became politically correct, "Better Than You," "Do it Yourself"—all the songs that were on the 7" were on there. We might have cut out a couple of crappy ones. Most of them were on there. It wasn't like we had an abundance of songs to choose from when we had to do the 7".

I think the first thing we actually put out before the 7" was on the *New York City Hardcore—The Way It Is* compilation. That was the first thing we put out, I think we put on "Better Than You" It was like, "I've died and gone to heaven now."

DAVE SINE

Gorilla Biscuits at Fender's, 1989.

That's the way I used to think of it. It was like, "All right we're going to do a band. First thing, let's practice." Then it was like, "Let's do a demo tape," and then, "Okay, we did that, let's try to play a show. If we can play a CB's show, I can die and say that we had a band." Then came the 7", then a tour. We took it one day at a time and set little goals.

And you were able to face the audience eventually?

Eventually, yeah, not very well for a while. For some horrible cosmic reason some fucking guy had a video tape of the first show and it's still out there in circulation. Oh my god, it's so bad! I'm in camouflage pants and a green hooded T-shirt from Virginia Beach with a seagull on it. I don't know what the hell was going on.

HIGH HOPES.

WHEN YOUR ON YOUR HIGH HORSE,
AND THINGS ARE GOING YOUR WAY
YOU REALLY DON'T APPRECIATE WHAT
YOU WANTED BAD YESTERDAY.
BUT, IF I LOST IT — I'D STILL BE THE SAME
IT WON'T BREAK MY SPIRIT - I'LL LOOK AHEAD JUST THE SAME
TIMES ARE HARD ITS TRUE — I'LL COPE
BUT IT WONT GET ME DOWN CAUSE I GOT — HIGH HOPES
WHEN YOUR ON THE BOTTOM THE PLACE TO LOOK IS UP
WHEN THINGS ARE GETTING BETTER DON'T STOP
DON'T SAY ENOUGH -
WHAT YOU ACHIEVE - THATS FOR YOU TO CHOOSE
YOU CAN ALWAYS - REGAIN WHAT YOU LOSE
SOMETHING SHITTY HAPPENS & IT HURTS — I'LL COPE
ITS TIME WE ALL HAD — HIGH HOPES
SOME PEOPLE CAN'T REBOUND
WHEN HARDSHIP HITS THEIR LIFE
WHEN THEY LOSE SOMETHING THEY LOVE & THEIR FRIENDS
HOLDING THE KNIFE, PICK YOUR HEAD UP
GET OFF THE GROUND. THESE HIGH HOPES
THAT I HAVE KEEP ME FROM GETTING DOWN.

Gorilla Biscuits lyrics

"BIG MOUTH"

FRIENDSHIP-
TO YOU IT MEANS NOTHING
TIME & TIME AGAIN YOU BETRAY FRIENDS
WITH LIES — AND YOUR GOSSIP
THE STORIES YOU TELL CAN HURT LIKE HELL!

IT'S YOUR BIG MOUTH & ITS GETTIN ON MY NERVES
YOU KNOW I WISH YOU'D JUST SHUT IT UP.
IT'S YOUR BIG MOUTH & THE SHIT THAT COMES
OUT HAS NOTHING TO DO WITH WHAT
YOUR TALKING ABOUT.

YOU KNOW I WANNA TRUST YOU BUT, I CANT
YOUR WORDS NOT GIVEN ITS LENT.
MY ADVICE TO YOU — IS TO START SOMEWHERE
WHY DON'T YOU SHUT THE FUCK UP NOW —

IT'S YOUR BIG MOUTH & ITS GETTIN ON MY NERVES
YOU KNOW I WISH YOU'D JUST SHUT IT UP.
ITS YOUR BIG MOUTH & THE SHIT THAT COMES
OUT HAS NOTHING TO DO WITH WHAT
YOUR TALKING ABOUT.

Are you regretting that wardrobe choice?

Yeah, it wasn't the hottest outfit. At the time, I guess it might have been a hot outfit, but I don't really remember.

We're doing a video tomorrow and we all bought mod suits—pegged high waisted pants and jackets that button high up and are tight.

What is this new band you're doing all about?

It's basically everybody that was in Gorilla Biscuits, but it's just going to be called "Civ." Revelation Records is going to put it out.

I have a friend who does production and film and video for a company, and he has a lot of connections. He's making this $60,000-$70,000 video for us on a shoestring budget by pulling every favor he has. We're building a talk show set. It's going to be a parody on talk shows, kind of a little funny film. The song is more of a background rather than us just standing there rocking out, so we're pretty psyched. I'm pretty nervous, actually...

TIM OWEN

What does Civ sound like?

Like Gorilla Biscuits, it's kind of where we left off, some pop hardcore stuff like we've played, but then some really hard stuff, still in a very hardcore vein. You know, giving the kids what they want. It's kind of like what the kids wanted in 1987. We're just giving them that stuff again. I've played it for a few diehard Gorilla Biscuits kids who never saw the band and hang out in my tattoo parlor. They were like, "Thank god it's good, man, I'm so glad it doesn't suck!"

How long was Gorilla Biscuits together after "Start Today" came out?

That came out in '89, I think, and the band stayed together until 1992. That's when I started tattooing, after the band broke up. We were still together, but we weren't really playing shows or anything. We'd play shows here and there. We actually started writing songs for a new record.

Yeah, what was up with that? What about the rumors of "the lost GB record?"

It's in Atlantis. We recorded a few songs from practice on regular tape. We just had five or six new songs pretty much down, and Walter was doing too much Quicksand stuff.

Did any of those songs turn into Civ songs?

No. Most of the songs are new songs. We might use a Moondog song, but the two songs that we're putting out on Revelation are brand new songs.

JOHN MOCKUS

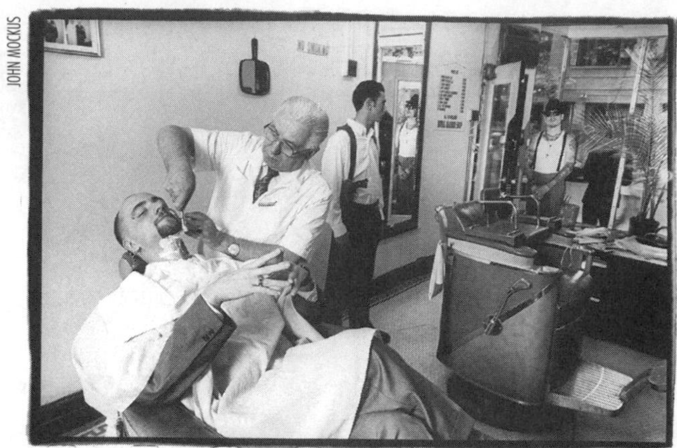

Jordan Cooper

Jordan in New Haven, CT, 1988

Jordan began Revelation Records in New Haven, Connecticut in 1987. He has since relocated the label to Huntington Beach, California. He is a complete workaholic, and he is also one of my best friends in the world. We conducted this interview on 26 August 1994.

The idea for the WarZone record? I asked Ray (Cappo) if he thought it was a good idea and he said that we should start a label to do it. We started thinking about names, and we came up with a long list. It came down to "Schism" and "Revelation."

How did you know that WarZone had a recording?
We were going to ask them to record. I didn't even have any concept of recording or anything like that. I just thought, "Let's do a record for them." I didn't know what it entailed ...

Well, what were you thinking?
I wasn't thinking. I was just thinking "record." I wanted a WarZone record in my hands.

So you said, "I'll just make it myself?"
Yup.

So how did you learn how to do everything? Did you have any help from anybody?
Kane, who did all the BYO and Positive Force pressings helped out a lot. Ray met him through Kevin Seconds. Kevin Seconds ran Positive Force and put out the Youth of Today *Can't Close My Eyes* 7". Kane worked in a pressing plant so I sent him all the tapes and stuff, and he had it mastered and got it pressed.

Side by Side / No For An Answer ad

Did you intend to make a label that would keep putting out records?

I thought of just doing the WarZone record, and we just came up with more and more ideas. I was into it. The *Together* compilation came up, and then Ray talked to Sick of it All.

How did you know about pressing records? You just learned that from the first records?

Yeah, from dealing with the different plants. We started out at Macola (where Kane worked) then, when they went out of business we used one in Texas or Arizona. I can't even remember—they went out of business. Then we used one in Long Island City that did the *Sick of it All* 7", and that place was pretty good. I just learned about everything as it was being done. A lot of the people that we worked with were really helpful and explained how things should be done.

How did you learn about contracts?

I didn't know anything about them. I just copied one from a book and used that. There are a few books available on the business side of music that cover legal issues. Those were pretty useful.

Let's chat about some of the early Revelation releases. Why did you do the Sick of it All 7"?

Because the music was awesome and the lyrics were sincere. They were, and are, a great band. Ray knew them and they were into doing the ep. Then Gorilla Biscuits was going to do a record with Duane (of Some Records), and somehow Ray talked them into doing it with Revelation. After that came the Side By Side 7" and the No For An Answer 7" at about the same time. Side By Side were from New York and No For An Answer were from California.

Revelation: 7 was the* New York City Hardcore—The Way It Is *compilation.

This was one of my favorite records we ever did. Somehow we got a lot of the hardcore bands at the time that were regularly doing shows in New York together on one album. The idea came from our second release which was actually called *Together*. That was a 7" ep with a few of the bands mentioned above on it. Basically what I did for *The Way It Is* was expand on the *Together* 7". We picked a few more bands, and I put that album together during my lunch breaks at work.

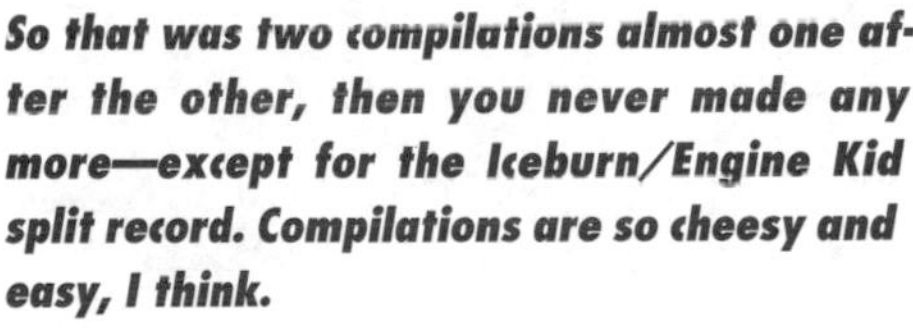

So that was two compilations almost one after the other, then you never made any more—except for the Iceburn/Engine Kid split record. Compilations are so cheesy and easy, I think.

Not really, they're the hardest, because you have to deal with way more people.

Well, it always seems like, some songs are good, some songs are fast-forwarded over.

Not that comp, though. That's a great one, easy for me to say, but I like it.

What was Revelation: 8?

That was Youth of Today *Break Down the Walls*, which was a remixed version of their record that came out on Wishing Well. Basically Ray wanted to do it on Revelation because they never got paid from Wishing Well.

Did you do it without their permission?

The band had the right to do what they wanted with the record and they did. You would have to confirm this with Ray, but he told me that Youth of Today paid for the recording so they really owned the tape. They wanted the record on Revelation where they felt they had more control.

And then along came Bold.

Yeah, we talked Bold into doing the record on Revelation instead of on Wishing Well. They had the artwork

Supertouch,* The Earth is Flat *ad, 1990

and masters for "Speak Out" for a long time and it didn't seem like it was ever coming out, so we talked to them and ended up releasing it on Revelation.

And then Chain of Strength. And they're from...

California, Upland. Basically the Inland Empire/Riverside area. Ray and Porcell knew them from the Youth Of Today tours.

Revelation: 12 is the Gorilla Biscuits album.

Yeah, *Start Today*. That is the most popular record we ever put out and it was one of the biggest projects for me. The band put so much into that album and I wanted to do the same with the artwork and packaging. The first pressing had embossed lettering on the album cover. That was the first record we released on CD as part of the standard production. The funny thing is that I paid for the recording with the money I got from a car accident settlement.

"I have nothing to do with straight edge, other than some behind-the-scenes vinyl shuffling."

Where did that one get recorded at?

Don Fury's.

Tell me about the* Chung King Can Suck It *record.

Judge recorded at Chung King Studios. I don't know why. They might have thought it was a good studio. Everyone liked the record and then half way through the tour—we were on tour in Europe

JUDGE

No Friends
No Hope
No Sweat

·shelter·

·shelter·
PERFECTION OF DESIRE

Early Revelation Records stickers

Bad
Bonus
~~Polluted~~ Pollluted
Kevin's
Cack
Crust
Hernia
Short
Ear Wax *
Secret
Extra
Used
Dee
Headache
Bypass
Follow up
Folded
Squelch
Beat
Free

(Left and right margins) Jordan and Ray's list of possible names for the label

with Youth of Today—Porcell and Sammy were calling Mike once in a while.

Three quarters of the way through the tour they decided that they were going to re-record it. Even before I'd left, people had ordered the new Judge album because it was advertised as "coming soon." So we worked out something where we pressed a certain amount of the records to send to people who had ordered it beforehand and then replaced the vinyl with the new recording, but in the end there was a couple of different songs. Two of the songs got cut, and they added a different one to replace them so we totally had to do a different thing. So we just called it *Chung King Can Suck It* and put out a hundred of them and sent them out to those people, and that's the whole story.

Did you call it* Chung King Can Suck It *because the recording was so shitty?

Yeah, they blamed the studio, so that's what they called it. Plus "can suck it" was kind of an "in joke" on the tour.

I want to talk to you about your definition and your views on straight edge.

No!

Come on!

I don't think it's very pertinent what I think about straight edge, because I have nothing to do with straight edge, other than some behind-the-scenes vinyl shuffling. Didn't you talk to Ray about that?

I can't put that in the book, Jordan.

Why? I put that in every interview that I've done about straight edge. I think that the reason a lot of people get into hardcore and straight edge has to do with their sense of self and identity when they're young, and they grow out of it whether they remain straight or not. I don't smoke, get drunk or take drugs but it's not my religion and I respect a lot of people who do some of the above. Lines being drawn doesn't make sense to me. If someone explained that they don't drink, smoke, fuck or take drugs and their reasons for it that's cool. What I didn't like about SE was the in-club, preachy, self-righteous side of it.

Do you think that it's good?

No. You could argue that it's better than following a trend that leads to self destruction, but a trend is a trend, a clique's a clique and you could just as easily argue that it might limit some people's experiences and growth even outside the realm of drinking, smoking and drugs.

Do you think it serves any purpose?

Yes, it gives them a sense of belonging, a sense of identity, a sense of separation. It puts them on a high horse to look down on others from, not in all cases mind you. I just think in a lot of cases. As I see it, a personal choice about drinking, drugs and sex to be an aspect of one's personality or music is fine, but for it to be the basis of it or an obsession is silly.

Rubber
Arm+Hammer
Dusty
Relief
Revelation
(o)(u)
Impact
Crucial
Hopeless
Remedial
Remedy
Bother
Buried
Reality
Frickin'
Harsh

Do you think that it's contradictory to what punk rock is all about?

Yes, although I think a lot of punks have a similar attitude about a lot of other things as well.

Was there ever a point in your life when you were sold on straight edge?

Never. I have never had an "X" on my hand. I have never called myself "straight edge." I have never purchased a straight edge record, other than before I knew what straight edge was and I bought the SSD *Get it Away* record and the Minor Threat record. I'm not into drinking or drugs but I'm not into straight-edge either.

Are you going to put out another straight edge record again?

I may. I may reissue the Chain of Strength record. Everybody keeps asking me to do it.

What are you going to do in the future with the label?

Just keep putting out bands I like. I want to start a good distribution along with the label.

Judge "Bringin' It Down" ad

JUDGE
BRINGS IT DOWN
WITH THEIR
HARD-HITTING DEBUT

JUDGE 'BRINGIN' IT DOWN'

AVAILABLE ON LP, CASSETTE, CD
FROM REVELATION RECORDS

P.O. BOX 1454, NEW HAVEN, CT 06506-1454
SEND S.A.S.E. FOR CATALOG

DIST. BY VENUS NYC, CAROLINE NYC, IMPORTANT NYC

© 1989 REVELATION RECORDS

Is there any other record company that you would like to model Revelation Records after?

None that I can think of. There are hundreds of great labels, but none stand out to me. It's the bands that make the label.

How long do you think Revelation Records will last?

I don't know, maybe twenty years.

Twenty years total, or twenty years from now?

Hopefully twenty years from now.

Right now Revelation Records is nine years old. Did you ever think that this was what you were going to do with your life?

No.

How do you feel about the way it turned out?

I think I missed a lot of good opportunities and a lot of fun while I was working, but other than that it has been cool.

Bold "Speak Out" ad

Do you feel successful?

Yes, but I also feel stupid. I wasted all my time on this. There are so many people that do so much more in much less time, business-wise.

I don't think it is a waste of time. I think that you built a successful business.

Success is relative. I am satisfied with the label, but for nine years? It's no big success story. I don't think it was a waste of time, but I wish I could have done it while enjoying my life along with doing what I did.

How do you feel about young kids that bad mouth Revelation Records?

It depends on what they're saying. I hate when people make judgments on us based on false rumors.

What bands are you going to put out in the future?

Whirlpool, Shades Apart, State of the Nation, Texas is the Reason, Iceburn and Farside.

Don Fury

This interview was conducted on 27 November 1995. Don Fury owns and operates Don Fury's Demo Demo Studio in a New York City storefront where he recorded many of the important records of the day.

JUSTIN BORUCKI

Don Fury in his studio

In 1979, I had a little rehearsal studio, and I was doing part of the punk rock scene, including Richard Hell, the Voidoids, and James Chance. Other bands were starting there, like the Bush Tetras, the Outsets, generally speaking, the east village punk scene—not the Ramones, not Johnny Thunders but people around that scene. We couldn't stay in that building because there were problems with other tenants, and we had to get out.

With the money that I made on the space there, I came to this space with the express idea of setting up what I have. The idea was to set up a little studio like Sun Studio, the old rockabilly studio where Elvis recorded. I wanted a little place where local bands could come and make records. At that time, hardcore wasn't really smashing through here in New York yet. It was 1980, and I guess in about 1982, I got involved with Agnostic Front on *United Blood,* and that's what started it off.

We did *United Blood* four track, and then nine months to a year later, we did *Victim in Pain* sixteen track, and that was it. Once those two records were out, the hardcore scene was revolving around this place. Straight edge, which came along later, just naturally followed Agnostic Front and the other bands that were recording here back in the day.

How were the straight edge bands different from the other bands you had been recording?

It's hard to remember how they were different, except that they were really young. I recorded Sammy, the drummer for Civ and Side by Side. He was 14 when I did his first record. Walter from the Biscuits was 16 the first time they came in and recorded. All of those cats must have been really young. Arthur, who's now in Civ, who was in the Biscuits...they were just kids—literally. That was the main thing. The other bands were a little bit older.

Straight edge itself did not impact on me in the studio. It was a slightly different kind of sound that was coming up, and we sort of evolved with it all together. The sound was a little bit more sophisticated in terms of its arrangement, in terms of its chord structure. It was a little bit more sophisticated in terms of its lyric content usually. Its social comment also was a little broader, including things like vegetarianism and animal rights and the various other straight edge peripheral arguments. It was a cleaner kind of presentation of the music. It wasn't as dirty as some of the hardcore stuff I was doing. Those other bands had a dirtier sound, generally speaking.

Do any of those bands' recording sessions stand out in your mind?

The Gorilla Biscuits single—the session doesn't stand out in my mind, but as a record it had an incredible impact. Once that record was out, everybody wanted to be like the Biscuits. I'm kind of making a joke, but in a way, that's really what happened. There were other bands out there contending around the Biscuits that were on the same scale, but there were many, many other bands out there that idolized the Biscuits and wanted to be just like that. As a result, I had a lot of bands coming in to me saying, "We really love that single. That's what we want to sound like." For me, it was good to work with all of these bands, but it got a little tedious, kind of formulaic after a while to do the same type of things for each band. But that's what they wanted, so it was kind of hard to get out of it for a while.

"It doesn't necessarily mean you're selling out because your ideas change."

The next one that rings a bell is the Gorilla Biscuits album. That was a pretty wild event because they actually had money for the first time. They had started working a big studio, 24 track. I was very small at the time. They were working at Chung King, taking off hours, working with assistant engineers and not being happy with the results and spending thousands of bucks trying to get the work done. All of the sudden I got this call from Walter saying, "Fury, we got to come in. We're going to re-cut the album." I was 8 track at the time. I asked, "Are you sure?" He said, "Yeah. I'm sure." So they came in, and we cut the album 8 track.

Walter had to go on tour with Youth of Today in Europe. We tried to cut vocals with Civ while Walter was away, but Civ had a pretty bad respiratory infection, either that, or some vicious cold that would not go away. We had a hard time with it. We got a lot of vocals down but nothing that was going to make the record. When Walter came back, we re-cut all of the vocals, bit by bit. That was very painstaking, but it paid off because the album was a big hit.

Agnostic Front "United Blood" 7"

What other straight edge bands did you record?

Youth of Today. I did a bunch of different things for them. I didn't do their biggest records, but I did a bunch of stuff with them, including re-mixing and re-recording *"Can't Close My Eyes,"* their last EP, and compilation things for them.

The last EP they put out was a pretty wild affair. We had all of the music down, and this was a time when the band's future was uncertain, and Ray was not always available. I think he was already into the Krishna scene at that point, so it was hard to get a hold of him. Getting the vocals down was really difficult, just to get him into the studio. We did three different vocal sessions. On the last vocal session we weren't nuts about what we were getting from Ray yet. We had done two sessions already. Ray was holding back. He was being more modest because of his new affiliations and his new role in the world as far as he was concerned, which had to do with Krishna consciousness. He wasn't really ripping the way he could.

Finally, me and Porcell just said, "Come on man, you just got to get into it!" Sure enough, he did. My studio is not that big. The main room is only 15 by 20 feet, and part of that is taken up by a drum room. He got into it, so into it that he was literally running across the room with the mic, singing, jumping off the walls. Not in front of the walls, not near the walls, he was jumping off the walls, like a skateboarder. It was really hysterical. Basically speaking, most of those vocals are what made it to the record.

Do have anything to say about how you've seen musicians as they go on and leave straight edge and do other projects?

This is difficult to say. Somebody could say this about me in the same breath, but as you go farther up the business scale, some of the cool shit that was around you falls away. I don't like to watch that happen. Let me just speak about what I try to do to keep that from happening, although I can't prevent it from sliding entirely. I try to keep both ends of the spectrum open. When I'm working with Civ or Quicksand and doing something for Atlantic Records or Island Records or something like that, I try to keep the very bottom of

Gorilla Biscuits "Start Today" ad

things open if something comes up that looks really neat. It's not even so much the size of the project that counts. It doesn't have to be super small, but it just has to be something that I think merits a look. It would be nice if these cats—and I think they do—keep some of that together, but I do think that some of those concerns that they had when they were younger tend to change as they get older and get more involved in what they've been going through. And that's natural. What they replace them with and how honest they are about it, I think that depends entirely on who it is.

I have less of a problem with people who are a little bit more up front about it, who say, "Look, I'm different than I was as a kid. I'm into doing this for the music's sake" or whatever the story may be. People have made comments about bands growing up and selling out, but you can't be 16 forever, and it's nice to get your music out to a broader spectrum of people. It doesn't necessarily mean you're selling out because your ideas change.

Mike Hartsfield

I met Mike in Huntington Beach, where he runs New Age Records and also co-runs Network Sound Records. He is a former member of Freewill and Outspoken. This interview was conducted on 18 May 1995.

DAN ADAIR

Freewill 1988

One of the first times I saw Uniform Choice was with Nuclear Assault, that was how I kind of ended up getting into hardcore, because I was a metal kid growing up. So I got exposed to that stuff, and it was really cool. It's really weird because you can't see that now. I think back about how everyone got along a lot better back then. There were all sorts of different kinds of people at shows; punk guys, hardcore guys, all sorts of different people. It seemed like everything went a lot smoother, and now it's a lot more fashion and a lot of people concerned with a lot of nonsense. That's actually not the only thing I look back on, but it's the thing I've thought about lately.

When and where did you first start going to shows?

I think the first show I went to was at Fenders in Long Beach. I think it was in '87. I just started going because I basically got asked to play bass for this band a long time ago. These guys I was kind of hanging out with were like, "Oh you can play bass, we got this punk band." I was still a metal kid. The stuff they were doing was kind of cool, and then I just started to hang out with them and it brought on a whole new thing. I saw a lot of differences in what I was into, and it definitely interested me a lot more.

Did you get into those hardcore metal bands when they were crossing over into metal?

Like DRI? Not really, because there was one day that I just hung up the hair. I was kind of getting out of metal anyway, but I can still appreciate the good metal. The first shows I started going to were Fenders shows.

DAVE SINE

Drift Again in Simi Valley, CA

What bands were playing there?

Half Off, No For An Answer, Uniform Choice, Straight Arm, Blast!, mostly local bands. Uniform Choice was definitely my biggest thing at that time.

What was Uniform Choice like, seeing them play live all of the time?

It was completely like, "Wow!" They were the first band that I was able to get records for and know that they were playing locally, and I would actually get to go see them. When I saw them the shows were just crazy. I remember just looking up and going, "Omigosh." It was like this omniscient energy force being put out from the stage, and it was just incredible. It was just so exciting, right when everything was going on. It was just amazing.

Did you get into Dischord stuff at all, more national things, or was it local mostly for you?

Well, it was mostly local because that's the only stuff I knew about. Then, through hanging out with different people, it would be like, "Oh, here's a tape of No For An Answer," and that was more local stuff. Then I would think, "What label are they on? Who else do they put out?" It just kept going. I would look on people's "thanks" lists to see who they thanked, figuring that if they were friends with these guys, then they must be good, too.

Did you get to see any of those bands?

Yeah, because they all played this huge show at Fenders in '89, and that was the biggest deal. It was the first time I saw Youth of Today. It was kind of cool, those East Coast bands coming to the place where I had started seeing all the West Coast bands, and where my first shows were. I used to think, "Wow this place is magic." It's been closed down for a couple of years.

Did you completely embrace straight edge right off?

Oh yeah, yeah. I wasn't much of a non-straight edge guy to begin with, so it kind of wasn't a big drastic change.

When did you first start getting into straight edge bands?

In '87, because as soon as I was getting into hardcore, I was like, "Wow, what is this stuff?," finding out the differences like, "Oh this is straight edge, this isn't straight edge...What are these guys into? What do they believe in?" At that time, I looked forward to straight edge bands and the things they were singing about.

How does Freewill fit into it?

Freewill started with me and this guy Paul. He wrote to me once, and I saw where he lived, and it wasn't that far. I ended up hanging out with him and he was the guy who had been setting up shows. So, I started going to shows that he was a part of in a totally different area that was kind of far from here. He was playing with this drummer, and he was a singer. They had a guitar player who wasn't really working out. I told them, "Well basically, I know a guitar player,

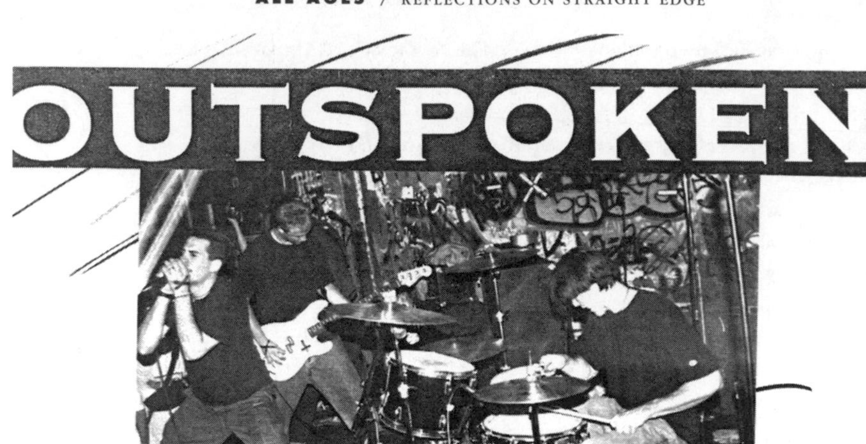

this is goodbye.
I've come to the conclusion that I'm just too sentimental. I thought it would be cool to do
something like this just for the simple fact that I wish some of the bands that I have seen
come and go had done something like this. Well basically, here it is. I asked everyone (I
didn't get jae's in time) to write something about Outspoken and their feelings. Out of the
bands I had been in previously this is by far the most attached I'd ever become to any. I
thought it would be nice to do this and I hope no one gets the wrong idea and thinks it's
"rock star" or anything like that. My good friend Norm even wanted to write something. I
hope all the guys, and you as well, think this is a neat little collection of feelings and
thoughts we hoped to express, and not "just another one of Hartsfield's dumb ideas" (like
all those samples I always talked everyone into). Goodbye

michael gavin hartsfield

To the left of me sits a silent t.v. with an assorted group of moving pictures they call "cops". To my right, Outspoken are practicing for what may very well be "the last time". I can't tell if that means anything to them, or if they even realize the significance. I'm just looking at things from a unique vantage point in history right now, and I'm trying to reflect.

It seems almost ironic that I, of all people am the one writing this. I live across the country in a small apartment on east 10th. street in new york city. It's not even half the size of "CLUB LATES", the practice studio slash home of Mike and Travis. Yet I can recall very well the beginnings of this southern california outfit. Even some 3000 miles away.

My friend Matt sent away for the "Look Beyond" demo in 1990. We listened to it in his car on the way to a show at the old anthrax club in connecticut. The band was good, I thought, and looked forward to the time when we'd drive to the anthrax to see them, it never happened.

I was excited for the "Survival" ep, but again without coming to the east coast, my enthusiasm dwindled. It wasn't until the summer of '92 that I first saw outspoken.

The show was in riverside, the flyer read: "don't call it a come back, they've been hear for years". I was inRessurection at the time, "A Light in the Dark" just came out, and I couldn't believe I'd finally be seeing outspoken for the first time. Much in the spirit of many of the late 80's east coast shows, the crowd was lively and the bands didn't disappoint. I do believe I mentally crowned the band the reigning kings of Southern California. Of course as I got to know the band personally, their real special points became obvious.

band stuff aside, I love these guys. Whether it be Travis' ability to crack a smile on my face, Mike's big hearted hugs or Dennis' occasional slaps of sobriety, the individuals involved are full of dedication and spirit. The kind of people the inspire me on a daily basis. The kind of people I try to surround myself with as much as I possibly can.

They finally got to play in new york city, some four years after the fact. Good turnout, and a great response to boot. I help but think I watched it unfold I can't believe I'm watching it end.

In a nutshell, I don't know all the lyrics and I don't know all the songs, but I damn well know who my friends are, and I sure as hell can spot a sincere heart.
Outspoken to me are both.

norm arenas
anti-matter
august 26th. 1994

Outspoken's epilogue

and I play bass, so let's try to get something together." It was the very end of '87, and we started practicing right at the start of '88. We played our first show in February.

We were all really into it and started doing things as Freewill. Then we got a deal with Wishing Well. We tried to do a lot of stuff—we were going and playing Gilman, we went to Arizona, playing around as much as we could, getting some shows with Uniform Choice and No For An Answer. At the start of '89, I was not getting into it anymore. I wanted to play more hardcore stuff and they were going a little more the Verbal Assault route. It wasn't such a drastic change. We were always being compared to Dagnasty and Verbal Assault. It was not a bad thing, but it's what I want to listen to, not necessarily what I want to play. So I said, "Hey guys, I'm out." They changed their name to "Stone Telling" and ended up getting a new bass player. They played a couple of shows and they broke up.

What did you do after that?

I went from playing bass in Freewill to playing guitar for Against the Wall with Mike Madrid. He had called me and said, "Do you want to play second guitar for Against the Wall?" I didn't even know how to play guitar. I had barely known how to play bass. He said, "Oh, we'll teach you how to play." I borrowed guitar equipment and I went to Against the Wall practice. Joe, who was also playing guitar, taught me how to play.

It was going really well. We had gotten on some really good shows. We had actually broken up and kind of started getting back together, but Joe didn't come back and the bass player didn't come back. We ended up getting Randy Johnson to play bass and Travis Hunt was playing drums, who is now in Mean Season. We did stuff as a four-piece and that grew old kind of quick.

When that was over, I started playing with Dan O'Mahony and Gavin. I had heard that No For An Answer needed a bass player. They were one of my favorite bands, so I called them up. They said that No For An Answer is not really going to do anything, but they wanted to do something new. I was completely up for it, and I started jamming with them. We practiced a couple of times. It was both of those guys, plus Steve from Insted, and me playing bass. It worked out well a couple of times. They had previously recorded the Carry Nation 7" and they said, "Oh Carry Nation is not going to do anything, this is our new band." It was basically Carry Nation with me instead of Frank, who was playing bass for Carry Nation.

All of the sudden, these Carry Nation shows came up and they said, "Oh, it's just a couple of shows. We're not really going to do anything with it." It turned into their new band and I was kind of left

Friday, March 26th 1993

Outspoken • Farside • Process
Unbroken • Mean Season

at Russo's, 2395 Hammer st., Riverside
Take 91east to the 15north. Exit 2nd st.. Turn left.
Turn right on Hammer. Located on the corner of 3rd st. & Hammer.
$5.00. For more info.:Bob (909)272-9322.

wondering, "What do I do?"

So, I called up John Coyle and we ended up forming Outspoken together. He was a guy that I'd hung out with and a guy who I'd like to be around, as far as the band. So I called him on the phone once. He was the guy down here that was in touch with everyone, as far as Huntington Beach and Orange County. He had been in Back to Back and Straight Arm and all sorts of bands. He was definitely a guy that I wanted to do stuff with. I called him and said, "Let's do a band together" and he said, "OK!" That was in January of 1990.

John and Dennis had written some stuff before we came along, and it was exactly the stuff we wanted to do. We recorded the demo within a month or two. John wrote the demo and the 7". Dennis and I were writing stuff; we did the later releases. Everything was just really good at that time, everything was really rolling. Then John graduated high school in 1991 and moved to San Francisco.

We thought we couldn't keep the band going with someone living in San Francisco, and so we tried out a couple of guys. We ended up getting a guitar player, and I decided to sing. That didn't work out so well. I didn't like it at all. So, we went back to me playing guitar, and we asked John if he wanted to commute. We kept going with him living eight or nine hours away. We would send him practice tapes, and he would call a couple of days later with the lyrics.

Didn't it feel really separated, as if he wasn't part of the band?

Oh, completely. I would think, "Wow, we wrote this thing—I hope he likes it." He would be working and going to school all week and trying to come down on the weekend. We were cramming in practices at one or two in the morning at his Dad's warehouse. It was really hard to keep everything going. We had just replaced our bass player, Jay, with the new bass player, Jason. Things were going really good, and he was great to work with. We were still as happy with it, I think, as we were before, but it was kind of like, "You know what, if we're not going to do this right ..." We were getting tour offers and we were writing stuff that we were really happy with, but being frustrated because we couldn't do anything.

We had talked about breaking up before the last tour. It was Dennis'—no it was my idea—and I said, "Yeah, let's get it over with." Dennis said, "No, no, no, let's keep it going." I said, "OK we'll see how things go."

When we got back from tour, John called up Dennis and said, "I don't want to do it anymore." Him making the decision was kind of strange, but we said, "OK, one last show."

We played the last show in August, and it was a totally emotional experience. Once we decided that was to be the last show, everything went so easily. Practices from then on were so much fun. It was a burden about to be lifted off our shoulders.

Where was the last show?

It was at the Icehouse in Fullerton. I had set up the show with the guy who owned the place, and I told him that we wanted to get all of the opening bands. So, I purposely got the four least known bands I could think of so our last show would hopefully bring people who wouldn't normally see them to the show. We made booklets that said, "Outspoken 1990 - 1994" with all sorts of pictures from tour, like Dennis pumping gas in the middle of Nebraska, us fixing flat tires and pictures from shows in New York and Utah or San Diego or wherever we happened to be. It was really neat. Each of us wrote a little paragraph about the band. We made five hundred of them and we handed them all out at the show.

The show was just incredible. It was the biggest show that we had played since *The Current* 7" had come out. Before we played the last song, we said, "OK everyone, this is the last song we're going to play, and so just have a good time!" Everyone was on stage, and it was completely crazy. After the show everyone was completely bawling. My mom was there, and it was the first show that she ever got to see, and so that was really cool. She came down with my brother, and my brother had never seen a show before.

What did she think of the whole thing?

She had never seen a stage dive before, so she was like, "Oh my god!" We were throwing guitars all over the place and there were drums flying around…It was a really good way to go out.

How did you first become started with putting out straight edge records?

I had friends who were writing music and doing things, but there were basically no local labels around at the time, besides New Beginning. There wasn't really a local label that was able to put stuff out. So I just started calling places, like pressing plants that offered like "1,000 7"s for $700" or whatever little deals that were going on. I basically just started calling places to find out if it was possible, and it was. So I contacted bands and said, "Hey! Do you want me to put out your record? I've never put out a record before, but I'm going to try!" So, it basically started from that.

I was working two jobs to get up money to do it, contact a printer, contact a pressing plant, completely blindly trying to put something out, and it worked out well. The bands were happy and I thought, "Wow, that's really cool, I put out a record. I wonder if I should put out another record?"

What was the first record you put out?

This band from the L.A. area called Walk Proud.

How many records are you up to now?

Mean Season was 24 and there's up to 27 planned.

When did you start New Age Records?

At the end of August of '88, Walk Proud recorded.

So it's eight years old.

Yeah, it's really weird I remember all of that stuff pretty vividly ...

That's because you were straight edge, Mike (laughter). Did you ever think that that's what you were going to end up doing for so long?

Oh no, no way. I was delivering pizzas and trying to answer mail when I would get home at 11:00 PM. I had no idea what I was going to end up doing in five or seven years. I don't even think I was thinking about it. I was just living every day, and it just turned into this.

So what do you see happening in the future for it?

I don't know. Since day one, all it's done is grown. Every day there's more and more stuff going on. There's more and more work to do every day, hiring more people, buying silk screening stuff and dealing with new stores and distributors. I can't see it doing anything but, hopefully, continuing to grow.

Do you think that it will always be primarily straight edge bands?

Yeah, because that's just what I'm into. That's what I started the label doing, and that's what I want to keep doing because it's what I'm still into after this amount of time.

Do you think you'll be straight edge forever? Realistically?

Yeah. I definitely do.

True till Death, huh?

Yeah, just because I have no desire to do anything. I don't feel like I'm missing out on anything. I don't have the itch in the back of my mind to do anything. It just doesn't exist. Even when I had experiences with things like that in junior high and the start of high school, I never had any great experience to look back on. I never thought, "Wow, that one time, weren't things great?" It was more like, "No, that one time I got real tired, and I went to sleep."

Do you ever feel any sense of responsibility for playing such a big role in straight edge by putting out records and being in bands? Do you ever feel like an influence on the kids?

I have a feeling that things are, but it's not pre-meditated. I don't think, "Oh you know, I want to write *The Current* 7", and maybe it might influence some bands." I'm just so happy doing what I do. It doesn't go much further than my own enjoyment. If I'm happy doing something, then that's the most important thing to me. If other people like it, or gain an ounce of anything out of it, then that's awesome. I think as far as the label and stuff, promoting the bands, those are the bands that I'm into. Those are the bands that I feel have a great message that I'd like to see people getting into.

SOUTH COAST AND JUST 4 FUN present...
YOUTH OF TODAY
SHEC
SHEC
IN THE CAL STATE STUDENT UNION ROOM
INSTED
NO FOR AN ANSWER
HARD STANCE
COME EARLY AND SURPORT DA' LOCALS!
HUNK A MANIA
FREE WILL
SAT. APRIL 2
AT CAL. STATE SAN BERNARDINO SHOW STARTS AT 7:00
$6 whudda' bargin
CAL. STATE SAN BERNARDINO
COLLEGE PKWY
NORTH PARK BLVD.
STATE
215
INFO: CALL SCOTT (619) 249-3887
FOR US, FOR THE HALL AND FOR YOURSELF...
NO ALCOHOL!

GLYNIS HULL-ROCHELLE

SUSAN MARTINEZ

Glynis Hull-Rochelle
Spring 1986

Glynis was one of the first friends I made in the hardcore scene. She lived in New Haven, Connecticut and worked at the Anthrax. She is currently living in Prague in the Czech Republic. This interview was conducted on 27 March 1996.

I was never straight edge. Even though I had been a vegetarian from childhood, I smoked cigarettes, which ruled me out categorically anyway. But more pertinently, I wasn't involved in straight edge because I couldn't think in those terms; because straight edge didn't involve me. The demographics of every single straight edge practitioner I knew were completely alien to me: they were almost all young white wealthy suburban boys who were athletically and musically inclined, or tried to be. Their world was insular, and straight edge was borne of this particular makeup. Therefore, its composition could only reflect its base. I don't mean that these were membership rules explicitly set forth; in fact I don't think that those boys could even comprehend how exclusive their straight edge "movement" was. But I certainly had no thread there to grab hold of.

For instance, a sort of obscure and strange form of male behavior was held in great esteem among the straight edge scenesters. This was described by the adjective "hard." There was a rating system of worth which was dominated by this word. "Hard" didn't mean exactly physically strong but mentally persevering, durable of spirit, as well. "Hard" implied a superhuman aspect, a secret knowledge or concept that mere mortals could not grasp. And hard, needless to say, related to maleness. Male genitals. Male behavior. Male minds. We couldn't exactly fit ourselves in there. Even if, as girls, we may have felt strong in the hardcore scene, we weren't that kind of "hard."

Girls in the hardcore scene at large, and in the microcosmic straight edge scene, as elsewhere, were basically ornaments. They were just messier-than-average ornaments. You could be a hard girl, but you were always that—a hard—girl. Boys were just hard. They made the regulations as to what was hard, what was respected. The activities they enjoyed were by definition hard. They, their normal habits, their natural interests, were the essence of hard. And it was meant to be scintillating to us all, but a lot of the girls really did not know how to react to this intense otherness, how to relate with this male inner world.

Many of the girls I knew who called themselves straight edge lived under the umbrellas of their boyfriends. The girls were smart, or pretty, or whatever, but it was the boys who had the energy. There was always something uncomfortable about the image of a straight edge girl. I knew only a very few girls who asserted themselves as straight edge, asserted that it was something they could lay claim to. I didn't find those girls particularly individualistic either, since they followed the straight edge rule book with a special fervor, but it was certainly a brave position to take. A minority of them were booking agents, or played the guitar, or skateboarded. Some of them were very loud and outspoken. Those I applaud.

I must say that I did feel as though Minor Threat and a couple of other straight edge bands had a certain respect for women. This was proven in different lyrics and in a general willingness to deal with the hot women's issues of the day, chiefly, abortion, rape and battering. In DC there were always benefit shows and that sort of thing, just more attention paid to such topics. Embrace was, and Fugazi remains, commendable on this point. This sensitivity was not visibly part of the NYC scene, nor the Boston scene as far as I could tell. I lived in Chicago off and on, and there too women were fairly invisible. In most scenes, lesbians were particularly anathema, even though nobody would admit their homophobia. You just knew not to mention it much. Also Verbal Assault, forever on the periphery of straight edge (I think by choice) also had an attitude of respect for women and concern for "women's issues." But most of the rest? One word about feminism or powerful women, and the room got quiet. It was difficult for hard boys to handle.

Girl bands, by the way, had to work ten times as hard to get half the recognition. They had to be that much more clever and entertaining. And they had to be musically gifted or be immediately disregarded. Well, in any event, there were no straight edge girl bands. As I said, it was just so far out of the realm of girls' comprehension. You see, it's rare that someone tells girls how fun it is to have an independent hobby, one that doesn't involve nurturing, like playing a musical instrument or working on a methodical, challenging task. No one tells girls that diligence of this type, systematic learning, is stimulating to the mind, the soul, the ego. No one tells girls how incredibly exciting it is to be external creators. Boys are told this all their lives, and they are encouraged to act on it.

Many of the straight edge boys were my friends, and they were interesting and likable people, but it's true that they could have been loosely termed "fanatics." I figured that it was better that they were obsessed with something healthy than with something not healthy, violent, or otherwise damaging to their person or to other persons' persons. Most of us took the "lesser of two evils" approach to the concept of straight edge. Because it really was in your face. Relentlessly. Staggeringly. Had I ever said so much as one hundredth about women's rights or feminism as these boys said about straight edge, I would have been burned at the stake as a castrating dyke witch bitch.

"... a sort of obscure and strange form of male behavior was held in great esteem among the straight edge scenesters. This was described by the adjective 'hard.'"

In all fairness, though, some people did want to hang the straight edge crew. That reminds me of Crucial Youth, a band from New Jersey whose sole purpose was to take the piss out of straight edge bands. I actually think their members were straight edge, but they had the width of mind to have humor about the aggressiveness of the straight edge movement. The serious straight edge scenesters were absolutely incensed by Crucial Youth, and that indicates that they played an important role in challenging the pervasive notion that straight edge practitioners were somehow more virtuous, or of a purer breed, than others. I think that perhaps a lot of their intended compassion and sharing got lost in the translation, when often the straight edge movement ended up sounding like an enforced-conformity plan to dominate the world. It often did seem as though they had a superiority complex. And they expressed themselves without apology. So it wasn't all cake and ice cream for them. I think they were trying to forge some other road to divert themselves from the ease and indulgences of their comfortable suburban realities. I think they wanted to try to understand their maleness, their humanness, in a different way, and this was a very commendable act. I don't know if it worked, but it was an important effort.

Mike Judge

Mike was the formidable front man for Judge. He also played drums in Death Before Dishonor and Youth of Today. He is now doing an acoustic project, Mike Judge and Old Smoke. I must admit, this was my favorite interview to conduct. It was probably because I had no idea what to expect and by the end of the interview I was convinced that Mike was one of the raddest people in the world. I spoke with Mike on January 24, 1995.

DAVE SINE

Judge at Fender's

How I got involved with hardcore? I guess it was the same way everyone else did, I was looking for something a little different when I was in high school. I met up with some kids, who I guess you'd call them punk rockers or whatever. They were older than me and they were going to shows in the city in I guess 1980-1981, and they took me with them. I got real involved in it from then, I really loved it and all. Me and some guys at home started a band called Death Before Dishonor. We played a lot of shows with Agnostic Front.

That was with Mark Ryan wasn't it?
Yeah.

Who else was in that band?
There were two brothers, Jimmy and Steve Yu, and me on drums and Mark Ryan on vocals. Mainly, we just played. It wasn't a real big time thing back then, you know. It was more just opening up for Agnostic at CBGB's or playing A7 a lot. We played A7 just about every weekend. I guess we kept that band together for up until, I don't remember exactly what year it was.

Mark Ryan was friends with Ray Cappo and Porcell and they had just recorded their record, *Break Down the Walls*. He introduced me to them, and I really dug them. They needed a drummer to tour with for the *Break Down the Walls*, and I tried out and joined up with them.

Is that how Death Before Dishonor broke up?
Well, I had left the band. They changed their name to "Supertouch," that all happened around the same time. There was a little bit of

hard feelings there between me and Mark because of the way I left, but after a while we worked everything out.

I went on tour with Youth of Today, and me and Porcell became really good friends. We shared a lot of the same ideas about what we wanted out of music, music we really wanted to play.

Through the tours that I did with Youth of Today, I saw how things were changing a lot around the country, and even in New York I could see how the whole straight edge seemed to be taking a beating from all sides, especially Youth of Today. I don't know whether it was because Youth of Today was more outspoken than the rest of the straight edge bands were, but they were really taking a beating. I thought it was really weird because Youth of Today was always about trying to be good to yourself and good to the people around you, and here were these people who were really putting us down for that. I guess towards the end...I think all the frustrations came through, and we wound up breaking up the band.

COMING JULY 18th.
FROM NEW YORK CITY
JUDGE
FOR INFO CALL 733-2434
A RATED X PRODUCTION
BRINGIN' IT DOWN

At that time, I was also writing music and songs for something I wanted to do. I didn't know what I was going to do with the material, I was just writing. Youth of Today had broken up, and I told Porcell that I'd been writing these songs and I have music and lyrics. Porcell at that time was doing Schism Records with Alex from Gorilla Biscuits and he said, "Why don't we get together and record and release them?" I thought it was cool. It was going to be my first time singing, I was always a drummer.

Why did you stop playing drums to sing ? Why didn't you do both?

Well, on the first Judge EP, I did do both. I played drums and sang, and Porcell played guitar and bass. We weren't really setting out to start a band. We were just setting out to more or less put out these ideas that I had.

The ideas that I had were kind of negative at that point because I was a little pissed off the way Youth of Today was treated. It was kind of stupid of me, I guess. I was mad at these people who were saying that we were these elitist, Nazi-type straight edge guys. Instead of trying to do something to prove that they were wrong, and that we weren't like that, I guess I went the full other circle and decided to give them a little bit of what they thought we were about. I think maybe I took it a little bit too far on the first record. I made more enemies than I did make friends. I don't know what it was, but we decided that even though there were a lot of negative things about it, and there were a lot of people who hated it, there were just as many people who liked it, at least in New York from what we could tell. If it could make so many people feel all these different things, it would be worth it to make it a real band. So, we turned Judge into a band.

Who was in the band besides Porcell?

In the beginning, it was me and Porcell, Jimmy Yu from Death Before Dishonor on bass, and Luke from WarZone. We gigged around the city and started writing for a full length record. We also changed drummers, too, because Luke was already in WarZone and Gorilla Biscuits and that's when we got Sammy. That was pretty much it. Judge was set for a while that way and we did a few tours, a lot of short weekend things out on the West Coast, things like that.

Did you drive out there or fly out?

A lot of times I just flew out because I had a lot of work here, where I was. Those guys would drive out. It would usually happen if Bold was on tour, then they'd set up shows where we could play with them on the West Coast, and that's what we'd do. I'd fly out there, and we'd do the West Coast with them. We did a lot of shows with Gorilla Biscuits at that time. In the different places we played, we could feel the scene changing around us.

How was it changing?

It just seemed that things weren't, not they were *ever* unified, *ever*, but, it just seemed that things were getting worse. People had these perception of what I was about and what Judge was about. In some cases they might have been a little bit right, but they just expected something different than Judge, or what Judge was. When we got there, there was a whole lot of fights everywhere. Things were just really taking their toll.

Money was taking its toll, too. It was costing us. It was costing me personally more money to tour, and I was at a point in my life where I really had to have a job. It was getting harder and harder for me to take a couple of months out and tour and not make any money. I'd come home, and I'd really be in a hole. Everyday things in life just seemed to be weighing down on me.

There was so much violence at all the shows. That last tour, by the time we were pulling into Florida at the end of the tour, I pretty much knew that these would be the last couple of shows that I would do with Judge, because emotionally I couldn't deal with it anymore.

I thought my words were being twisted in weird ways and there wasn't anything I could say about it. If I tried, it just fell on deaf ears. I had pretty much told people what I was about in the beginning of Judge, and more and more, I felt myself trying to get away from the guy that I made myself out to be in the beginning. I figured the only way I could do that was to totally wash my hands of it and just split. That's pretty much what I did after Judge got back home after the last show. I pretty much just split. I came back to Jersey and I hid out for a couple of years, didn't talk to anybody, didn't look anybody up, just tried to get my shit together.

What did you do during that time?

A lot of my old friends from the city who wondered what I did, and why I did it those couple of years, think that I only did it to them. But, when I came home, I pretty much hid myself from everyone I knew, except my family. Even my friends here, who are removed from the whole scene, who just know me as me, grew up with me, even they didn't know what was going on. I just basically worked and stayed in my room. In those two years, I was still writing a lot of music, but it was music that I wasn't writing for a band, so it seemed to me that it represented more of me. I knew out of all the things I've been through music-wise, I knew all the mistakes that can be made, and how things can affect other people. It seemed that I wasn't making them anymore, that deep down I knew how things were working.

"Every time I would let my mind get off on me and start beating me up a little bit, instead of letting myself take it out on me, or take it out on someone else, I just told it to my guitar and together we put in on tape."

I spent a lot of time writing. Basically that's all I really did. I started playing guitar. I learned how to play guitar then. I wrote a lot of music, a lot of lyrics. I got myself a four track and recorded all these songs. I've got shelves and shelves and shelves of all these tapes that I've done. That's how I kept my act together. Every time I would let my mind get off on me and start beating me up a little bit, instead of letting myself take it out on me, or take it out on someone else, I just told it to my guitar and together we put in on tape. It was a weird little therapy that I had going.

Is that where the Old Smoke record came from?

Pretty much, yeah. I wasn't even expecting to start Old Smoke. The rhythm guitar player for Old Smoke, Todd, who was the roadie on the last Judge tour, had pretty much seen everything that was going

Youth of Today

on. He hadn't seen me after the tour for a couple of years. Off and on he'd see me, but never really talking or hanging out. Every once in a while he'd stop by, and I'd let him hear some stuff that I'd been doing, how I'd been passing my time. He was a Judge fan in the beginning, so I never really knew if he was impressed by the songs I was doing, or if he was just impressed that I was doing music again period.

Once he found out that I had music that was completed, he was the one who called Jordan and said, "I know what Mike's doing and I have a feeling that if you talked to him, he'd come out and you could do something." Jordan got in touch with me and told me that he figured it would be worth it to take a chance on me doing my own thing.

I was a little bit worried at the time because I didn't know if Jordan realized that I wasn't doing hardcore or anything really heavy anymore. It was more acoustic based. I have deep roots in folk music and I was doing what I felt. I was playing music for me in-

Judge publicity photo

stead of writing music I thought I had to write. I was writing music for myself this time. He said he'd like to do it, and that's how Old Smoke happened. That's what I'm doing now, still plugging away with Old Smoke. Musically, I don't think I've ever been more happy, playing the music I'm playing now.

What would you like to see happen with that band?

Well, I think Old Smoke is a great band. I think they're kind of a throw back to the way music used to be, by way of no one is exceptionally talented in the band. For me, it seems that Old Smoke can't go on if one of the members were gone. It's just the feeling that I get when we're playing together. It feels to me that it's the way music is meant to be. It's not extremely polished. It's not heavy in the sense of how Judge was heavy, but to me it's ten times as heavy as Judge was just for the sheer emotional content of what's going on in the music. The words are more personal. I would just love everyone to at least take a chance and just listen to the band. I think the band has a lot to offer. I'd love to take Old Smoke as far as I could take it. I'd love to make Old Smoke my main thing.

As I'm getting older—I'm twenty eight now—it's getting harder for me to give 50 percent to a job, and 50 percent to every other aspect of my life and then still look inside of me for another 100 percent to give to my band. I would love to only have to do music everyday, that would be my main thing. That's what I dream about. I still think that day might come, and that's what I keep myself going with everyday. When I'm doing something, and I get myself a little down, I just say, "When this happens, things are going to be great." I just keep thinking about that, and I keep plugging away. I constantly write. I'm constantly looking for something better and trying to do the best that I can do. I try to do my best, and I know that the guys I'm with, for the most part, try to do their best. I'd like to see it pay off for all of us. I think all of us really have a lot to offer if someone would just listen.

Have you been playing a lot of shows?

We started playing last summer. It took a long while for me to find the right members to be in the band. There were a lot of different lineups for Old Smoke until I found one that I could be in sync with. It took a long time for me to get comfortable with my job as being a guitar player and a singer and a lead guitar player and song writer. With Judge, all I had to do was show up with lyrics. The music was there for me, already figured out. Now, I'm building songs from the ground up. Pretty much everything that goes on, everyone looks to me. If they have something that they want to do, they say, "Here's what I want to do, what do you think?" So, I have so much more responsibility than I've ever had. It took me a while to get used to that. When I finally did, that's when we started playing out.

I was out of it for so long, that when we did start playing in New York and things had changed drastically again for me, that threw me off a little bit. But now I pretty much understand the way the whole music scene is. I guess I thought maybe there was going

to be a little bit of a payback when I started again. Now I know that nothing is being given away and that there are no breaks for anybody. You just got to go and do what you want to do and not expect anything for free.

Were you worried at all about how the straight edge kids were going to perceive something like the Old Smoke record coming from Mike Judge?

I was really worried about it. That's what put the whole band on hold for a few years. I was really excited to record because that's pretty much my favorite part of the whole thing, being in the studio and building something in the studio. I was really excited about all

Youth of Today

that, but when it was all done and all of the sudden I had this finished product in my hand, and it was time to go out, that's when it hit me. The big feeling I had was that I didn't want to let people who looked up to me and respected me for what I did, to feel like now I'm letting them down or that I turned my back on something. I remember how I felt when bands I really loved, or looked up to as I was growing up, changed their direction. I knew how that made me feel and all of the sudden, I found myself in a position where I said to myself, "I'm doing the same thing that I hated other bands doing." That's what really turned me off. It scared me a lot. I didn't want people thinking that, in one way or another, I deceived them, or that I'm just trying to get over on them. I knew that this music is a total opposite direction than what I've done. I knew when people think of "Mike Judge," they expect *this* and then all of the sudden I'm giving them *that*.

I was really worried about that but everyone around me said, "You know there's nothing you can do about it. This is music that is coming directly from you. Every aspect of this music is coming directly from you. This is what you love. Just because it's not a part of you to do another version of Judge, it would be unfair to you to say, 'OK, since I can't give you another Judge, I can't do music anymore.'"

So when they put it to me like that, I just said, "To hell with it. If I just do my best, hopefully, they'll take it a little easy on me."

What I found out was that all of the worrying wasn't worth it. I think it took so long for me to do this, that the word was out already that I wasn't doing a hardcore record and that I was doing this acoustic thing. I think the people who liked Judge and didn't want to hear me do this didn't buy it. That's perfectly fine with me, I totally understand. But then there's some people who loved Judge and did buy the Old Smoke record and really liked it too. Then there's people who bought the Old Smoke record because it was a new band.

I don't expect anyone to be a full-fledged Old Smoke fan because I was in Judge. I just want people to like Old Smoke for what it is—it's a good band.

I think it was a great move on your part.

It wasn't even a move. I love to do music, and this is the music that I love. It wasn't like I was looking for more money playing this type of music. It was never anything like that. When I got home from a Judge gig, I'd come home and I'd bang on an acoustic guitar. That's what I did. So when it came time that someone gave me a chance to do something that I was into, that's what Old Smoke is.

So, if you wanted to get away from Judge and everything that was happening with that, why did you do the Old Smoke record on Revelation, the same label that had Judge on it? Weren't you trying to distance yourself?

I wasn't trying to distance myself. They were so many years apart. I like things that are familiar. Like I said, I don't feel I could do Old Smoke if one of the original members was gone. It wouldn't feel right to me.

Jordan to me was more than just "the guy who ran the label that Judge was on." Jordan was a guy that I hung out with. We talked a lot, he was a friend of mine. So, when he told me that he would like to put the Old Smoke record out, I never even thought, "I'm doing something for Revelation again." I thought, "Here's Jordan helping me out. He has the ways and means. He knows what he's doing." It was never like, "Jordan expressed interest, and if Jordan expressed interest, maybe there's another label that might do the same thing for me." I consider Jordan a friend, and he was willing to do it. I was happy to do it for him.

Actually, I give Jordan a lot of credit and respect for doing it because I'm sure he took a lot of shit for doing something so different. When most people talk to me about Revelation, they talk about their straight edge bands, or their hardcore bands. All of the sudden, Jordan's putting out this. As far as I'm concerned, he was taking as much of a chance as I was, so I give him credit for that. He deserves respect for that.

When I say I separated myself from that scene it wasn't because I hated what I'd done, or hated it. A lot of the best times of my life were on tour with Judge. I'm sure that some of the best times on stage that I'll ever be able to think about was when I was with Judge. It was a great time of my life, but it came a time when it just got too heavy for me. It wasn't only the band that was weighing on me, and it wasn't only the people around me and at shows that were weighing on me. It was things at home. Everything at that point was coming in on me and I wasn't ready to handle it. I didn't know how to juggle it all, and it freaked me out a little bit. I cut out a lot of things in my life, I kept cutting things out of my life until I thought I had a handle on what I had to do. I tried to get to a point where I was comfortable enough to say, "Now I can take care of business."

As far as I'm concerned, I have nothing to be ashamed of with Judge and with Youth of Today. I think both bands put out great music and influenced a lot of kids. I'm sure that out of those two bands and the music they put out, they probably put the idea in people's heads to start their own bands, and that's the main thing. There's always going to be someone else after Judge. There's always going to be another great band. I think Judge was a really important band for its time. I think they were ahead of their time, in a lot of ways, musically. I don't look back with regret on anything I do. I don't say I'm sorry. I never say I'm sorry for anything. If I fuck up, I'll admit it, but I'm not going to apologize for it.

What are some of your best and worst memories of Youth of Today and Judge?

My best memories were playing shows with Gorilla Biscuits and Bold. It was a lot of fun to be in other cities and have that be the lineup—Judge and Gorilla Biscuits, stuff like that. When we were together, it just felt so good, it felt so right. But, there were a lot of bad shows, too. It really opened my eyes to the different kinds of people that there were. There were a lot of intolerant people. Their one-sidedness used to blow me away to the point where I just couldn't believe how some people thought. I would have never

DAVE SINE

Judge at the Country Club

seen that if I had just stayed here in Jersey, or if I just stayed in New York. I experienced that from being on the road with Judge. Even though those times sucked, that was a great time, too, because not everyone gets a chance to experience that firsthand. So, those were great times. In every bad time, there was a good side of it, anyway.

I guess the worst time was the last leg of the last Judge tour. It was just about as close to hell as I could get. I just felt so alienated and alone, even in my own band. It was no one's fault but mine, it was just the way my mind was working at the time. It was things that I was getting myself caught up in outside of the band. I guess the worst time of it was not being strong enough to handle it, and letting it fall apart, not being smart enough to know how to keep it together. I do think Judge had a lot more to give, and it ended prematurely, so I pretty much blame it all on myself.

Where did the name "Judge" come from? That's a pretty heavy name.

And that's pretty much exactly how I came up with it. I wanted to piss people off. I didn't want the people who were condemning bands like Youth of Today and all the positive bands getting a laugh out of it. If they wanted to spread all this bullshit, and make up these things about the way these bands were, then I was going to give them a band that was exactly what they thought we were. I was going to shove it right in their face. I was going to give it to them. That was the beginning of Judge. I was thinking. They want something elitist, and they want something militant, then what could be more militant and elitist than calling the band "Judge?" And it worked, I caught hell for it.

So why do you keep the name now?

I keep the name now because a good friend of mine named me it, and he was the first one who started calling me "Mike Judge." It just became who I was, it was the way I was known. Even if I didn't go by "Mike Judge" anymore, I'd spend everyday saying, "Hey, that's not my name."

Was that Porcell?

Yeah.

Do you still use that name when you meet people just hanging out that have nothing to do with music? Do you introduce yourself as "Mike Judge?"

Yeah, I introduce myself as "Mike Judge" to everyone, especially cops.

The infamous Chung King Can Suck It

Chung King.

The *Chung King* record, that was going to be Judge's first full-length record which we were going to do for Revelation. I didn't necessarily quit Youth of Today. It was a mutual thing that we were breaking up. That's when I committed myself to getting Judge off the ground with Porcell.

After we recorded our *New York Crew* record, Youth of Today got back together and they were doing well. They recorded another record, and they were going to tour Europe. We wanted to record our record before they split, so that when Porcell got back from the Youth of Today tour, our record would be out and we could go out and support that.

We got together with Jordan and told him that if we could book a weekend at Chung King, we could record the full length record. Porcell was leaving on a Monday or a Sunday night. That's what we set out to do. It was a total rush job.

The people at the studio really didn't care about us. We were just stupid kids who had no right being in their studio in the first place, and that's the way they treated us, and that's the way they made the recording sound. When I finally got a copy of it, I thought the quality of it was awful. I thought the performances were too rushed. They could have been ten times better. I was really disappointed, and I was sitting on this thing for awhile.

One day Porcell called me from Europe to see what was going on, and I said, "Hey, I think this record blows. I think it sucks." We talked about it, and we picked it apart, and he agreed.

We talked to Jordan and he said, "If you think you can do something better, go for it." That's what we did. When Porcell got back, we booked time in another studio in Rhode Island. That's when we set out to record *Bringin' it Down*, which was going to be the *Chung King* record. By that time, we had a couple of new songs, we dropped a couple of songs that were on there and we re-wrote a couple of songs. We went in, and we did it right, and *Bringin' it Down* was released.

The *Chung King* record was going to be shelved, but Jordan decided to put it out as a limited thing. It was just a way to get his money back, which is understandable because he gave us the money to record that record, and we didn't like it. Then he gave us money to record the new record. It wouldn't have been fair to him, to make him eat this whole thing. So, he put it out as a limited edition called *Chung King Can Suck It*. That's pretty much that. I seem to catch a lot of shit for that one, too. People write me or call me and say, "Your record is going for a hundred bucks" or whatever, "How do I justify charging a hundred bucks?"

I don't know where they're seeing it for a hundred bucks, I have nothing to do with it. I don't make prices for record stores. What record stores want to charge, they charge. I caught a lot of hell for that.

How do you feel about straight edge and what's going on in it today? Do you follow it at all?

I really don't know. I haven't followed it. I don't know what the state of it is now. I know that at the time that I left, which was '91 or '92, I can't remember exactly, it was getting pretty strange. It was getting really militant, the hard edge thing. It's really strange. I don't know what it's like today.

Do you ever get approached by kids today who know who you are?

I run into a lot of them today. There's a bar down the road from me that puts on all ages Sunday matinees. The engineer at the studio that we work with runs the shows, so a lot of times, I stop in and hang out with him. I see a lot of kids, straight edge and all. They know who I am, but they don't approach me for whatever reason. After I leave, they'll go up to the engineer and ask him questions about me and I'll find out about it the next day. It seems that they think I'm unapproachable, or that I'm a nasty guy, or something. I don't go out of my way to say, "Hey! I'm Mike Judge, remember me?" I just try to blend into the wall and do my thing. The only time I'm up front is when Old Smoke is playing, and there's never really any hardcore or straight edge kids at Old Smoke shows.

In doing interviews for this book, you are probably the one person that everyone else is asking about. Seeing as everybody wants to know what you're doing now, what's your average everyday experience?

I'm a driver. I drive a truck and pull pretty much short little things. When I'm done with work, I come home, go to the bike shop and check on my bike because it's getting rebuilt at this time. When I get done with shooting the shit at the bike shop, I come home, grab something to eat, pick up the guitar and go to the studio and play over there, where I'm recording at this time. Right now, this is my happiest time. I love being in the studio. I love taking the idea of a song, putting it in the studio and building it up. I'm in the studio just about every night.

HILLY KRISTAL

CHRIS TOLIVER

Hilly Kristal is the owner of the legendary New York club, CBGB's. I interviewed him on 22 March 1995.

Hilly Kristal

Seeing as CBGB's was hosting most of the important straight edge shows that were going on, how did you perceive the straight edge scene that was happening in New York during the late 80's, early 90's?

Well, I don't think we had much in the 90's. I think I stopped having hardcore as such because I had too much trouble with hardcore here generally, whether it was straight edge or thrash, anything, skinheads, it just didn't matter. There were too many people who latched on to it who were very unsavory and caused trouble, and I couldn't control it. But as far as how did I perceive straight edge? I know with a lot of people, the social thing is the most important, but to me, music is the most important. So, I'm not crazy about or against any kind of music, and I don't think that the music of

Sunday matinee
8/12/84

straight edge was any different than any other hardcore music that I could see. I think their behavior was more temperate, obviously, no alcohol, no drugs, no cigarettes, which was refreshing. The followers of straight edge I don't think were any nicer or less nice. I think they were part and parcel of most of the hardcore kids. So I don't really see that much difference. Of course I didn't have any long conversations with straight edge people, so I don't know. I was mainly interested in the music, so that was important. I did like the idea, as far as I knew, of what it stood for.

A lot of the big talk around the straight edge scene was that one particular straight edge show was the cause for the end of the Sunday matinees. Is there any truth to that?

One specific show, no. It was building up. It really had nothing to do with the crowd that came, it was some people who latched on to the crowd. Well, of course they were part of the crowd, but some people who latched on to the crowd, these were people who came and beat up people. Straight edge people, is that their habit? What do you think? I don't know, but it's other people who came in, and I just couldn't have these shows anymore.

First, I had to hire 10 security people. When I started doing hardcore, the place was jammed with Agnostic Front and Murphy's Law and all those people. I had one girl sitting up front. I didn't need any security. Everybody took care of everybody else. It was really a great scene.

In the early 80s, up through '87, it started getting rougher and rougher. I had to hire people to keep others from stage diving because they'd break ankles and arms and legs. I had to stop it because I didn't want people to get hurt and also insurance reasons, too. I started getting people suing (chuckles), at least the parents did or whatever, and I had to stop that as much as I could. The more out of hand that got, the more security I had to have. The real problem I had was when these groups of people started coming around and causing fights. They'd pick on one or two kids and just beat them up. We had to always stop that. At some point, I said, "I don't need this anymore."

If the bands, especially the big bands, can't handle it themselves, group together and tell people, "We don't want any of this. You people are not welcome to hurt other people," then I didn't want to have it. That's my feeling. I'm not here to have people hurt other people. It's enough, the stage diving and controlling that, that was fine, but the other, forget it.

Ian MacKaye

Ian MacKaye is a former member of the Teen Idles, Minor Threat and Embrace. He is currently in Fugazi. The record label that he helped to found, Dischord Records, has been responsible for numerous classic records for over a decade. I spoke with Ian on 3 January 1996.

How did you get involved in music in the first place? Who were your influences? How did it come about that you were associated with straight edge? What do you think about straight edge today?

My initial interest in music was, of course, when I was a kid and really young, listening to Jimi Hendrix and the Beatles and that kind of stuff. But it quickly became clear to me that I was not talented enough to play music in the practice of a band. It seemed like professionals only, and it didn't seem to me that I would ever be able to do that. So I gave up pretty early on, but I still listened to music all the time.

I was a skateboarder from 13 to about 17. I was skating listening to a lot of Ted Nugent, which was, at the time, one of my favorite people. One of the things I liked a lot about Ted Nugent was that he was straight. Because I was totally straight as a kid, basically I didn't do anything. All of my friends were constantly getting involved in drugs and alcohol and getting fucked up, and I just wasn't interested in it. In fact, I was definitely not interested in it. So for me, skating was a perfect kind of past time because it didn't involve the party aspect of socializing—it was just going out and skating.

When I was 17 and in high school, at this point I was the only straight kid and had a reputation for being pretty outspoken about it. They used to call me "the group conscious." I was pretty much constantly being ribbed about being straight, but I had kind of an attitude about it because my feeling was that I didn't understand why I was getting so much shit for being straight. Now you have to keep in mind that this was in the context of the late 70's when virtually every teenager was smoking pot. Everyone I knew drank or smoked pot and people who were straight were really considered totally the goofiest, nerdiest motherfuckers and I was not interested in getting high. I just was not into it, and I did not appreciate the fact that I was made to feel a fool, so I responded by being aggressively straight. I was like, "Yeah, I'm fucking straight, do you got a problem with that?"

It was right around 1979 or 1978 that I first heard about punk rock, and at first it seemed incredibly nihilistic to me, the way the Sex Pistols were being portrayed in the American media. As I said, I was a major Nugent head—so the two didn't seem to really mix too well. Some close friends of mine were really getting more and more into it and they lent me some records and I started listening to it. I was really struck by the fact that this was completely non-commercial music. Most of the bands I was listening to in the beginning were from England, so they had no commercial relevance here whatsoever, even though they were popular there. Here, Fleetwood Mac was popular— so hearing a band like The Jam or Generation X was insane. It was a radical departure from what was over here.

I got into punk rock because I went to see The Cramps, and it was one of the most mind-altering experiences for me because suddenly it was what I thought rock should be. This completely cathartic show where...it was dangerous, it had this feeling of unpredictability. There was this real energy in this room that was packed with people. Things were breaking, people were standing on tables, and they were collapsing. The show was just this side of chaos. It made me think that was the way shows should be because it was about the moment. I noticed, all of the sudden, that there was this huge underground community that existed in punk rock that I had never realized.

I really felt comfortable because at this point in my life I was thinking about college and I didn't really want to go to college because I was not interested in the normal life whatsoever. I was interested in just living my own life in the way I though it should be lived. I did not want to go into the mill with all my friends, and it just seemed so planned out and predictable at that point.

Punk rock introduced me to this whole underground, and in that there was this incredible array of ideas, philosophies, approaches to life—I was challenged on all these different levels. There was philosophical, theological, sexual, political, musical...all these ideas, an incredible assortment... and there was room for everybody, and it was open to everyone. So of course it totally made sense for me to be like, " Yeah, well I'm a punk rocker and I'm straight," and no one could believe it. My friends and I would say

"Yeah, we're straight punk rockers," and it was unheard of at the time because everybody felt punk rock just meant that you were totally self-destructive and that was it.

It really upset the status quo within the punk scene because suddenly there were these little teenage, punk kids who were straight, and they didn't know what to do with us. We were going to these shows where everyone was always falling down drunk all the time. So we formed a band. The first band was called The Slinkees, and I played bass in that band. We had a song called "I Drink Milk" which was what the whole song was about. (Singing) "I don't care what people say, I drink milk everyday." We were totally anti-drug. We had a song called "Deadhead" which was about boring pot smokers. A lot of what we did was full of humor. Later on, people who read my lyrics took them way too seriously. We were having an enormous amount of fun with it, and we were definitely pissing off an enormous amount of people.

It was so easy to piss off people. At that point just put on a dumb pair of sunglasses and the world hates you. That realization that so much hatred and instant prejudice existed was such an incredible lesson to learn, man. That the world was so perverted at this point that people would just hate you for the slightest deviation in appearance. It's really changed. Appearance deviation is really not that big of a deal now I am telling you straight up, that at that time, I would be at some fucking restaurant and find myself instantly in some huge fucking fight because of the fact that I had on a pair of children's sunglasses or something. People were not prepared for that, and they had the worst attitude.

In the real world, in the big world, we were out there pissing them off because we were non-conformist punk rock kids. In the punk world, we were pissing them off because we were straight kids, and we were being made fun of. I thought that the punk world would embrace us, which it did in a way, but a lot of people made fun of us even more. The punk rockers just thought that we were hilarious and ridiculed us. They called us teeny punks, little Georgetown punks, but we fucking meant business, and were very serious about what we wanted to do.

At that point, the drinking age in Washington D.C. was 18, and we were all 16 and 17 years old Punk bands started coming into town, and we were jumping through hoops and barrels trying to get in…getting fake I.D.'s, sneaking through the back door and all this stuff. It was a real slap in the face that all these bands that we invested our beliefs in, that bands that really spoke for you, that they would come to your town and you couldn't see them because you weren't born in the right year. When you realize that this is a situation that was really predicated on the sale of alcohol it really aggravated us because we didn't even buy alcohol. It was ridiculous, the

SS DECONTROL

XXX ALL AGES XXX

FROM Washington, D.C.:

MINOR THREAT

SAT. June 12, AT 6:00 PM

XU

AND GUESTS

NEGATIVE FX, + PROLETARIAT

AT GALLERY EAST

24 EAST ST. / Near South Station Behind Hotel Essex

fact that we weren't going to buy alcohol made us not welcome at these music events, it was fucked, it was totally the wrong thing.

So we were battling that and what we found out being straight and singing about it, that there were these other kids who were straight that started coming out of the woodwork, who were just, like, "we just want to drink Coke —we're not trying to get fucked up—we're just goofy punk rockers like you." We were all just goofy punk rockers together, and we sort of formed this family.

The Slinkees became the Teen Idles after we changed singers. We still did the song "I Drink Milk" and I was writing songs like "Sneakers," which was about kids acting older than they were. Those songs were the groundwork for the next band, which was Minor Threat. We were trying to get shows. The Teen Idles went to California where we got two shows, one in Los Angeles and one in San Francisco. Six of us took a fucking Greyhound bus across the country with just our guitars and drumsticks and managed to get on these two shows. Henry Rollins was our roadie and we went out there together. He grew up in Washington D.C. He was our main roadie guy.

We were in San Francisco, and we played a place called Mabuhay Gardens. They asked if we were going to drink and we said, "no," and they put an "X" on our hands. So we came back to Washington D.C. and went to this nightclub, the 9:30, and said, "Hey look, we're not going to drink and we will put this "X" on our hand. If you see us drinking, you can throw us out forever. We are not going to drink, we just came to see the music."

They were in a peculiar position, there is a loophole in the law in D.C.—it says that minors are not allowed to be in bars, but there is also a law in D.C. that says if you're going to sell alcohol then you must sell food. So technically in Washington D.C. there is no such place as a bar, there are only restaurants. The reason clubs were not admitting people underage was that they knew the penalty for serving alcohol to minors was far more severe than discriminating against them by not letting them in. The second reason was if you have a bar, and a kid can't drink, they're not going to buy a drink and it would be an economic faux pas to let them in. So we found out about this law and went down to this club, and we basically said "Hey, legally we can be in here, but we know we can't drink. So we're not going to drink, and to prove it we are going to put these X's on our hands. They dug it and said, "OK." So we did it, and it worked.

The Teen Idles' first single, which was the first record that our label, Dischord, ever put out, the cover has a pair of hands, crossed, with X's drawn on them. Now at the time, it wasn't supposed to signify straight edge—it was supposed to signify kids. It was about being young punk rockers, and that was the ear markings of it. It represents youth. The markings on the hands were just what kids in

Washington D.C. had to deal with just to see music, to be free.

So then I was playing bass for these bands, and I was writing a lot of the words, and my songs were about teenagers, and this other guy, Nathan, was singing them, and I really wanted to sing. The Teen Idles broke up, and I said, "I want to sing, I don't want to play bass anymore. I've written these lyrics, and I want to sing them."

At that point, things were getting a lot more aggressive in town and were heated and a lot more violent and a lot more angry. The music and the bands were a lot more aggressive and angry as well. Minor Threat was definitely a lot more angry than Teen Idles, and I just started writing songs. Jeff and I, Jeff was the drummer, were trying to figure out a name for the new band. I wanted just to name the band "Straight," because we were going to push this thing even more. We didn't end up using it for the name of the band, but I ended up writing a song about it, and it was basically a song which was, in my mind, championing the individual. The idea that, "Yeah, I don't get fucked up, but I am a person, and I am an individual and legitimate in that I don't think that I should be punished or made fun of or ridiculed or dismissed just because I don't go along with the status quo." I was fucking pissed off at that time in my life. I'm still pissed off, but I just have different ways of dealing with that. At that point I was really angry at the way Teen Idles were ridiculed, my friends, this family of punk rockers that I belonged to, the way we were being treated...so we just came back even more aggressive. That is when I wrote the song "Straight Edge," and people picked up on it insanely. People would sing along, they were amped, they were totally pumped up on it.

When the Teen Idles record came out, people bought it all over the country, there were really regional scenes at that time. There was the Washington D.C. scene, there was not much of a New York scene at all. New York was trying to wake up from its late 70's, English junkie phase. But there was Detroit, Los Angeles and San Francisco—we were in contact with people from all these different scenes, and there were people we could relate to in all these other towns. The next two bands that got into the whole straight edge stuff were, obviously, 7 Seconds and SS Decontrol.

I met Kevin (Seconds) in 1982 or 1983, and they were really a great fucking band. I remember Kevin drank Pepsi all the time. It was sort of a running joke because I drank Coke all the time and Kevin drank Pepsi. A lot of soda was being ingested at this point. Kevin was really into the straight edge thing, and I loved his band.

Meanwhile, up in Boston, SS Decontrol appeared and Al (Barille) and those guys were way more hard core, way more aggressive. It was kind of funny because they had a really heavy pose. They came off really like bad guys. They were sort of thugish and big, and everyone wore black and headbands, and they had read about straight edge and taken in to militant extremes—whereas we were straight in Washington D.C. I mean, we were bad kids, we got into fights and stuff, but we were nice and sort of goofy.

We didn't go out looking to kick someone's ass all the time. Even though there was all this talk about gangs and straight edge kids in Washington D.C. knocking beers out of people's hands it was total bullshit. People who were involved with Minor Threat and the D.C. hardcore scene, people who were supportive of the straight edge scene, were totally not straight at all, they just were into it and supported the idea that kids should see shows and that alcohol should not be the deciding factor. They respected our decision, and they were our friends. It was more about respecting each others individual choices, rather than getting totally obsessed with distractions.

When I met Al and them they were much more on the militant tip. Their thing was much more intense on that level. It was kind of weird because it wasn't something that I was really into. They were my friends and I like those guys, I think Al is a great person. I respect him quite a bit, but it was a different thing where they were coming from. If you have ever seen a Minor Threat video, you know that there is a certain light heartedness to it. It wasn't all really grim. Whereas, SSD was pretty grim. They were really hard.

I think that a lot of the New York scene, like Ray (Cappo) and all them the Connecticut crew—was more picking up on what Boston was about. I think SSD had a much larger impact on them. I think it appealed to them much more—it was tougher. When I first heard Youth of Today, I thought, "Wow, this is like SSD."

7 Seconds was way more melodic than the New York hardcore bands. Kevin is a melody freak, and he loves it—even if you listen to their earliest record, even their demo tapes. I remember when I first started talking with Kevin, and he sent me a bunch of tapes, of just him and his brother playing in his bedroom. They were fucking great. They are fucking great tapes, I can still listen to them and enjoy them. They are just so melodic—he was so into Sham 69—as I was, too. Sing-songy kind of stuff.

That was the biggest thing for me, I wanted nothing more than a room full of people singing together. I thought that would be a great way for people to meet, to come together and do something. It was such a great feeling. If people could just get involved in a gig, then they could forget other stuff. I don't want to get into a severe analysis of it, but it was a real important thing in my opinion. All of these kids having a place to go, and to get together in a room and to create something that has so much power. To me, that's what music is all about. It's this opportunity for a band and a audience to conspire electric moments. You can't buy those things. They are not consumer items. They are the result of a lot of combined efforts. It is a totally amazing moment, and it can be reached, but it takes work.

Minor Threat toured and played all over the country. We played two really big tours and did a bunch of smaller ones. We played New York quite a bit and all of the sudden found ourselves in the middle of a big deal. People were really down with it.

As a matter of fact, last night I had a friend in town, she was one of the original Philadelphia BYO people—BYO was the Better Youth Organization. They were doing gigs, it was sort of a bunch of different groups in all the different cities, punk groups who were putting on gigs and getting active and putting out records and stuff. There was the BYO label in Los Angeles, but then they started other chapters of BYO. This woman, who is an old friend of mine, was living in Philadelphia, and put on a gig at Buff Hall in New Jersey. It was Minor Threat, SS Decontrol, Agnostic Front from NY and Flag of Democracy from Philadelphia. It was one of the first really big meetings of everyone on the East Coast getting together. We watched a video of that show last night, and it was really weird.

Actually, the night of that show I got hit by a car. I was standing outside of the gig—it was a pretty bad neighborhood, but everyone was out skating and stuff. Al from SSD pulled up in their black van, and I walked up to talk to him. I was standing at his door talking to him, but there was plenty of room on the street for cars to pass and stuff. I looked down the street and saw this car and said to this kid who was skating, "Hey you'd better get out of the street." This car was coming fucking fast. I squeezed myself as close to the van as I could to give the driver even more room—even though there was plenty for him to pass—and he just centers his car and hits the van head on with me just standing there, totalled Al's van, totally cracks this one kid in the head and totally knocks me 10 feet. We still played the show that night though!

Agnostic Front was kind of down with us. I think of those guys as being one of the prototypes of the New York straight hardcore bands, even though I don't think they were ever straight edge with the same gusto as Ray and all them.

Minor Threat was together for about three years, and we played all over the god damn place. More and more people were coming out and you saw a lot more "X's." I guess the movement had sort of started, but in my mind I wasn't interested in it being a movement. It ran conversely to my initial idea that it was a concert of individuals, as opposed to a movement. I felt like a movement had to have some sort of aim. The only aim that I could think of that the straight edge movement ever had was to try and get people to stop drinking or whatever. But from my point of view, if someone tried to get me to start drinking, I'd be fucking pissed. What I look for in life is people who I respect, living and teaching by example, and I trust that human beings can make up their minds and make the right decision for their own lives. It's not my fucking business to be telling people what to do with their own lives.

One of the more aggravating aspects of the straight edge thing, is that later on, people really got in their minds from reading about the straight edge thing is that I must be some sort of fucking fascist and that I was totally intolerant. Lord knows there was all those sort of weird offshoots of the straight edge thing, like people who are homophobic or people who are pro-life or ultra-vegans or whatever. There are all these different things going on and all of the sudden, power was a big part of it.

From my point of view, I am not interested in intolerance. I am interested in respect for people's decisions in their lives. I have my own opinions, and I live my own fucking life by those opinions. If someone leaned on me, told me what to do, I would tell them to fuck off. People who did that really pissed me off.

I wasn't a vegetarian until 1984 or so, and I had vegetarian friends who gave me a lot of shit, and it made me really fucking angry. It made me feel like they did not respect me. I had a couple of people that I really respected and really loved, and they never gave me a hard time. They just lived, and I learned from them.

I think that vegetarianism was a logical step for straight edge. For me, it was logical. To me, it's a process. The idea in my life, of the process that is, is re-examining things given to me and seeing if they work and constantly working to try and make myself better—do a better job in the world. So it just seemed to make sense, it was logical. I can remember Ray (Cappo)—and he may dispute this, but I swear to God that I had this conversation with him—Youth of Today were playing The 9:30 Club, and I had heard of these guys. The New York straight edge thing had started up, so I went down to see them, sort of to figure out what the fuck was up. So I met up with Ray, and he goes, "What's this about the vegetarian thing being straight edge?" I swear to God we had this conversation. I had done this interview in Flipside, and Ray said to me "That's insane, what does that have to do with being straight edge?" I told him that I was speaking about my own ideas on straight edge and how it made sense, as did the vegetarian thing. It was like I was making up new rules or something, which I wasn't trying to do. I was just speaking my mind. It is funny now, of course, since Ray is a Krishna now.

The militancy of the New York thing was pretty intense. At that time I was in a band called Embrace, which I think, at first, threw a lot of people. It was totally not what they were expecting. The thing about Embrace, which I don't think most people understood, we were entrenched in a war to reclaim a community down here.

In the mid 80s, the skinhead thing really, really set in. The Cro Mags were happening and the whole skinhead thing was really kicking in down here. At the gigs skinheads were just being mother fuckers and picking on people for the dumbest reasons, beating them up for wearing red shirts or whatever the fuck—all this stupid moronic stuff. We—and in "we" I mean the older punk community, the people who were around in the early 80's—found ourselves in a position where we were totally unhappy. We thought that these shows were disgusting and that this community was fucked because you go to a show and everyone just ends up fighting and getting beat up. These people were morons. My friends and the original punk kids started to drop out because they were finding it dumb and no longer wanted to be a part of it anymore. We all got together and talked about it. We decided to reclaim this, but instead of trying to reclaim the punk scene, we decided to start our own fucking punk scene, another one. That's the way Revolution Summer started.

Revolution Summer was the name that we placed on the summer of 1985. We decided everybody has to get a band and start playing and create this new scene, a new community within this bigger community. We were going to create this new fucking scene, and we fucking did it. It was Rites of Spring, Lunch Meat (which later on became Soulside), Mission Impossible, Embrace, Gray Matter, Beefeater, Kingface, Fire Party—all these bands, it was a conspiracy. We were like "Everyone's got to start a band, and we have to create something new." It wasn't that we were going to try and fix the skinheads, not try and take anything away from them, we're just going to create something new that they are going to hate. The reason they are going to hate it is because we're not going to act like a bunch of tough, fucking macho assholes. Skinheads hated Embrace because they wanted Minor Threat. It just really turned them off. There was this song, "Said Gun" that was directly about the whole skinhead thing. I had a lot to say then.

A lot of people were questioning me about the straight edge

TIM OWEN

Ian MacKaye, Fugazi

JORDAN COOPER

Porcell (guitar) and Ray Cappo, Youth of Today

DAVE MANDEL

Kevin Seconds

CHRIS TOLIVER

Sammy Siegler

Ray Cappo in India

DAVE MANDEL

Richie Birkenhead

BETH LAHICKEY

Gus Peña with tattoo

BECKY'S MOM

Becky Tupper and Ray Cappo, senior prom

BETH LAHICKEY

Jordan Cooper

LAURA PORTO

Glynis, Anthrax

MARC HANOU

Walter, Porcell, Ray (Youth of Today) and Jordan (Revelation), on a tram in Amsterdam

Bold in Disneyland

Gorilla Biscuits, Safari Club, Washington DC, Winter 1990

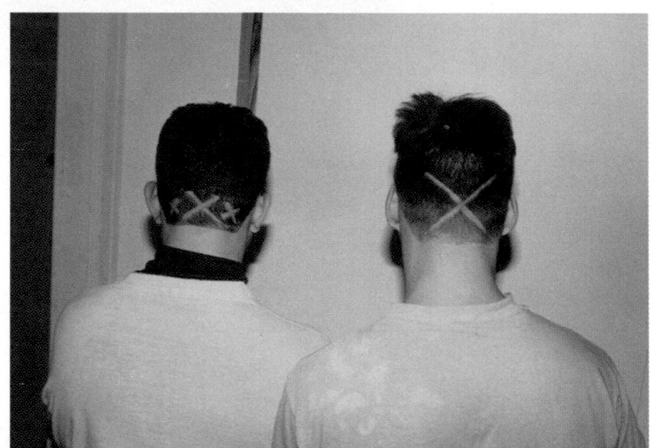

Sammy and Porcell

GREG METZ

Mike Judge live

DAVE MANDEL

Supertouch

TIM OWEN

Porcell with Shelter

TIM OWEN

Walter and Tom with Quicksand

JORDAN COOPER

Walter, Ray and Martin (tour manager for European tour, 1989)

CHRIS TOLIVER

Walter Schriefels, Gorilla Biscuits

CHRIS TOLIVER

Civ—Charlie, Walter and Arthur, Limelight NYC, 5/21/95

DAVE MANDEL

Mike Hartsfield with Outspoken, Simi Valley 1994

JORDAN COOPER

7 Seconds, Albany

BECKY TUPPER

Youth of Today with Glynis and Walter. Albany, NY

thing and there was a lot of pressure on me. The people in Embrace didn't want to be known as a straight edge band—it was just too overbearing. It kind of, not trivialized it, but just sort of formatted it. To me, classifications make you dismissable. If there is a name on you, then they can easily file you into a drawer, and we didn't want to be filed into the straight edge drawer. Punk rock was kind of amorphous. It was big enough, and even hardcore to some degree, and it covered enough ground. But you get into a goth band or an Oi band or a mod band or a ska band or a straight edge band or krishnacore or whatevercore. It's gotten so absurd now.

At the time though, those guys really didn't want to be known as the next Minor Threat. At the same time, it was important for me to let people know that I was not backing down from my original point of view. I think in "No More Pain," I addressed that. A lot of people I knew who were straight early on really changed a lot. For me, it was never a fucking joke. I was never kidding around about it. I know that for me it was always important when people I respected were consistent. There were some people that I really respected who later on did things that were totally hypocritical, and it really kind of fucked me up a little bit. It didn't destroy me, but it did fuck me up a little bit. Already by 1983 or 1984 there were so many rumors about me being a junkie or whatever—these rumors just go on and on and on. I wanted to respond to it, but I didn't want to be pandering to it—so I wrote and sang about it a little bit.

The New York straight edge kids at the time, I don't think thought much of Embrace—but I think they respected me. Later on, I know that a lot of people got into that band. But at the time we were playing, let me tell you, we were not a favorite band. It was hard at shows—we never really played out of Washington—well we played Baltimore once and that's about it. I think we only did about 14 shows.

We played our first show in, I think, August of 1985, and we played our last show in March of 1986. The reason we broke up, the reason the band didn't work, is that three other people in the band were in another band together called Faith, which my brother, Alec, sang for—I think this was 1981 through 1983 or so. So Chris, Mike and Ivor had already been in a band together and already gone through major throw down fights. It was kind of happenstance that we all actually ended up in a band together. It wasn't like I went to them and said, "Let me sing for you." It was more that all the bands had broken up and everyone was looking to get bands and I was playing with Mike for a little while, then I was playing with Chris for a little while, then Mike, Chris and I played with another drummer and then that drummer quit and Ivor was looking for something. So all of the sudden it was me with Faith.

It was doomed from the beginning—those guys really had a

problem with each other and it drove me crazy because I wanted to fucking play music and the internal conflict was so intense. I remember we had a show in Boston booked, and I had gone to England for about three weeks. I told those guys that they had better practice while I was gone because we were going to play in Boston two days after I got back. So I got back and they had not fucking practiced at all, and I was like, "Fuck this." These guys didn't like each other, and I got sick of being the kingpin, the one to keep them together, so that was the end of the band. Actually, it took quite a bit of cajoling to get that record out because initially they didn't want the tapes to come out. I really wanted them to come out because I had worked hard on those lyrics, and I thought they were good songs.

And then Fugazi. With Fugazi, the straight edge thing gets picked up on so much. If you're a writer and you write about music, you know that it's impossible to write about music, and it is much easier to write about the pomp and circumstance around it. I think that straight edge is just something that is easy to write about. So I think that's why it gets a lot of press and a lot of ink. Of course, we kind of get tied into it all the time, but I don't think that we are part of the straight edge movement so much. Maybe we are in a weird way, I don't know. A lot of the people I have met who are straight edge, who are really down with the movement concept, are really cool and are trying to do good stuff with their lives. A lot of people don't give those kids a break because they consider them just stupid straight edge kids. My feeling is that when you are a kid, you are having a tough fucking time, and anything you can do to get through it without getting totally tripped up is totally OK by me.

"To me, that's what music is all about. It's this opportunity for a band and a audience to conspire electric moments."

People have asked me how it feels to have created this monster, and I tell them I don't think that I actually created it. It is not as though I was the first key holder, I just happen to be one of a whole line. Secondly, if I did anything to inspire kids, I am glad that I inspired them to be straight. I'd much rather inspire them to do that than to go shoot people or to shoot heroin. I am glad I'm not Lou Reed, or whatever. I like Lou Reed, don't get me wrong. I respect a lot of what he did. The junkie aesthetic is all good and well for intellectual society, but there are a lot of people who follow things on the fashion tip and sometimes don't make it back.

Of course, the same could be said for the straight edge thing. Some of these guys, these hard edge guys, or whatever they are called, it is just ridiculous, it is really fucked up. I remember reading these lyrics that were so totally over the top, so extreme like, "We give you lessons about veganism and the right to life, and if you don't accept these lessons then waive your rights, that we can kill you." What was up with that? Who the fuck wrote that?

Who did write that?

It was literature in Memphis that I saw four or five years ago. I think it is part of a record—I think an insert of a record, but I cannot think of who—I have so many fucking records. I couldn't believe it, and I felt really ashamed that if anything I had ever done had come down to this. This is so completely the opposite of everything I ever wanted in life. I really felt bad. I read this Canadian fanzine that actually blamed me for it, and I blew up—I just couldn't fucking believe it. I made the cardinal sin of actually writing a letter to a fanzine. You never should respond to a criticism. If you get dissed in a fanzine, just forget about it. Don't ever respond to it because they get back to you and respond with the last word. But I decided to respond and shouldn't have done that because then the guy really went off on a really major rant about how much he hated me. But the hardest thing was that it was not a good situation.

A lot of the religious stuff—there is a lot of Christian straight edge stuff and, obviously, there is a lot of Krishna straight edge stuff—I don't really have an interest in either one of those things. I don't really believe in the right way, theologically I don't think that there is a right way. I think that people make decisions in their lives, they have to deal with it, and if their spirituality is a way to deal with that, then that's cool, but I am not interested in proselytizing, and I am not interested in being sold a religious package. I respect people's religions, but not if it is for sale.

What do you think the next progression of straight edge could be?

That's a good question, I don't know where it could go next. I bet that it could tie in with rap. The rap thing and the straight edge thing—with skaters—already kind of crossed over. The rap aesthetic, hip hop aesthetic, is straight edge now. I am surprised that there is not more rap-straight edge stuff. One thing about straight edge I'll say, and I'm sure you're clearly aware of—that this is something that is extremely "boy" oriented.

By boys, for boys and about boys?

Right, but that was another element of it early on. That was another element of it for me, early on. When I first got into punk rock it was open to everybody, the women and the girls and the boys and everybody were all working together, and women played a big, big part in the early punk scene in my mind. When the Minor Threat thing was happening, things were getting more and more angry, and it seemed at the time, really like we were under attack. Our community was under attack, fighting all the time. It got more and more aggressive, and there was this cycle of things. I am not removing myself from this—I was definitely fucking fighting. It just seemed like things were getting more and more insane, more violent. What I started to notice was this drift—women at the front of the stage drifting towards the back of the room and eventually out of the fucking room. That was the other element of Revolution Summer, which was that what happened to punk rock was violence and boys, and we felt like women played too much of a crucial part of our community to be just dismissed like that. That was what Rites of Spring and Embrace were about—our whole thing was like to bring women back to the front of the stage again. Stop with the fucking stage diving, stop with the violence, and let everybody get to the front and have a good time. That was a really big part of it. But I guess I understand why straight edge is such a boy thing. I am often surprised by how many women were involved with it. A lot of fanzines were done by women and a lot of shows were put on by women. But there weren't a lot of women on the stage. I was trying to actually think of a single, straight edge woman singer. I couldn't think of one.

Washington has had women in bands for a while now. In the early years, it was harder for them, community support-wise. It took Dischord a long time. We had one band in 1981 that this woman, Toni, played bass for, but it took quite a while for us to start getting women in bands. Now there are so many bands with women in them you don't even think twice about it anymore. That's the way it should be.

I think the straight edge thing really appeals to a lot of jocks too. Which is weird again because I am not a jock. I was never down with that kind of stuff. It's weird, I don't know what the fuck I am. I am not really sure where I fit because I'm not a computer geek, not a jock, just sort of a normal guy.

People over the years were so hardcore, fucking jump down my throat because they feel I am not vocal enough or hard enough. I had guys saying, "I can't believe you fucking play places that sell alcohol, " or, "I can't believe that you play places where people smoke cigarettes." I had this one kid say to me—I was outside the van drinking an iced tea—and he says to me, "I can't believe you're drinking ice tea." I was like, "What?" and he said, "In my book, caffeine is a drug." I said, "Fuck you." These kind of people were so hard and so ready to attack me because they didn't think I was hard enough—where the fuck are they now? I'm not trying to be so smug about it. But I am 33 now, and I don't give a fuck about all the rumors. I don't drink. I don't smoke. I'm not into dope. I don't do it. I never did it. It's not a fucking game. It's not a joke for me. I never had done it. I drank when I was twelve. I never smoked pot in my life. I don't like the fact that I constantly have to pull down my pants to show people that my underwear is clean. That annoys me. But I understand why they do it, and if they're polite, then I might just pull them down a little bit. But if they are not polite about it, then I will tell them just to fuck themselves.

They need to respect me as a person.

The Bad Brains, to me, were like the godfathers. H.R. and them were like my mentors and really an important part of the unity concept. The 1980 version of the Bad Brains, to me, were the greatest band of all time. The early demo tapes were the best, coolest fucking things on earth. Our first New York show was opening up for the Bad Brains. It was at Irving Plaza. The Bad Brains were the greatest.

I met John (Bloodclot) in 1981 or 1980 at a Bad Brains show in Washington D.C. There was this kid sitting on this bench outside the Wilson Center. He was just hanging out, and we went up and talked to him because he was a punk rocker. If you saw a punk rocker then, you talked to him. So we were talking, and he told me he just went AWOL. Later on, he went to jail for that AWOL stuff. I knew Harley when he was in the Stimulators, I haven't seen him in years. He was a tough kid.

Youth of Today, they were all right, they didn't do much for me. I liked Supertouch. I think Revelation put out a compilation with one of their songs on it.

"Searchin' for the Light"

Yeah, that was a great song. That was cool. I thought the Gorilla Biscuits were pretty good. That whole thing, though, didn't really do much for me. They were all so formulaic, going for the mosh part in the middle. I felt like Minor Threat was a great band, I like the songs a lot. It's been twelve years, so I am removed from it. With Embrace, people would ask me why I was doing it, and I said, "I don't want to do another Minor Threat."

I kind of felt like the kids in New York and what was going on then—I can dig why they were doing it—but I was also like "Don't cheat yourselves of creativity." Break it out—do something more. They ended up defining a new sound, but to me it is heavily based on SSD and Minor Threat. You wanna know who else was an important band? Verbal Assault. Pete lives in Seattle. He was really a big part of all of that too. I produced a record for those guys—the *Learn* album. Most of those bands, the later New York bands, were okay, but I wouldn't play their records. I know that they were speaking to a community, but it wasn't really speaking to me. It was weird to me to hear it because it sounded so much like Minor Threat to me.

BETTER YOUTH ORGANIZATION PRESENTS. .

DIRECT FROM WASHINGTON D.C.

CHANNEL 3

AGRESSION

SUICIDAL TENDENCIES

AMERICA'S HARDCORE

$6.00

SAT. APRIL 2, 7.00 P.M.

ROLLER WORKS

9400 OSO AVE. (IN CHATSWORTH) info: 701-1053 or 654-0214

Take The Ventura Frwy. West To Winnetka. Go North 3 Miles, Then Left On Plummer, & Left On Oso.

PLUMMER
OSO
WINNETKA
CORBIN
NORDHOFF
ROSCOE
VENTURA FRWY
SAN DIEGO FRWY
N

Susan Martinez

Susan was another of my early friends in hardcore. I used to stay with her in New Haven, Connecticut on the weekends and it was she who first introduced me to the Anthrax.

Susan and Beth

Minor Threat, 7 Seconds and SSD records spun on my turntable, but it was never more than music to me. The re-emergence, popularity and progression of straight edge bands in the mid to late 80's was astounding. All of the sudden, handfuls of boys I had hung out with for a few years regrouped or formed new bands whose popularity broke out of the tri-state area. My personal involvement with that phase of straight edge was purely as a spectator. I had friends with X's on their hands and others with beers in their hands. At the time, I was too interested in those things straight edge kids denounced to ever consider enlisting in the "youth crew."

I don't remember the first hardcore show I ever saw but can remember the first I ever listened to. Black Flag was playing at Toad's Place in New Haven, Connecticut in the winter of 1983. It was not an all ages club or show. As hard as I tried, I could not get in. I ended up standing by the back door and just listening for half an hour or so.

All ages shows started creeping up on New Haven. At a show in 1984, my friends and I met a bunch of skateboarding boys that were in a band called Violent Children who told us about an all ages club in Stamford. Shortly thereafter, I frequently started taking 50-minute train rides to see a variety of bands play on a four-inch-high stage, located in the basement of an art gallery.

I probably spent more hours at The Anthrax than I did in school. The Anthrax was unlike any other club I have ever been to. Perhaps because of the size of both the building and the Connecticut scene at the time, it was a place where everyone knew each other's names or at least recognized their faces. There were no barriers between the bands that played, and shows were only $3 or $4.

There was a refrigerator filled with sugary beverages with only a cigar box on top for kids to put their quarters into on the honor system. After a while, this system did not work too honorably anymore, and I was inducted as the Anthrax's first "juicy—juice girl."

I met a lot of people through the almighty hardcore network which meant going to New York City, Albany, Poughkeepsie, Providence, Baltimore, Boston and other places to see friends, bands or just hang out. My most vivid memories of those days have nothing to do with straight edge bands. I have seen thousands of shows in the past 14 years—and a lot of them have merged into brief, fuzzy memories. I guess it's more associations of feelings connected to memories rather than the actual visualizations themselves. I bet the straight edge kids remember so much more.

I saw Youth of Today play their first show. Honestly, I guess I just didn't think much of it—just boys I knew with a plethora of catchy choruses. Because they were friends, and because we shared many mutual friends, I ended up seeing a lot of Youth of Today shows. When I lived in D.C., I went to go see them at Rock Against Reagan during the summer of 1986. I was psyched to see some familiar, warm faces but wasn't prepared when kids starting asking Ray for an autograph.

"... it's as though corporate America is now embracing the very things they once scorned us for—and it feels like a big kick in the ass."

When Jordan began Revelation Records, I helped him a lot on the exchange system. I stuffed WarZone 7"s in exchange for Naples Pizza. Though it seemed I always had more paper cuts than pizza slices.

Being a girl at shows was extremely alienating at times. Girl bands or even girls in bands were so rare, and even then, mocked by boys. Look at pictures from old shows; the majority of the immediate audience around the stage was male. I rarely left the front of the stage at shows and remember punching and/or kicking more than a couple of boys who groped me.

As in any subculture, there are reflections of mainstream politics that ripple through its boundaries. It freaked out a lot of boys that girls could be aggressive, or have energy, or be in the pit or jump off a stage. Girls were displayed lots of times by boys as ornaments or prizes. We were not taken seriously for who we were, but by what we looked like. Yes…I am making generalizations, and there were exceptions, but it was fairly common. Girls were always the supporting cast, never the stars. That is one aspect of the old days that I was psyched to see change.

I guess one of the most intriguing parts of the hardcore scene all together, for me, (besides the music itself) was that it wasn't something that Teen Beat or MTV was trying to cram down my throat. Hardcore wasn't a concept created by a corporate executive, and it wasn't accessible to everyone. It was created by kids, net-

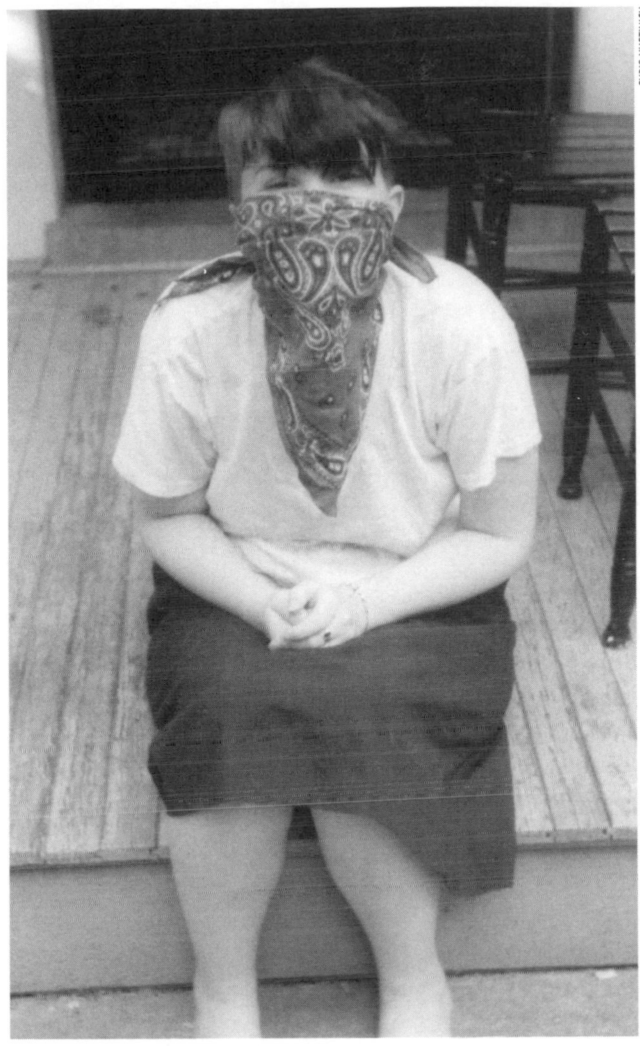

Susan Martinez in Baltimore, MD

worked by kids and for kids. There was no bigger scheme to appeal to, and best of all—it was all ours.

I remember getting stuff thrown at me on the city bus because my hair was fire engine red or purple or whatever—this was only 10, 11 years ago. Granted, I wasn't the only teenager to discover creative fun with vegetable dyes—but to those other kids on the bus, or in the mall, or on the train or whatever—it made me different than them, and I was happy for the distinction. In retrospect, I guess I never wanted to play by the rules as to what a teenager was and with the hardcore scene I could safely burrow myself into a community that adults were rarely a part of.

My passion for hardcore began to lessen halfway through college as other interests broadened. I still listen to some of my old records—and even re-invested in a handful of them on CD. Musically, my taste has expanded, and I have more of an interest in other kinds of music. I still make an effort to see certain bands play when they are around. I must admit it is strange to see some of them infiltrate the mainstream. Don't misunderstand me, I think it is wonderful that they continue on. After all these DIY years, they deserve the opportunity for growth, expansion and exposure on a larger scale. However, it's as though corporate America is now embracing the very things they once scorned us for—and it feels like a big kick in the ass. Seeing the Bad Brains reunite to be on Madonna's label floored me.

Last year, I worked at a record store within an all ages club called the Tune Inn in New Haven, which gave me an opportunity to become acquainted with today's straight edge scene. It is great to see young kids with so much energy about music. However, I have encountered a lot of closed minds within that lot (and, oddly, an abundance of X's on 13-year-old hands holding cigarettes).

Yes, it's a personal choice to label yourself straight edge, and it is encouraging that there are circles where kids don't feel pressure to drink or use drugs. However, I feel that it also can limit their choices and options because they are conforming to a standard they did not create. For many kids today, being straight edge means listening and seeing mostly straight edge bands, wearing certain clothes, eating specific food and having particular friends. This secludes them from experiencing so much that doesn't require them to grab a bong. I guess it bothers me that kids continue to label themselves in order to fit in somewhere.

I overhear (and have argued with) a lot of kids who are upset because they feel their hardcore heroes have fallen by either selling out to a major label or because they are no longer straight edge. I feel those opinions aren't that well thought out and are rather brash. First of all, I haven't seen anyone in those bands who have gotten signed to major labels denounce their roots or turn their backs. They also aren't 16 years old anymore and I think it rocks that they are able to make a living by creating music. Secondly, I find it really hard to hold someone accountable for a position they held when they were 15 or 16 years old People change and grow in different directions. Although I feel fine about who I was when I was a teenager, I am glad she is not all of who I am now.

Dan O'Mahony

DAVE SINE

No For An Answer at the Whiskey, CA 1989

Dan O'Mahony was the singer for No For An Answer, one of the first West Coast straight edge bands. He recently published Three Legged Race, *a personal account dealing with his life since his straight edge days. We spoke on 25 September 1995.*

I went to my first show in September of '82. It was sort of a weird situation where my friends and I always dressed like punk rockers and stared at everybody mean and sort of tried to play the part, but there was really nothing behind it. Another guy at the high school that I was going to asked me to take him to a show because he had never gone to one before, and he was afraid. He knew I knew what I was doing because I went to shows all the time, which I really didn't. And that was sort of my baptism.

Where was that?

It was in a classroom at the University of California, Irvine. It was a Social Distortion show. The woman I went with got hit in the head by Mike Ness's guitar. Every time people fell down on the dance floor, the whole room ran over and kicked them. This gang in Orange County rushed through the door and knocked over the table that was taking the money and beat everybody up and scared the hell out of me. It made me never want to go to another show again. But somehow I got talked into going to a Vandals show a few months later,

where the Vandals threw a rat in a blender and threw it all over the crowd, and I never wanted to go to another show again. And then I got talked into it again, and I guess it just wore me down.

I wanted to be allowed to have fun and have some reason for trying to strike terror into the hearts of those around me. So I started going regularly. The next thing I knew, I started running into slightly more intelligent bands and started meeting more of the people around me and getting caught up more in the philosophical angle of the thing. I would say that's when I sort of developed a regular diet of hardcore.

The first thinking band, the band that sort of put me in the direction that showed itself when I started doing music, was 7 Seconds, who I saw for the first time maybe in—I have no idea what year. I know I was pretty young. They were still a three-piece. Kevin was really the first singer I ever saw who talked and seemed to be vocal about some slightly more constructive things. Some of the things that I actually hated going on around me were things that I heard him chanting down right there in front of me. That had a pretty big effect on me.

What were some other bands that got you interested?

Well, the funny thing is, is I remember going to shows the year that Minor Threat came out to California and laughing about everybody getting excited about this American band. Up until 7 Seconds, I really only considered British punk to be valid. I was right there while the band that probably had the biggest impact on me was playing, laughing at their existence, and really not getting into them until maybe a year or two after they were gone.

To this day, I would say Minor Threat has probably had a bigger impact on me than any hardcore band. In terms of providing an emotional release and finding a place to vent sort of darker aspects of my personality, Black Flag was a huge issue with me too. But Minor Threat philosophically was probably the first band to really angrily vent my attitude at the time towards chemicals and things and towards the basic dependency diseases that were ruining my family's life.

How did you get into straight edge?

Well, the weird thing is "straight edge" was just sort of a word that sort of jumped on my back. You're a kid, and unless you fall in with the wrong types, you may very well make it all the way to your twenties without ever experimenting with chemicals at all. You may be at a pretty responsible age before you actually step towards that stuff. I mean, I came from a family where my mother was a relatively responsible human being, but her smoking killed her. My father is a recovering alcoholic and recovering heroin addict. My sister is a heroin addict. All the people around me were just sort of crumbling as a result of their involvement with unhealthy chemical input. It was just real easy for me to say, "God, no, not me." Coming into the hardcore scene, there was really no place for me to vent that. When it did sort of come along or when it became something I was aware of, it was almost a word that was hung on me before I ever really embraced it.

I can remember during my junior year in high school somebody having an "X" on their hand. I guess this would

JOSHUA LANE STANTON

No For An Answer

be 1983 or '84. I had no idea what it meant, even though I had already started telling people that I was straight edge when they would ask me if I wanted a drink. I had heard about straight edge via Minor Threat, but I didn't own their records. I didn't really hang out with people who labeled themselves as such. I remember feeling like such a fool when somebody explained to me what that "X" meant. It was never anything I really ran out and became a part of and educated myself on, so much as that it was a word that applied to the way I felt personally as a result of what was going on in my family.

Did you ever fully embrace it and call yourself that outright? Well, sure. At every Uniform Choice show, you could count on the bands getting in fights with the skinheads in the audience and with whatever troublemakers were there. A very clear, very obvious "us against them" mentality started to form. I'd say I started to wear the word as a badge. I started to mark up my hands and started to growl and keep the shaven head and try and look as muscular and angry as possible around people. The point at which I would say I was wearing what would be called fashionable straight edge wear and openly embracing the philosophy was a time in my life when I was trying to be confrontational, when I was trying to push people towards the outside. And it's a fact that labeling yourself and openly embracing symbols of some kind of group does invariably push everybody who is outside that group away. Eventually, it left me to feel a real distaste for the word, not so much for the philosophy or the whole attitude towards chemicals, but towards the group mentality.

I don't think the mutual support and group support really does anything to help a person, to help an individual build character. I think a person's got to stand on their own, and any time they claim to be a part of anything, that's not what is going on, at least from where I stand. Again, that doesn't really address the whole issue of drugs, that just really addresses the tag.

How do you feel about straight edge today?

It's a weird thing. I mean, on one level I think, OK, there is a 14-year-old kid living in a suburb somewhere. Everyone around him is too young to drive and constantly drunk off their asses or all of his friends are getting stoned during lunch hour or whatever. I don't think that's necessarily good for them. It's an extremely formative period in their life and a place where they can really learn some discipline and establish some sense of self reliance. The first time anyone takes a drink, they don't have a taste for alcohol. They're responding to the suggestion of someone else or the pressure of someone else, particularly when a young person does it. I don't think that's ever so good to capitulate to outside pressure.

What eventually led me to mess around with alcohol at all was actually a huge curiosity spawned from years of putting it down. That and maybe subconsciously some need to—you know, they always say, "monkey see, monkey do" or "like father, like son." I come from an addict family. Sooner or later, I guess I wanted to know what all the hubbub was about.

411 at Gilman Street

DAVE SINE

How do I feel about straight edge today, though? I mean, I wouldn't call myself straight edge. Not a snowball's chance in hell. I'm not really familiar with that many of the bands doing that music today. The bands that I like that were the third generation spawn of the bands that I liked 10 years ago. What has become of the people and all the earliest hardcore bands is still stuff that really excites me. A few of the things that are going on with some of the older generation people from New York interests me. But as a whole, as a movement, I feel no kinship to it at all. I still, I would say, very much identify with my hardcore roots. I remember how important it was to me to be pure of mind and body and to draw that hard line between myself and people who were, I felt, disgracing themselves or behaving irresponsibly. I have just become really, really uncomfortable with the concept of participating in a scene, with the concept of affiliating myself with something that pushes other people, absolute equals, so far to the outside and which sets such a moral mandate. The idea of the young mandating to anybody what is "the lifelong applicable philosophy," is obviously silly. There are very visible problems with it. While their points may be correct, their belief that it is so all-encompassing is sort of dingy.

How old are you, and what are you doing with your life now? What can I tell the kids when they ask, "What happened to Dan O'Mahony?"

Well, I'm 27. I'll be 28 next Monday. I order all of the alternative music merchandise for a shop in Berkeley, California. It's sort of a big old music store. It's nothing particularly interesting. I do direct mail order on my book, on the first book, on *Three Legged Race.* I sing for a band called Both Hands Broken, which actually has its first shows booked right now, so we're sort of becoming an active on-stage band as of this winter. I've got another book done, but not yet released, and a third

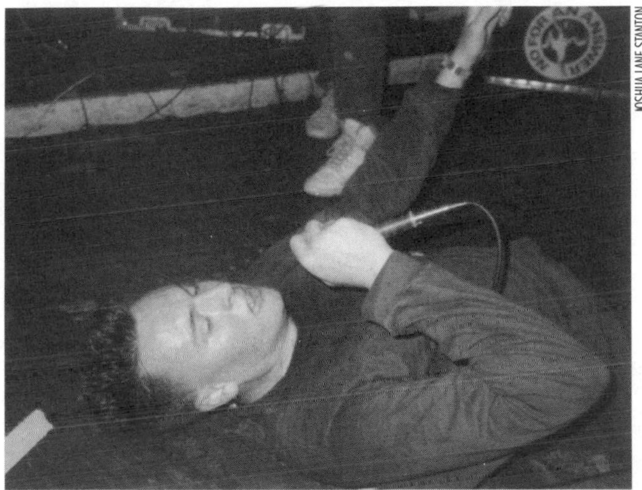

JOSHUA LANE STANTON

No For An Answer

book about halfway in the can. Writing is my first love these days, music second and probably physical fitness third.

Do you have any interesting stories about being on tour, like playing with other bands or anything that really sticks out as a positive or negative memory of being straight edge?

Oh, God, I've got a lot. I can remember when 411 finally went out on tour it was always really, really disappointing. I would say the central theme in 411 was one of openness and was one of self-exploration. All of our songs were sort of about tearing down the facades, about not embracing any obvious mechanic for self-marketing. In other words, not embracing something that was an obvious tool to put yourself over with others and to find yourself a niche but rather to develop some self-understanding and then to be open with others about it and hope that in doing so you could find genuine communication in your hands as opposed to some false sense of kinship. But then we would go out, and here it was two or three years down the line, and they looked like No For An Answer shows. While I'm not to a point where you don't want all your old fans to come see your new band—I mean you very much do want that to happen—you want to believe that they're growing right alongside with you, that everybody's going through these same stages, and we've all momentarily gotten caught up in these different facades, and that's not necessarily true.

I can remember being in Pennsylvania and being horrified looking over at someone's shoulder and seeing my own tattoo. I remember seeing a white power skinhead with the No For An Answer guy, the bald guy, jumping up across his back. I would say that was sort of a negative experience. It made me sort of never really want to embrace overly muscular bald male energies again in my graphics.

No For An Answer publicity shot

The positive experiences are almost too many to mention, and the negative experiences are almost no fun to walk backwards through. I mean, they're negative enough that I don't like to think about it.

I miss it. Doing music for five, six, seven years straight had a really positive and negative impact on my psychology. I think that the straight edge movement, in particular, endows a lot of people with some sense of having become a savior, and people see themselves as being these moral standard bearers, which I just don't think is really logical in one's adolescence.

I think it was very bad for me in the sense that I came to really only understand who "Dan For An Answer" was and not "Dan O'Mahony." After my mother died, and after several other remarkably sobering events took place in my life, I started looking in the mirror and having no idea who I was. Being just the singer of a relatively popular hardcore band didn't mean much in the grand scope of things.

Interesting choice of the word "sobering."

But I mean, that's a very real delirium. I mean, that's one thing. A lot of people become horrified when they find that I've gone through periods over the last two or three years where I was drinking, where I was drinking quite a bit. And they seem hideously disappointed in me. I can understand that, and I can see the obvious hypocrisies between that and my past. I can also see that when I was four I used to suck on my big toe. There are a lot of things that I don't do any more. I'm not saying that it's quite the same, it differs in degrees, but the analogy has an obvious worth. The whole thing about drinking is that there are some things about it that are obviously unhealthy, all right? But at the same time, when I think about some of the things that have happened during periods of heavy drinking in my life, there are things that my friends and I still laugh

about that were in some sense positive experiences inasmuch as what comes out is. Drinking does not create an evil in the individual. If there is an evil in the individual, drinking might limit the person's ability to hold it back, and you've got to be responsible about introducing such a thing into your system. It's hard to be responsible about it once you put it in because your hands come flying off the reins. Inasmuch as that's true, I see it as a bad thing.

But I see straight edge, potentially, as being an even more terrible thing inasmuch as it allows people to focus a massive amount of energy on one of the more overrated evils in this world. There are hideous, horrible things going on. There are brutal things, totally, permanently scarring things that go on in every human relationship that are virtually ignored in hardcore literalism. That's terrible. Because you have the scene that's supposedly so introspective and so morally based that it really doesn't concern itself with common everyday cruelties. Everybody's very willing to get involved in the plight of animals, but not in the plight of their fellow human being on anything other than an obvious black and white racism/sexism/homophobia level. There is no real intense analysis of human behavior going on, and I think that's sad.

I am glad that somebody finally said that in an interview. How was the East Coast/West Coast straight edge—

Different?

How was it when they mixed together?

Uniform Choice used to just rule the roost out here. Pat would run back across the stage, being about 200 pounds, intensely muscular, screaming at people, and everybody wanted to be him. The same way they wanted to be Stallone if they went to a Rambo movie.

Then one night 7 Seconds and Youth of Today played on the same bill. In fact, I think Half Off played, I'm not sure. Youth of Today didn't even have their own drummer with them. The drummer from 7 Seconds played drums on some songs and Kevin Seconds played drums on some songs, but you just had these two crazy short guys with big old noses just going out there and being flat out overt,

JOHSUA LANE STANTON

No For An Answer

massively confrontational and pretty verbal about exactly what was on their minds. It was just such a display of audacious, straightforward resentment, that people just had to leap onto it. It went one step further than what Uniform Choice was doing at the time, which was that it made very clear statements about exactly what it was pissed off about. Uniform Choice were really great for saying, "We care, we care, we care, we care," but they could never tell you about exactly what.

Then Ray and John came out to the West Coast and said, "This is exactly what we're pissed off about, and you want to fight? We just might." Great. It was cool. If you're 17, 18 years old and someone comes out and verbalizes that on stage in the biggest club in Southern California, it's going to catch on.

So what happened when the East Coast came West was everything that was supposedly West Coast straight edge went out the window. The next thing I knew, everybody that was a generation behind, like myself and Gavin Ogelsby and Joe Foster and Casey Jones, like Billy Rubin, like the initial nucleus in Orange County, you know, Pat Dubar and Pat Longry, all of those people, sort of became the East Coast. All the next generation kids, you know, immediately it was shaved heads and sweat shirts. It was, you know, Bermuda shorts and Nikes.

Really, it's never looked back. I see the East Coast as being infinitely more influential on that scene than the West Coast. Being from the West Coast, that's sort of embarrassing, but it's just true.

I remember we were really caught off guard when we finally

took No For An Answer to the East Coast. Here we were, a bunch of guys wearing Vans and big baggy black surf pants and two long-sleeved shirts and things and not really being the East Coast concept of straight edge, and still getting a really pretty good response and being treated pretty well by the people and being shown some respect. That's not something we ever really thought would happen. And from what we understood, it didn't really happen to too many other West Coast bands because before you knew it, the only West Coast band that really broke big in the straight edge thing after us or Uniform Choice was Insted, you know. Insted were —as much as I liked those guys, and I consider them to be totally well minded individuals—essentially an East Coast spin-off band. They were visually and musically doing everything they possibly could to emulate the East Coast.

It's funny. For a while, I got really caught up in that New York energy. It was really fun to be friends with all of those people but now here we are, you know, nearly 10 years down the line. If I put on Uniform Choice *Screaming for Change,* or something like that, it's amazing to realize how different that stuff is and how much I had just lost track of that stuff and all the energies that really carried me through high school. That whole scene has been redefined and has a completely different identity than what it did, simply because of a few bands from the opposite coast.

"The idea of the young mandating to anybody what is 'the lifelong applicable philosophy,' is obviously silly. There are very visible problems with it."

When I went back a few years later in 411, we played ABC No Rio. We played a lot of all ages shows in bars in New Jersey and in Upstate New York, really weird atmospheres. I like the East Coast better in that sense.

And finally going to Washington DC, which in my opinion is really the birthplace of the whole thing, I finally met people I had always wanted to meet. I'd known Ian for a few years, but I finally got to meet Amy Pickering and a few other people. We met the Jawbox people and they were great. We played with Bikini Kill at St. Stephen's Parish, I think is the name of the place, and it was a huge experience. Bigger for me than anything I experienced in New York. Those to me are the two main places to be on the East Coast. DC, being that I'm a little bit older, was a much bigger deal to me, to finally make it there as a musician.

What about Boston?

Boston's cool just because I like the Slapshot guys. They're old friends, and we always had this sort of parody confrontation going on, this sort of fake tough guy growl thing. We always had audiences thinking that the bands were on the verge of fighting when the fact of the matter was we were the best of friends. It was always fun when 411 went out, a couple of years after No For An Answer, to stay with those guys. They came to our show with Shelter and completely hassled us and everything else. It was the best.

The point at which No For An Answer really started to know that we didn't want to be involved with the whole New York straight edge movement was when it occurred to us that all you ever heard from New York was "tough guy" stories. You'd hear, you know, so-and-so goes to shows with an eight ball in a sock and, you know, smashes people in the face. Could Mike Judge take this person? Could so-and-so Death Before Dishonor take Raybeez? I would think, "You know, Christ, on the West Coast on a daily basis we're dealing with having trouble loading our equipment into shows because there are Crips standing there eyeballing our van," and things like that. It just started to seem kind of hokey.

No For An Answer stepped into a different lane early on. I'm not trying to be self-important. I mean, it may have been that we shot ourselves in the foot. We were West Coast kids slowly but surely getting sucked into an East Coast thing and we couldn't really identify.

Gus Peña

CHRIS TOLIVER

Gus, then known as "Gus Straight Edge" was a fixture at every straight edge show. He lives in New York and is on the staff of "Chord," a national music magazine. We spoke on 1 December 1995.

Ocean of Mercy

In high school, the difference between me and everybody else was that I didn't play sports or watch them or even aspire to. I also had an insatiable curiosity about the city. I would look at the skyline every day on my way to school and wonder why I lived only five blocks from my school. I lacked the adventure of daily voyage. So I invented my own.

Me and a friend would sneak off into undiscovered territory, emulating Lewis and Clark. Eventually, we worked our way into the Village and discovered its nightlife. I loved 7 Seconds and Agnostic Front as well as The Exploited. Reagan Youth were a favorite too. Around this time, I tried a few different drugs. Mostly, we just did the alcohol thing.

One afternoon at CBGB's, I heard about straight edge. Youth of Today played and they said something or another about it. I asked my friend what it was and he gave me a Minor Threat 7". I used to wear X's on my hands, but I still smoked. I thought that it was OK. I later found out that you weren't supposed to smoke, so I quit. The more I got into hardcore, the more I liked the idea of straight edge. I was already vegetarian, so this just followed suit. I was about 15 by the time all of this was going on.

The idea of a "youth crew" was something that appealed to me. I don't know what I expected it to do for me, but I thought it was a good idea. Maybe it gave me the sense that I belonged to something that was important. I thought of it as separate from vegetarianism. How they got lumped together was a little beyond me. I mean, I know that it makes sense, but I think that it makes straight edge even that much more exclusive. I thought that everybody should be able to be straight edge regardless of what they ate.

I had my fanatical stages, but mostly I was just doing it for myself. I felt as though I should do this. All along, I was friends with people that weren't straight edge, even people who were the farthest thing from it. I lost all feeling of it being a "movement" shortly after getting into it. It was a social thing, and it was a lot of fun. It gave me the opportunity to express myself in a loud and obnoxious way. Big black "X"s on my hands and a shaved head, yelling, feeling very righteous. Actually, it was almost dangerous.

JOSHUA LANE STANTON

Gus and Alex Brown

It was great to be part of a generation rebellion. If I was going to part of one, I'd rather it was that. I think when I'm old, I can look back at it fondly. I don't mean to minimize it to just some youth culture uproar. It was, and is, omnipotent then and now, and it definitely felt like we were doing something.

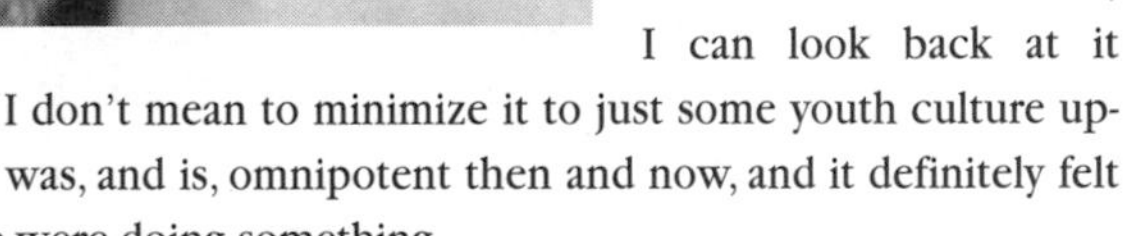

Of all the titles one can get, I liked being called "straight edge." I know that even nowadays, I still look for that type of energy that we all had at that time. In my mind, I'm not sure if it could ever be recreated. Not that it's downhill from there, but it set a good precedent.

Today, I still don't drink or anything like that. I'm not sure if I qualify as "straight edge." At heart, I would like to think so. I have gotten more into spirituality, like Krishna consciousness. The fact that I don't do any drugs is probably more due to that than any claims of straight edge, these days anyway. Also, I didn't acquire a taste for any of it. I had my stints of doing intoxicants, but they didn't last long.

Porcell

Porcell is a former member of the hardcore bands; Young Republicans, Violent Children, Youth of Today, Project X and Judge. He is currently in Shelter. I interviewed him on 10 May 1995.

Youth of Today in Boulder, CO

I was always into punk rock, ever since I was a little kid. I went from listening to Kiss in fifth grade to jamming out the Sex Pistols in sixth grade. Then, I got into hardcore in junior high and never looked back. It was ninth grade or so when I first went to the Anthrax. That's when I started getting into straight edge. Some of my favorite bands were Minor Threat, 7 Seconds, Youth Brigade—bands that were inspirational, bands that had something to say. That's what attracted me to hardcore and punk—the music had integrity and honesty. It wasn't like the lame stuff my older brother was listening to, like Rush, AC/DC—that kind of thing I really couldn't relate to.

I learned how to play a few bar chords on guitar and managed to put together some punk bands when I was little. Then when I met Ray, I joined Violent Children. We were into the same kind of music—straight edge, positive, but the other guys in the band were totally off in another direction. Me and Ray wanted to do something serious. Basically what we wanted to do was start a serious hardcore band with the power of Negative Approach, but mixed with the positive message of bands like 7 Seconds. And that's exactly what we did. At the time, all our favorite bands, like Minor Threat and DYS, had broken up. Speed metal was the next big thing. We weren't into it because a lot of the pretension and stupidity crossed over from the metal scene along with the music. In retaliation, we were going to start the hardest hardcore band around. We even picked a generic name—Youth of Today. It was simple, basic and to the point. We drew big X's on our hands and set out to conquer the scene.

Most of the people in the scene drank, except us, so we were definitely the minority. Being straight edge in the high school I went to was practically unheard of. I went to John Jay High, the same school the guys from Bold went to. When we first got into the straight edge thing, there was so much peer pressure to drink and do drugs—

JORDAN COOPER

Violent Children at Sal D's

not just from kids in school, but from the punks in the scene also. So we decided to reverse the peer pressure. We were straight—loud, proud and outspoken. I remember Ray even had a jacket that said "Straight Edge in Your Face" on the back of it. Once, when the Dead Kennedys played, I jumped up on stage and grabbed the cigarette out of the bass player's mouth and stomped it into the ground. Sure, we were young and stupid, but at the time, it was our way of dealing with all of the peer pressure that comes along with being a teenager. It was our revolt against the mainstream.

After a while, Youth of Today really became serious about putting out a positive message. Music was powerful, and we knew that it had the potential to inspire others and change their lives. But I soon realized that intolerance doesn't change a thing. When you act that way, people don't listen or even take you seriously. They just get turned off, and the communication gap widens that much more. We had a message that we wanted others to hear, so we took a different approach. We tried to be examples of clean living. When kids see that you're sincere, that's when they get inspired—"Practice what you preach."

When we moved to New York City, I remember the first time Youth of Today played CBGB's. God, the scene was so drug oriented back then, kids sniffing glue and smoking dust all over the place. After we played, Johnny Stiff came up to us and said, "Oh, you guys are a straight edge band? You'll never make it in New York!" and I almost believed him.

Yeah, when I first got to New York, I hated the scene. Where was the punk, the alternative? I mean, the clothes were dirtier and people had weirder haircuts, but basically they were doing the same things that every burnout in my high school was doing—listening to music, getting drunk and getting in fights. They reminded me of my older brother, only he'd get plastered and go to Ozzy shows, and the punks would huff glue and go to CB's. So what was the difference? I had gotten into punk to get away from all that junk in the first place. I think that's why the whole straight edge thing caught on in the city. People were ready for a real alternative. They wanted something with substance, with a message, something that was going to help them rise above their miserable surroundings, not get them deeper into it. And man, straight edge caught on like wildfire. It was such an exciting time in New York.

All these other straight edge bands started popping up—Gorilla Biscuits, Side By Side...even WarZone went straight! I couldn't believe it! It all seemed to happen so fast. It was amazing, actually. The scene that was once so sunk into the drug culture had completely turned around. Johnny Stiff must've been scratching his head, wondering what happened. After Youth of Today put out *Break Down the Walls*, we toured the country, which was a pretty rare thing to do at the time. A whole straight edge scene was developing across the nation. We'd play gigs and hundreds and hundreds of kids would show up, and I mean, they'd be going nuts—stage diving and singing along with X's on their hands and everything. Even in Europe, straight edge was booming.

After the Youth of Today song "No More" came out, practically the whole scene went vegetarian. When we wrote that song, we weren't sure if kids would be into the idea or completely turned off by it. But we didn't care. It was such an urgent message, and we figured that if people were really serious about not poisoning their bodies and polluting their minds, they'd take to it. Pretty soon being a vegetarian became synonymous with being straight edge. It really inspired me to think that others were actually taking the message of the music to heart. Things were starting to change, and it really gave us a revolutionary spirit. We were out to change the world.

Then, somewhere down the line, things started to go wrong. Sure, straight edge was popular, but when something gets popular, a lot of kids get into it only because it's the "cool" thing to do. It became trendy and cliquish. Just like any other trend, it had its upswing and it had its downfall—and straight edge crashed hard. It was really disheartening. I'd say about 90 percent of the kids who had the edge in the "Youth Crew" days went to college and started partying. I became disillusioned with the straight edge scene. It was sad because after all the tours, after all the screaming, all the sing-alongs, it didn't seem like people were really changing. Just like Shakespeare said, "Full of sound and fury, signifying nothing." That's how I felt, and it broke me. I think that's why Youth of Today called it quits. Judge, too.

JORDAN COOPER

Youth of Today

By the time we went on the last Judge tour, the whole "tough guy" image was getting out of control. At every show Judge played, there'd be a lot of violence. The worst part of it was that the kids starting the fights were directly influenced by our band. I can't even count how many times these jerks would come up to us and brag how they just kicked some guy's teeth in and wait for a sign of approval from me or Mike—as if we were into that. It seemed everyone had this preconceived notion that Mike was a big hardline sort of character, a real rock. Even though he had that side, Mike's actually a really sensitive, caring person. He wasn't into all that stupidity. Yet Judge had this real violent image. It was weird. It wasn't a good feeling to know that indirectly we were responsible. So this whole thing with Judge had me and Mike really bummed out. After trying to convey something honest, after trying to be an inspiration, the whole thing was blowing up in our faces. And if that was the result, it wasn't even worth being in a band. So Judge broke up. It made me realize that when you're in a band and you get up on stage, whether you like it or not, you become a role model. And it can be a dangerous thing.

Our records were selling like 30,000 or 40,000 copies each, so a lot of kids were really taking them to heart. It's a huge responsibility because you have influence over their lives. Just like with the Project X record. We wrote it, recorded it and mixed it in about three days. We had no idea that it was going to get so popular. And more than once, I've regretted it because of all the violence and intolerance caused by that one record. That's not what I was about at all, so it was a lesson well learned. If I have some influence on someone, I sure want it to be a good influence. That's what music was all about for me—motivation towards something higher.

After that, I was in Gorilla Biscuits for a little while. That was a weird situation for me because the rest of the band mostly wasn't straight edge by that time. Yet, there we were, singing all of these straight edge songs, and I watched as kids sang along with full sincerity. I don't know, I felt a little compromised. I think that's when my disillusionment with hardcore reached its limit.

This was my crisis. Here we were all these years, screaming "Make a change, make a change, make a change!" And after all my ranting and raving about personal change and growth, I couldn't even change myself. Supposedly I was against the exploitation of women, and we'd go on tour and what would I do? I'd be scamming on girls. I was against dishonesty, yet I worked at a health food store and every night I'd steal about $20 out of the register and take home a whole bag of groceries free. One night I came back to my apartment after I had stolen this huge bag of food and it hit me—I was a hypocrite. It really made me re-evaluate my life.

I realized that you can't just talk about change. It's not enough to just shout slogans or wave your X'd up fist in the air. Before you can have an effect on the outside world, first you have to change the world inside yourself. And it was clear to me that my consciousness needed some work—on a spiritual level.

After some soul-searching, I quit my job, moved out of my apartment, sold everything I owned including my records—left all my friends and moved to a Krishna temple. I knew there was truth in the philosophy of the Bhagavad-gita, but I also knew that I'd never realize that truth unless I lived a spiritual lifestyle. That seemed like it would be an impossibility in New York—just too many negative influences for me there. So I moved to a Krishna-sponsored cow protection farm in Pennsylvania. Yeah, I had done it. I renounced hardcore and all its hypocrisy. I left behind all the envy and competition that comes with

JORDAN COOPER

Youth of Today

Youth of Today, Denver, CO 1988

Youth of Today in Boulder, CO

being in a band. I stepped down from the spotlight, and I felt some peace. Then out of the blue, Ray—well, by this time he was Ragunatha dasa—called me up and tried to get me to join Shelter. I told him flat out to forget it. I wasn't about to jump back into the fire. But actually in the Bhagavad-gita, Krishna says that it's not what you do, but it's the consciousness behind what you do that's important. So very cautiously, I set out to do hardcore again, but this time I was determined to do it in a spiritual way. And it's made all the difference.

So now I'm still in a band, still trying to make a change and trying my best not to fall prey to prestige and adoration. I find that if I let myself slip and think that I'm some big deal, it just brings back all those old bad feelings. Now I have to make sure my constant meditation is that I'm doing Shelter as a humble service to try to enlighten myself and others. In this way, I find that being in a band actually has some purpose and becomes satisfying. Instead of getting on stage to show how "cool" I am, I do it to spread spiritual knowledge, and this way the people in the crowd walk away with more than just a handful of illusions.

CHRIS TOLIVER

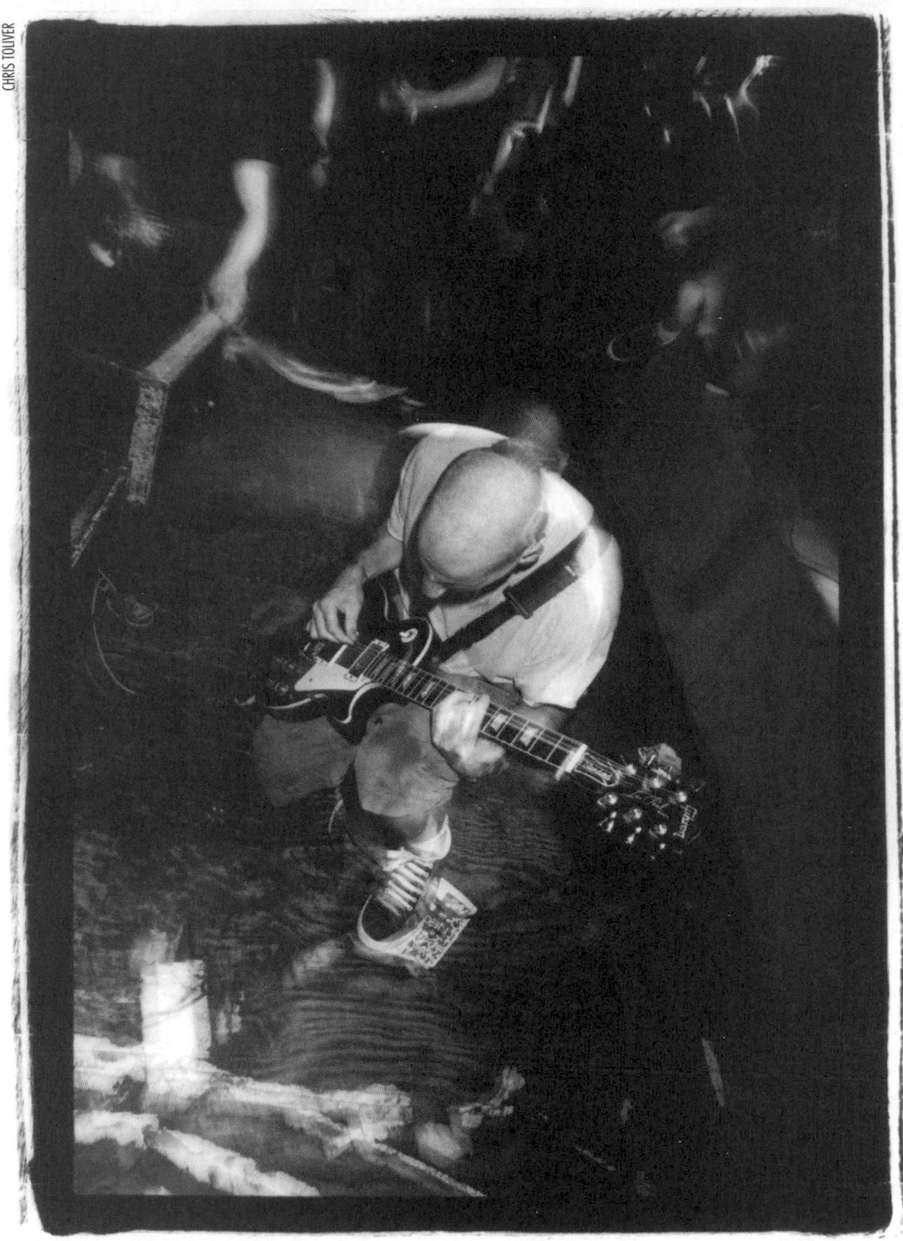

Shelter

RAYBEEZ

Raybeez was the singer for WarZone, a band that lasted for over ten years. He died tragically from an illness in September, 1997. We spoke in the wee hours of 17 September 1995.

How did WarZone start to get involved with straight edge? You were not a straight edge band originally.

(Laughter) No, we weren't.

You have had in-and-out involvement with it.

Yeah, in the beginning WarZone had a family thing going. There were a bunch of different apartments that we all lived in on the Lower East Side. The way it was, there was eight or nine people living in each apartment, and there were people that stayed over a lot. We were like our own little type of family. We would have dinners, like family dinners, over our house. What happened in the beginning was because everyone was always living together, people would always party together. What happened was that after the early 80s, people started dying. Everyone started partying a lot, people started overdosing, people just started getting really fucked up and going crazy and doing crazy shit. On the Lower East Side, what happened was in the early 80s—WarZone, AF, Murphy's Law and a lot of other bands—everyone used to do a lot of crazy stuff like steal cars.

After the early 80s went by and some of our close friends died, it was time to look at your life, to put things in perspective. In '85, maybe '86, I'm not sure, everyone just stopped doing drugs. Everyone got really kind of scared because people were dying around us. We went from being one way militant to the other way militant. No one wanted to die.

For us, it was a way of life. I don't want to minimize how people are today, in Europe and U.S. in straight edge, but sometimes it seems that a lot of kids just do it to fit into a trend or because of music. Back then, it was our life. Everyone stopped doing drugs be cause we were scared that we were going to die. It wasn't a joke. It wasn't a music trend. It was maybe even more militant, maybe more intense at first, because it was like a gang thing. We all decided to stop because we were scared for our lives. When you are on that level, it takes things to another point.

Did it support a decision that you had already made in your life? Whereas for many people, who may be taking it from a different approach, straight edge is something that they decide to do through the music, you had made a decision in your life, and the music supported it?

Yes, and this is the whole thing with WarZone, which made it really intense, which made us get a really big following, is that a lot of the songs that we wrote, like "Escape From Your Society" and "Wound Up," early songs that I used to write the lyrics for—it makes the difference when kids know that you're really living it. A lot of bands today might sing drug-free songs, it's cool, I don't want to put anyone down for that, but when you do it from the perspective from where your life is on the line, it's more intense like that. When Youth of Today and WarZone kind of hooked up for a while—we did a lot of shows together—it made it even bigger because Youth of Today came from a whole different scene than where we came from.

WarZone
NEW YORK CITY
W Z
Lower East Side

Yeah, that's an odd pairing.

You know what it was, was that me and Ray became really close. I love Ray like a brother, to this day, every time I see Ray I give him a big hug. I'd take a bullet for him. It just happened like that.

We started hanging out with the same people. There was this one girl, her name was Elise Mogenson. She was at that point in time, straight edge. She was part of the Youth of Today crew. We hung out and then dated each other for about two years. To this day, I still care about her. Me and Elise, that was like our "Sid and Nancy," but on the straight edge tip. That's how Elise and me were. Then she went away to Guadalajara to go to school, and we stopped seeing each other. You know, it's really weird, because a lot times guys in bands don't give—and I'm really saying this in a humble way, I really mean this—girls the respect they deserve. When we were straight edge, the whole Youth of Today/WarZone time, when we put the single out on Revelation, Elise was the backbone of everything WarZone was for me. She did everything for me, and everyone knew it. I totally gave her props.

DAVE MANDEL

There were a whole bunch of other girls, too. You had the WarZone women, but the whole thing with the WarZone women was they weren't girls that we were fooling around with, it was our family. They were a gang of girls—some of them were straight edge, and some of them weren't. It was a brother and sisterhood. Elise was the leader of all that for me because she did a lot. She was down with Side by Side and Youth of Today, and we all hung out together. Elise was really good friends with Sammy and Walter and Arthur. That's how we became all really good friends.

What about the New York/Boston rivalry?

Well, you know, it was really New York/Boston/DC. In the early days in the scene here in New York, in the early 80s, it wasn't straight edge. In the beginning, we were kind of Oi punk hardcore skinheads and we were into John Belushi Animal House partying. It was like a family. This was the way we looked at it, in Boston and DC most of the scene was made up of guys, the whole SS Decontrol thing in Boston, the Minor Threat thing in DC. In New York, the whole thing was 50 percent guys and 50 percent girls. That's what made it different. Where in New York, there were so many girls, punk and hardcore and straight edge girls, that part of the movement, that made it even more intense. Where in Boston and DC, you had the bands, all the guys, SS Decontrol, DYS from Boston, or when you had Minor Threat or the other bands coming from DC, it was all guys in the crews. With us, when we played shows, it was all guys and all girls. There was no macho thing, so I guess the whole thing

with the rivalry was they were so into being straight edge, but at that time, we weren't.

That is where the whole rivalry came up. Then what happened was a couple of years later, we all became friends. I guess everything kind of goes full circle, we all became friends later on. It's really funny, with the exception of Ian and some other guys, a lot of the guys who were straight edge in Boston and DC wound up partying later on, and then the guys in New York wound up being straight edge. In the end, we all became friends. After time, we all started playing together all of the time and the rivalry went away.

So, when these healthy, jock straight edge boys from Connecticut started coming down to New York City, what did the bands like the Cro Mags, Agnostic Front, all of those old bands, what did you think of them at first?

You got to understand, for a lot of us, we were hanging out on the Lower East Side every day, seven days a week in the early 80s, mid 80s. We'd hang out all night until five or six in the morning every night. What happened was when all of these kids that you talk about started coming, in the beginning, there was a lot of animosity because they would just come in for the show. It seemed like none of them were doing anything for the scene. All of us worked the clubs here. We all worked at CB's and the clubs that were here. We would hang out seven days a week through the dead of winter. It didn't matter what season it was. You could come down to Tompkin's Square Park and there would be 50, 75, 100 of us hanging out constantly together, all night long. So when you're doing that, that's kind of the base for New York City hardcore. Then people come from out of town and started coming to shows, and we didn't know them, so there was a lot of animosity because a lot of us didn't come from good families. Everyone came from dysfunctional families. Even if their families had money, a lot of the kids here turned out to be street kids. A lot of the kids who used to come from New Jersey or Connecticut came from well-off families and lived in houses, do you know what I'm

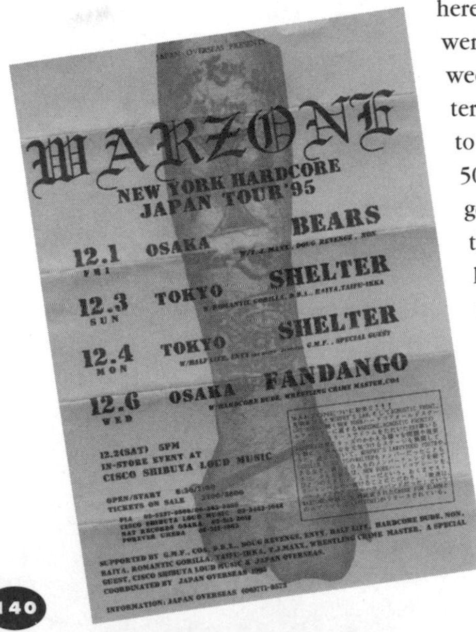

FROM NEW YORK:
AGNOSTIC FRONT
BACK FROM U.S. TOUR '86
WAR ZONE
CBGB and OMFUG
315 Bowery (at Bleecker) (212) 982-4052
$6
SUNDAY, AUGUST 24 3:00 PM

saying? So there was animosity about that, but that dissipated over time because we all started playing in bands together. I think that the best way to explain it is, if the scene is true in heart, then sooner or later, everyone comes together.

Do you think that is still going on with straight edge today from what you have seen?

Yes and no. It is in some ways and isn't. The scene went from being maybe a couple of hundred people in the family, now to being a couple of thousand. The scene now is worldwide. You have straight edge and hardcore scenes in Japan and Croatia and Serbia and Greece…it's all over the world now, so it's huge. When it gets so big like that, it loses it closeness, but there are still people in different parts who all write to each other, so in some ways it's still really close. The bands write to each other. We're constantly writing to people all over the world. There is a crew of people in every little country.

Do you consider WarZone a straight edge band at all now?

No way. The way it is now, the way it kind of formed into, now it's like a really big family. It's not even a band anymore. There are so many different people into WarZone. You have punk rockers into WarZone. You have Oi kids into WarZone. You have straight edge kids into WarZone. It's really weird, because now there's so many people in WarZone. Right now, we have about 20 people we could pick from to play in the band. There are so many people who have been in the band over the years. Now it has kind of turned into the Grateful Dead of punk hardcore straight edge. Everyone goes through their time.

I'm not an angel. I go through my periods where I'm totally straight, or I like to party a little bit. My goal in my life is to stay straight. As long as you have your head where you want to go, if you fall it's OK, as long as you can get back on the road. It's not as easy as people think it is, especially if you come from a partying lifestyle, or living in the streets and all that entails. It's not always so easy to be straight. It's just so big now that WarZone encompasses so many things.

With us being on Victory, it's a really good thing too because that's like a really

CREEPY CRAWL PRODUCTIONS
Presents
A Medical Benefit for BJ, Roger, Mike & Jimmy
Featuring
Murphy's Law
KILLING TIME
H2O
warzone
LEEWAY
SHEER TERROR
Skarhead
MAXIMUM PENALTY
25 TA LIFE
MERAUDER
REJUVENATE
Terrorzone
New Faith
DOWN LOW
$12
Doors 5pm til...
All Ages
September 2, 1995
"All proceeds will be split 4 ways"
Coney Island High
15 St. Marks Place
212 - 674 - 7959

big family to us. We all really support each other. Also, Tony, who started and runs Victory Records is 100 percent true when it comes to honesty and beliefs.

You play a lot of shows with those younger straight edge bands now.

We do off and on. We're going out to California this summer, we're going to play a couple of shows out there. At the end of this year, Tony Victory is hooking it up for Snapcase, Earth Crisis, Strife, WarZone and a bunch of other bands are playing two weeks together. We're going to put a video out of all of the bands on Victory. That's a really big thing for us. It should be cool.

How do you think those younger bands look at WarZone?

Well, I know the guys from Snapcase, Earth Crisis and Strife. When we see each other, we hang out and talk. We support each other. It's all a matter of respect for each other. There was a show a few months back where Earth Crisis and Snapcase played Wetlands. There was a point where Karl from Earth Crisis and (Daryl) from Snapcase and I were all hanging out on stage between sets talking to each other. We noticed that kids were looking at us and taking pictures of us and people were bugging. It's like 99 percent of the people who are in bands from the so called "old school" don't take the younger bands seriously. It's so important to reach out to everyone!

Snapcase is a great band.

Yeah, we really like them a lot. What's really good about Snapcase, Earth Crisis and Strife is that they are sincere. They're honest in what they do and what they say. You have to be honest in saying what you believe in, that's the most important thing.

What about all of those bands that used to say all of those things and then grew up and are now partying?

Do you know what I learned? You can't judge other people. You have to look at yourself first. I think what everyone needs to do is to look at yourself, and worry about yourself, and focus on your spirituality and where you're going in your life and not worry too much about other people. There's the people that you care about, I really love Ray Cappo and Arthur and Walter and Civ and those guys, but you have to look at yourself and concentrate on yourself. If you're doing good in your life, and you're surrounded by people who are doing good, if the other guys fall off the wagon once in a while, you just let them know that it's OK, they can come back, you're always there for them. It's so easy to talk shit about people. I think it's more important to support each other. I think it's really against what the scene is trying to do—keep everyone together. If people fall off, I think it's important just to let them know that you still care about them. I think you need to look inside people's hearts, and look out for each other. People go through a lot of heavy shit in this world.

NEIL ROBINSON

Neil is the singer for the punk band, Nausea. He also books shows at ABC No Rio and runs Tribal War Records. I interviewed him on 22 March 1995.

How did you perceive the whole straight edge scene when it was happening, since you were not really a part of it yourself?

To me, we were all the same. I didn't see any divisions. In New York, everyone would go to the Sunday matinees at CB's. There was no concern if you were straight, if you drank, or anything like that. It was just like one big group that was pretty much fighting for the same things at that stage. I knew all those people. We played with the bands, the straight bands. It was just like one big family then.

What was your involvement with it?

I was in Nausea and I was doing stuff on the Lower East Side what with Squat or Rot, we were putting on shows on around the Lower East Side.

How do you see straight edge today in terms of how it had been back then?

It's still got that fashion side to it, which I've never liked. A lot of the younger kids that I've talked to and asked, "Why are you straight?" Kind of the answer is, "We like the look" and this and that. There isn't any deepness. It was a fashion thing back then.

I have a lot of respect for the older kids who are still into it. I'd like to see more of the older punks talking about it. It's such a young scene. I'd like to see an older crowd getting into it. It seems like they get to 21, 22, 23, and the peer pressure starts. I was talking to someone about that today. He was telling me about someone who just gone off of being straight because he'd met this girl who's into going to the bar, and he felt pressured into drinking. I'd like to see people sticking with it. There's a lot of cool bands. Some of the beliefs that everyone seemed to hold back then seemed to have gotten lost in trying to fit in. The beliefs were the strong thing back then.

Mark Ryan

Mark Ryan is a former member of Death Before Dishonor and Supertouch. He lives in New York City and continues to play music. I spoke with Mark on 27 March 1995.

DAVE SINE

Supertouch at Fender's 1989

I just found some old tapes of old radio programs that I used to tape. I found one that had a demo version of "We Will Not" and the DJ says, "That was 'We Will Not' from the Bad Brains. That's not going to be on their new cassette," talking about the Roir cassette. Then they played Minor Threat and the DJ says, "This just out of DC —Minor Threat." That was from a radio show in New York called "Noise Show" during the early 80s. Since the late 70's, I had always listened to the college stations. I was interested in punk and new wave, like the Sex Pistols and even Adam and the Ants, The Plasmatics, The Pretenders, stuff like that. The Dead Kennedys came out and I started listening to them. That was really when I started thinking, "Yeah *this* is punk." I started getting into the Circle Jerks and Black Flag. I loved the Buzzcocks and Sham 69. That's basically most of the stuff I listened to. When the Dischord stuff started coming out, I started listening to that.

When Minor Threat came out, it meant a lot to me because it was a brand new music. When I was in grammar school, I drank and I was always one of those types of kids, always on and off. I did it all the time, but part of me knew it was a fucked up thing to do. I didn't want to become an alcoholic, that was the last thing I wanted to do. When Minor Threat came out, it was so strong and powerful that as soon as I heard it, I was like "I'm straight edge!" But it didn't always last. I was always on and off with it. I would be straight edge a month, not straight edge a month, straight edge for a week. Whenever I was straight edge back then, I was kind of militant. I wrote it all over my notebook. Then when I would go on my little drinking

BETH LAHICKEY

Supertouch at the Anthrax

binges, I would say, "Well you know I'm straight edge but..." I would always try to make up some crazy logic like, "... every once in a while I drink, but I'm not obsessed with it. I don't have to..."

A SHOW FOR AARON- ALWAYS REMEMBERED!

AT THE ANTHRAX SUNDAY JULY -9 '89

25 PERRY AVE. NORWALK, CT

$6.00 3:00 PM

ALL PROCEEDS WILL GO TO AARON'S FAMILY

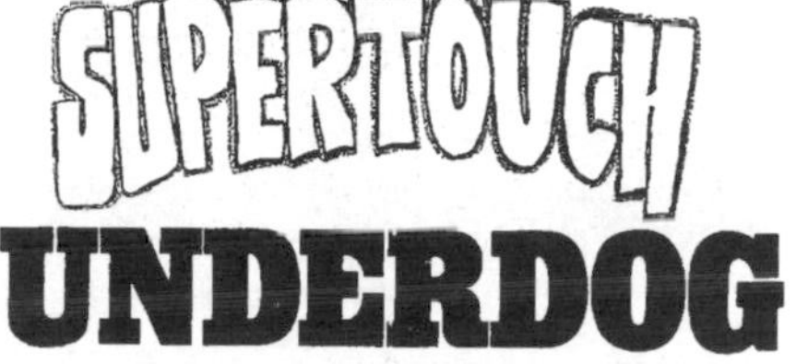

UNDERDOG

UP FRONT - WIDE AWAKE & MORE

A BENEFIT IN FAITHFUL MEMORY OF AARON STRAW

Were there straight edge bands in New York at that point?

Well, The Abused came out. They were kind of straight edge. They were New York style straight edge. I remember I was 14 years old playing quarters and smoking pot with the singer. Their big song was "Drug Free Youth."

It was such a strong thing that you wanted to be straight edge, but you were just so fucked up that it didn't last long. I think I've had periods of six or seven months where I was straight edge. I don't know, it's all kind of blurry. I was always cheating. The last time I tried straight edge was when that whole Youth of Today thing came around with their 7". When they moved to New York, I started hanging out with them a little.

At that point, I had been really bad with partying all the time, and I wanted to relive the early hardcore days. That was a special period of my life. I hated being in my house, it was one of those rough childhood things. All of the sudden, hardcore came out. I started going to the city for the weekend, sleeping on Avenue A, and all of the sudden, I was free. The music was all brand new. It was the greatest thing that ever happened. I felt like it kind of died out in a lot of ways, for me, that new spirit.

Once in a while, there would be a really good band that would get me psyched up, like with Youth of Today. They were really trying

to go for that early hardcore thing. It was kind of fun for a while, and then I realized it wasn't for me. I got kind of burnt out on it.

Supertouch was not straight edge, but you were always playing with straight edge bands.

I was friends with Bold, and we got lumped in with that. It was weird, especially since the first line on our record was, "I've been drinking all night," and a lot of times when we'd go somewhere people would expect us to be straight edge. They would be bummed out because we would be all fucked up. Sometimes people who would have liked us didn't like us because they thought we were straight edge.

Seeing as you saw a lot of shows in New York before the whole Youth of Today thing, did you think that they were going to be so popular?

No. Even though I thought it was generic, and I was already out of that style of music, it was good because a lot of bands went metal at that time. They had a lot of energy. It was fun to start dancing again. I had not gotten into that for a long time. But then, for me, it was a quick burst, and then it died out. I lost interest. They didn't hold up for me like the other bands held up, like Minor Threat did. I'll throw on Minor Threat now, early Dischord bands or Bad Brains, and still love them. Most of the stuff I like is early hardcore, before 1983. I think hardcore started getting fucked up.

Another reason why I liked Youth of Today at first was everyone was going metal, and that was the thing that fucked up hardcore the most. It was a bad combination. It seemed like a lot of hardcore bands, as soon as they learned to play their instruments a little better, they thought playing metal was the way to go. I think a lot of bands were more creative when they were hardcore.

What do you think of bands like Quicksand, insofar as hardcore mutating into something else?

I think it's cool. I don't think it should stay the same as what it was. I like bands with a hardcore influence as long as they do something different with it. But then, who am I to say that? If you're into playing the old style hardcore, then you have the right to do that, too.

Walter Schreifels

Walter is a former member of Gorilla Biscuits, Youth of Today and Quicksand. I interviewed him on New Year's Eve in 1994.

JOSHUA LANE STANTON

Gorilla Biscuits

I moved to Astoria and met some hardcore punk kids that lived in the neighborhood.Through that, I started going to shows in New York. I was into all kinds of stuff. I loved Minor Threat, Negative Approach, a lot of the Dischord bands, DYS, SSD and that kind of stuff. Eventually Youth of Today and Straight Ahead started playing in New York, those were my favorite bands. So, through them, I kind of got more into the straight edge scene. Even though I liked those bands, the older straight edge bands, I never was into being straight edge, even though I pretty much was anyway. When they came around, I just thought it was the coolest thing. Gorilla Biscuits had started around that same time.

We were kind of "punkier" or more goofy than Straight Ahead or Youth of Today, which were more serious type bands. I was influenced by those bands too, so the music of Gorilla Biscuits got more hardcore, straight forward like that. Some of the lyrics were more, not like goofy, well, they were goofy, some of them, but not as much about girls, but more about like social issues, such as a united scene or whatever. I became more involved in that. The whole scene just kind of took off on its own when Revelation started pressing up records like WarZone.

Someone was playing every weekend down at CB's or the Pyramid, bands like Sick of it All, YDL, Altercation, Side By Side, WarZone, Underdog, all these different bands

gorilla biscuits

Gorilla Biscuits publicity photo, 1989

playing together. It was really a tight-knit kind of thing. There were a lot of different people.

The few records that were coming out in New York people in the scene all got, or taped or whatever. So by the time that Youth of Today put out the second record, or Gorilla Biscuits put out the first album, there was a whole scene across the country of people interested in what was going on in New York.

Eventually, I think everything kind of frayed apart by '91, or something like that. CB's wouldn't do hardcore shows anymore, a lot of the bands had broken up or were kind of into different things or whatever. That's when I started doing Quicksand.

A lot of the same people that grew up with the bands are still around, but there's still a lot of new ones that will come up and ask me about Gorilla Biscuits or old shows. That's pretty cool, too.

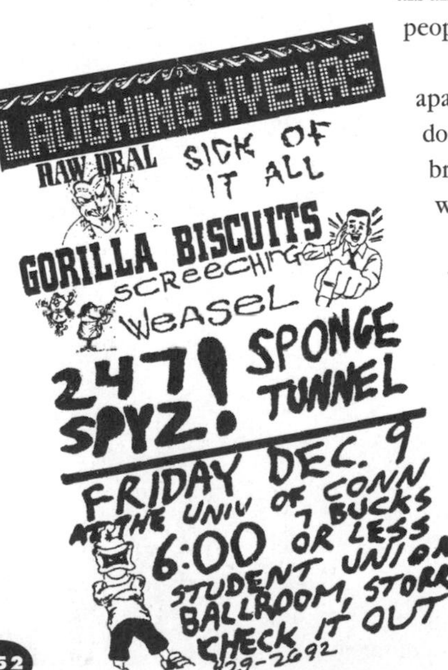

When did you start playing guitar?

When I was 13.

Had you been in bands before that?

Yeah, my first band was kind of a punk band called the Rodents. We never played in the City or anything.

I moved to Ohio for a year after that, and then I was in different kinds of wacky, not a real serious band. When I came to New York I started Gorilla Biscuits. That was my first serious band, really, where I was like, "Yeah, I want to play shows, make it happen."

RORFE KREVOLIN IN ASSOCIATION WITH THE RITZ
PRESENTS
A CONCERT TO BENEFIT AMNESTY INTERNATIONAL
HARDCORE BENEFIT III
AT RITZ
WITH
KILLING TIME
TOKEN ENTRY
SUPERTOUCH
SICK OF IT ALL
GORILLA BISCUITS
BURN
QUICKSAND

$10 IN ADVANCE
$11 DAY OF THE SHOW

FRIDAY AUG 10th
DOORS OPEN 8:00p.m.
SHOW STARTS 9:00p.m.

RITZ BOX OFFICE (212) 956-3731 54th ST. WEST OF BROADWAY
CHARGE BY PHONE (212) 307-7171 • (201) 507-8900
MUST BE 16 AND OVER TO ENTER • MUST PROVE 21 TO DRINK

How did Gorilla Biscuits come about forming?

There was a group of people in Jackson Heights and Astoria, a whole kind of punk crew. There was a real kind of scene in those two areas. Jackson Heights and Astoria are next to each other. Token Entry lived in Astoria, Murphy's Law lived in Astoria, Kraut lived in Astoria. There were a lot of kids in Jackson Heights that were into punk, and I hung out there a lot, hung out in Astoria a lot. I knew how to play guitar. There was a cool scene happening, so it just seemed like the thing to do. I knew Civ and wanted someone else to sing because I couldn't sing and play guitar, and he was down. We got the drummer from Token Entry to play for us originally, and Arthur, and that's how we started off.

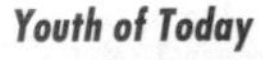
Youth of Today

TIM OWEN

So what is going on with the Civ project?

The music of Civ is a mixture of Sham 69 and Minor Threat. Thick, like aggressive, but cool, poppy in the sense that Sham 69 had a pop side to them.

How does that make you feel today when you see kids who are completely enamored of Gorilla Biscuits still in 1994?

That's cool. When you're doing it, you hope that it has an impact on people, in a sense, but you never imagine that it would be this far reaching. Sixteen-year-old kids buy this record, that's one of their first records to get into punk, the way I might have bought an Exploited record, or Suicidal Tendencies or Circle Jerks. I recently had a

GORILLA BISCUITS
WALLY'S PLACE
- PRESENTS -
SATURDAY NOVEMBER 19th
7:00 SHARP! $6
ALL AGES
NO DRUNK FREAKS!
INSTED
NO FOR AN ANSWER
NO FOR AN ANSWER
beyond

conversation with someone who said, "Yeah, the Gorilla Biscuits record got me into hardcore." It can only make you feel good.

What record was it for you?

For me, that got me into hardcore? There were a lot of them. The Buzzcocks and Sex Pistols got me into the whole idea of punk, and the Ramones. The first real hardcore I heard was Minor Threat, and that fucking just blew me away. I thought that it was the sickest thing I'd ever heard, outside of Suicidal Tendencies, who played fast too. Minor Threat just seemed so much more underground and fucked up that they really, really inspired me. So that was pretty much the main band that did it for me. If anyone feels that way about anything that I've done, that's so fucking cool, because I know what that feels like and how cool that is and what a special thing that is.

What happened with Crisis Records?

At that time, like '90-'91, something like that, one scene was kind of dying out, and I was hoping that another one could pick it up. I thought Quicksand was a part of that, for sure. I thought if there were some other bands that I could help out, put out records, that there was a whole structure there for

Arthur and Walter

JOSHUA LANE STANTON

JOSHUA LANE STANTON

Civ and Walter

me to do it. Jordan knew what he was doing. So I figured, get a couple of bands that are really new bands, that are trying something different, and promote them to try to get something else going, so that's what that became.

Outside of the initial few records I haven't had really anything to do with it, but I proposed the idea to Jordan, and he got it going. I think there's been some cool stuff come out of it. Farside are probably the most well known out of any of the bands that I started working with.

Why did you call it Crisis?

We had a couple of different names, but we thought "Crisis" was cool because there was a "crisis" in the scene. There was some lack of direction, and we thought that these bands were trying to fill the vacuum of the crisis in the scene. There were a lot of different things springing up. At that time, the ABC No Rio scene that was springing up in response to this vacuum that had to be filled by these bands not having a venue to play in anymore, like CB's. That was kind of a similar kind of idea, trying to fill the vacuum. That whole 80's thing had died out, kind of and that's about it.

When did Gorilla Biscuits go over to Europe?

When Youth of Today went in '88 or '89, no one else that I'd known had gone before. Six months later, Gorilla Biscuits went. Within those six months, from Youth of Today going to Gorilla Biscuits going, so much had changed. It was just so obvious. The next time

CHRIS TOLIVER

Youth of Today reunion

Gorilla Biscuits went back, it was even more so. Everyone was focused on New York hardcore. Within a period of two years, it totally changed the whole character of the European scene. A lot of people would say for the worst because they had a more political punk, squatter mentality over there, and now it's way more Americanized, consumer kind of scene.

When you joined Youth of Today, what happened with Gorilla Biscuits?

It just continued. It wasn't like either band was on tour all the time, so if someone was on tour, the other would have to hold off for a little while. Youth of Today was more active at that time.

Which band did you prefer playing in?

I like playing in both, that's why I did both. I was always pulling for both bands. In Youth of Today, I didn't have to play as much of a role, because I was a bass player. I was writing for the band, but I wasn't the main driving force in the group, so it was easier for me to take a back seat. Whereas with Gorilla Biscuits I was definitely more active, so it allowed me to have a lot of fun, basically.

Youth of Today in Boulder, CO

How did Gorilla Biscuits come to an end, and how did your leaving Youth of Today come about?

Youth of Today was about Krishna consciousness at that point and about promoting it. I don't believe in Krishna consciousness, or promoting it, so for me to be in the band was a little bit strange. I still enjoyed it and had a great time, and I wasn't against what we were doing, but it wasn't what I envisioned the band as, what I felt the band was about. That's how Ray felt, too. Ray wanted to do something that he felt sincere about, which was starting a band that revolves around Krishna consciousness, so that's what happened.

With Gorilla Biscuits, it was the same, but it was more of a musical style thing. I wasn't really interested in straight forward hardcore with really straight forward lyrics. I didn't feel that the people that were coming to see Gorilla Biscuits at the later stages of the band had an idea of what the band was about anymore.

You see a lot of bands that just kept playing and kept playing and kept playing because they had nothing better to do. They just milk the name of the group into the ground to the point where people think, "Oh god, they're playing again?" So it makes it special, bands that break up when they should break up. I think that Youth of Today did that and so did Gorilla Biscuits. We didn't go do re-

Ray and Walter

unions and things, we just broke it off, and that was the end of it, so people remember it fondly.

Didn't you just do a Youth of Today reunion?
(Laughter) Yeah, at City Gardens.

Why did you do that?
I was in town. Shelter had been playing Youth of Today songs in their set, so they asked me to. I said, "Yeah, fuck yeah, I'll go nuts." I think it would be stupid to do a tour, but to play five songs at City Gardens was probably a good thrill for the people that never saw the band, so it was cool.

KEVIN SECONDS

Kevin Seconds is the singer of one of my favorite bands, 7 Seconds, who I think have more integrity than almost any other band around. I had the pleasure of speaking with Kevin on 12 May 1995.

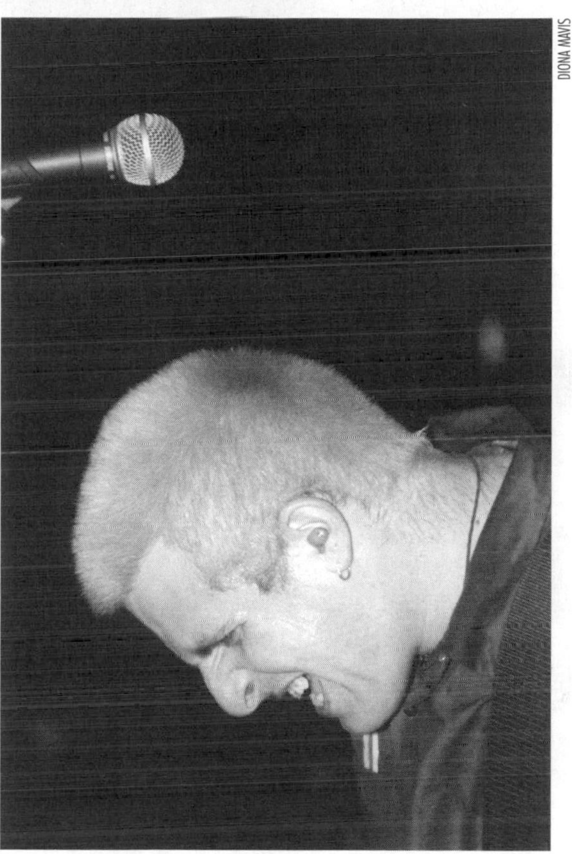

7 Seconds at the Pioneer Square Theater 2/10/96

Living in this shit hole Nevada which was very conservative, and there wasn't much going on, we decided that this was the perfect setting to start a punk rock band, so that's what we did. At that point, we didn't do drugs, and we weren't into drinking or smoking or things like that. We were kind of out of place with just about everybody that we came into contact with. We'd play parties. Everybody would be drunk, and we were playing our music. It was kind of frustrating.

Then we got a letter from Henry Rollins, then Henry Garfield, who was in a band called SOA from DC. We started trading tapes and writing to each other, and then we wrote to Ian (MacKaye) about that time. Minor Threat was really the first band. Because of the song, "Straight Edge," we connected. We were on the West Coast and we had similar views about the whole "no drug" thing. They were on the East Coast. We just kind of connected. They came out to the West Coast and we played a lot of shows together. We were kind of affiliated with Minor Threat and the DC/East Coast thing. We had more in common with those bands than we did with at the time the big L.A. hardcore bands like Social Distortion or the Circle Jerks. We were slightly different. I think we were faster. We were way against the whole drug thing.

At that point, we weren't really calling ourselves straight edge. We were outspoken about our views on it, but I don't think we were really preaching too much about it. I tried to stay away from that as much as possible.

We put out a couple of records and built up a following. We

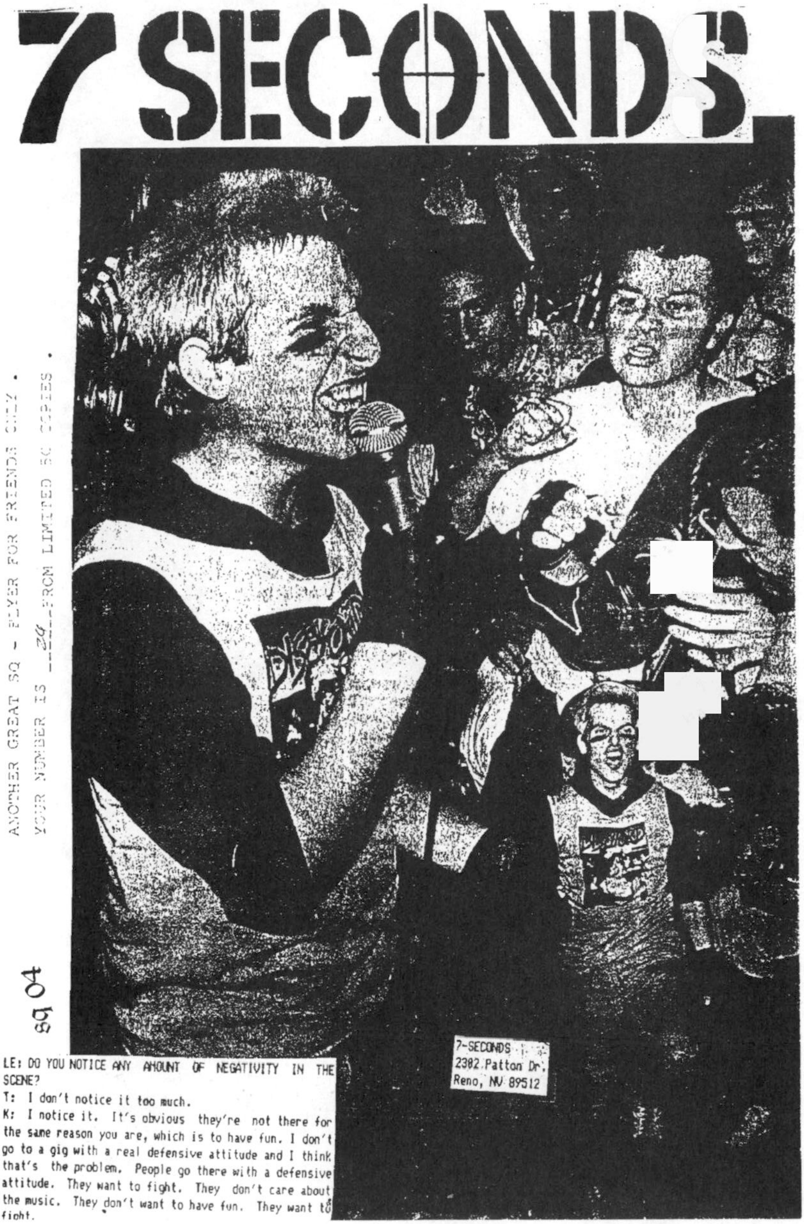

7 SECONDS
ANOTHER GREAT SQ - FLYER FOR FRIENDS ONLY.
YOUR NUMBER IS _24_ FROM LIMITED 50 COPIES.
sq 04
LE: DO YOU NOTICE ANY AMOUNT OF NEGATIVITY IN THE SCENE?
T: I don't notice it too much.
K: I notice it. It's obvious they're not there for the same reason you are, which is to have fun. I don't go to a gig with a real defensive attitude and I think that's the problem. People go there with a defensive attitude. They want to fight. They don't care about the music. They don't want to have fun. They want to fight.
7-SECONDS
2302 Patton Dr.
Reno, NV 89512

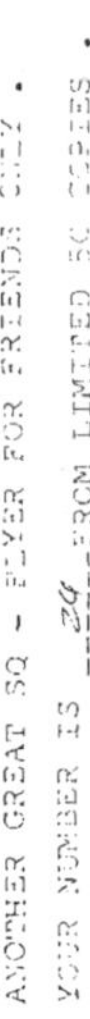

toured a few times. We came back one year, and the New York scene went crazy. There were a lot of New York kids who were picking up on a lot of the straight edge bands, like DYS and SSD from Boston. We played a show in Connecticut at the old Anthrax club. Ray (Cappo) was then the drummer for Violent Children. He came up to our show and asked to dedicate the song "Trust" to his girlfriend, and we did. He got up and sang.

Positive Force ad for Youth of Today Can't Close My Eyes EP

A couple of months later, I got a phone call from Ray. He said, "Hey I'm starting a new band called Youth of Today, and we're going to send you a tape." He sent me the tape, and I thought it was really cool. I was running my own label called Positive Force, and I guess that's where it all started with our connection to the youth scene, straight edge New York thing.

I'm just not into trying to lay down laws to people or telling people how I think they should live their life. For me personally, not doing drugs or not drinking is just a personal choice. I don't have a big political agenda behind it. It's a personal thing, and it works for me very well. At the same time, I have friends who drink or smoke pot or whatever. I'm not going to condemn them, that's their thing. I don't want to have to be bothered with it.

I'm kind of out of touch with the newer straight edge scene. I know some of the bands, and I like some of the music. It used to be more networked. People were writing to each other a lot, and I'm sure there still is. I lost touch with it, doing so much touring and moving around. I'll pick up a fanzine, and I'll read about these bands and think, "Oh my god, I don't even know anything about these bands!" There's this whole new breed of kids, but it's cool.

Do you get a lot of straight edge kids at your shows?

Yeah, we still get a lot of straight edge kids. We got flack. About eight years ago, there was a pretty significant change in our sound. We weren't doing totally fast stuff, and a lot of kids were bummed out at that. They stopped buying our stuff and going to our shows. But with that, there came a new group of kids who were still into the straight edge thing, but they were into more melodic stuff. There was almost like a new scene, at least from where we were at, for us. A lot of the old kids come out. I'll see them every once in a while. We'll be on tour, and I'll see someone from years ago, and it's cool to think, "You're still around, I'm still around, here we are!" It's funny to think that a lot of the kids that we knew from 10 years ago, a lot of these now are lawyers, or they're married or have kids. It's kind of cool.

But yeah, we still have a large straight edge contingent at our shows. In fact, we're doing a couple of shows coming up. We're doing a show here in town in a few weeks with Strife. There's two other bands, it's a complete straight edge bill. It's going to be very interesting. The Sacramento straight edge scene is small, but it's there.

7 Seconds in Denver, CO

RICH JACOBS

DIONA MAVIS

7 Seconds at the Pioneer Square Theater 2/10/96

7 Seconds 1985 tour sticker

Sam Seigler

TIM OWEN

Youth of Today

Sam began playing drums at 14 and eventually played with just about every East Coast straight edge band. He is now playing with Civ. This interview was conducted in two sessions, on Christmas Eve 1994 and 4 March 1996 from backstage after a show with Civ in the midwest.

How did you get involved with hardcore and straight edge?

My sister knew two guys who needed a drummer for their punk/ska band, Noize Police. We only played a few weird shows, like for a school trip on a boat and talent shows. I was about 12 years old, and was smoking cigarettes and pot and being punk rock. It was before I got into straight edge.

Did you play drums before that?

I started when I was ten. My dad, grandfather and uncle played, it was just around when I was growing up. I got more into it when I started playing in bands. After I was in Noize Police, I played in Gorilla Biscuits. My best friend knew Walter's younger brother. I only played one show, called the "Birth of Unity" show. It was with a whole bunch of great bands out on Long Island at this club called The Right Track Inn. I got kicked out of the band because I wasn't very good. My friend met Jules from Side by Side and hooked me up with them. We did a bunch of shows with Youth of Today. That's how I got hooked up with those guys. Porcell and I did Project X, and after Youth of Today broke up, we did Judge. We then played in Gorilla Biscuits, Bold and Shelter together. We were really tight.

You were in every band.

I was in the right place at the right time.

Were you in Side by Side from its onset?

Yes, I think I was the first drummer. I did my first recording with them, one song for the Revelation Records Together 7". Playing with them and doing shows with Youth of Today is what really got me into straight edge.

How long were you in Side by Side?

I think it was about two years. It's kind of a blur, everything sort of overlapped. I don't know why we broke up, but I got to play in Youth of Today after that, which was a dream come true because they were my favorite band. Their drummer Mike left to start Judge and Porcell was really pushing for me to join. They took me on my first US tour when I was 14 and my first European tour. I made my first full-length album with them. It was great.

How did it come about with you leaving Youth of Today?

After our European tour in '89, Ray wanted to do something else. He had become a Hare Krishna. I think he was tired of doing Youth of Today after five years, so he started Shelter. It all worked out because I joined Judge, which was a lot of fun.

Did you ever play in more than one band at a time?

One summer I played in Judge and Bold back to back for a 4-week tour and I think we were still in Youth of Today when Porcell, Walter, Alex and I did Project X. That was our full-on straight edge project.

How much did Project X play out? I remember only a handful of shows.

I think only six or seven shows. Not many. We only pressed 500 of the 7" and they only were available in this zine that Porcell and Alex did, called "Schism."

Which band do you think of mostly as the band you were in?

If not Civ, the band that I'm in now, I would have to say Youth of Today because we did so much. I think that we had a really positive influence on people's lives. It was much more than some hardcore band traveling around playing music. It was really special.

How was your rapport with the other drummers in the straight edge scene?

There was some level of competition. I would watch Drew or Luke play, and I would get totally inspired and want to get better, or I would want to throw my drums in the garbage. Everyone had their own style and was still growing a lot as musicians. There were also drummers like Mackie and Pete Hines that I totally looked up to. Some people were really good and others kind of sucked, but that was the beauty of that music. It didn't really matter if you were good or not, as long as you were sincere and had that energy. That was all that mattered.

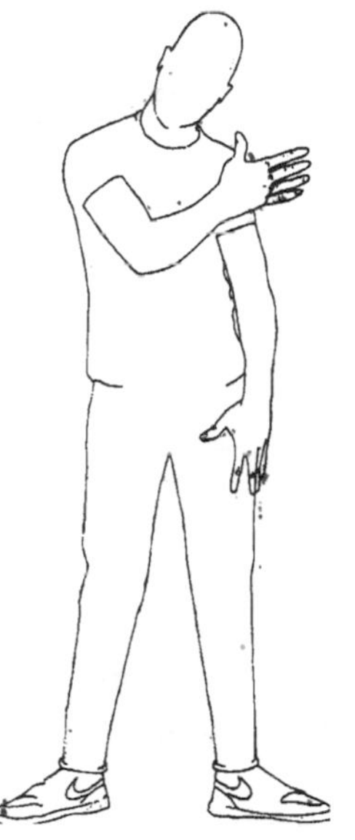

When you went to Europe with Youth of Today, what was that like for you?

Two months during the winter, in a little van, playing and sleeping in squats—it was kind of a hard tour. I think we were the first straight edge band to go over there and they definitely had a hard time grasping our philosophy. We were also getting ripped off, and were on tour with Lethal Aggression—a "drug-core" band from New Jersey. It was an experience.

Was it better when you went back with Gorilla Biscuits?

Yeah, it was a lot more organized. The shows were bigger and people were hip to the whole straight edge thing from the foundation that Youth of Today set up. It was also the second time that Gorilla Biscuits was there—Luke was playing drums the first time. We had more friends there and I think the weather was a lot nicer, which made a big difference. There was something special about when Youth of Today went. It was as though we were on some mission to bring New York straight edge to Europe. It was cool seeing the scene in Europe for the first time, playing in Yugoslavia and Czechoslovakia—it was a trip.

Did Judge tour the United States?

We toured twice. One tour I booked myself. It was supposed to be all around the US, but it kind of fell apart in some places. The other was the Bold/Judge tour from Los Angeles to New York. They were both fun. It was hard to go on tour a lot because Mike had a lot of obligations at home. We were supposed to go to Europe, but it got fucked up.

How did Judge break up?

To be honest, I don't really know. Porcell and Mike had a big conversation at the end of this one tour, and that was it.

You played on the Judge album Chung King Can Suck It. What did you think of that whole thing?

After we went to Chung King and recorded and it came out like shit, I was pissed. We thought that if you went to a big fancy studio and dropped a lot of money, you'd get a better sound. We were wrong. In the end, I think it all worked out. I thought it was cool for Jordan to do the Chung King Can Suck It album and explain on it what happened. We got to go to another studio and re-record those songs and we made a slammin' record.

Chung King Can Suck It got bootlegged.

I think so. A lot of those records did. I don't mind if they look and sound good and I get some of the copies. A lot of times the quality is shit, and I don't get shit.

Did you guys ever get paid for any bootlegs you were on?

Nope. When I went to Europe with Youth of Today, we went to our record company's warehouse and they had five different shirts that they made with the worst designs and they were on the cheapest shirts. They told us we weren't getting any money for them and that it was the norm in Europe to bootleg merchandise. We had always made it a point to use good, 100% cotton shirts with cool designs. Companies still pull that shit. Lost and Found in Germany puts out the worst quality merchandise and records, and rarely pays royalties—it's a joke. A lot of us just aren't in the position to run around suing everyone, so we get jerked.

"The reality is you do get older and things do change."

What did you do after you stopped playing in hardcore bands?

After Gorilla Biscuits broke up in '91, I started playing in a reggae band called 32 Tribes. It was cool, we played totally different clubs to different people. It was a nice change. The music was fun and the guys in the band—all six of them—were really cool. We played one show with Quicksand. It was cool to see the different scenes mix. We played with H.R. once. He had no band, so after he lip-synched his latest record, he jammed with us. I also played in a band called Engine, which was more of a heavy-rock thing. The singer, Ian, and I had too many problems with band members, so it didn't get far. We did do a two-week tour with Into Another, which was cool. I was also going to school for jazz in New York, but after a year and a half, I figured that I would be better off playing full-time in bands.

What do you think happened to straight edge?

I think a lot of the kids forgot that hardcore was about looking out for each other and supporting each other whether you were straight edge, skinhead, punk or whatever. The straight edge scene became really separated and more about fashion and gossip. That's what ruined it for me.

How do you think you've changed since then?

I'm a little older. It's easier for me to take things in. When I was 15 and going on tour it kind of flew by. Now I make it a point to slow down and enjoy every show.

Which recording are you most proud of?

I love the Youth of Today Disengage 7". I'm also really proud of the Civ album Set Your Goals. Bringin' It Down is cool, too. I can still listen to those three and get psyched.

How did the Youth of Today reunion show come about?

Ray and Porcell called me up because they needed a drummer for Shelter, they wanted to start writing some new songs and had a tour with Type O Negative. I did that and since it was me, Ray and Porcell—three of the members from Youth of Today—kids would always shout out Youth of Today songs and we didn't really want to do Youth of Today stuff because it was a different band. It's kind of cheesy when bands do that. So we just said that we were going to do it for once and for all, a real deal Youth of Today show, so we got Walter and did it.

It was actually a Shelter and Sick Of It All show at City Gardens in Jersey. We just got up after the Shelter set and just played. We opened with "Flame Still Burns." It felt good. I think a lot of bands in the past couple of years have been getting back together to tour Europe just for money or whatever. Their hearts are not in it. I think that there are some things that should be just left alone, just let them be. That is why we said we'd just do it once.

Did everybody just freak out when they saw you all come on stage?

Yeah, we got a positive response from a lot of people. I was worried. I think reunions are kind of cheap.

But it's kind of neat when you're at a show and something weird happens.

It just seems with Shelter, a lot of times people want to hear Youth of Today stuff. We played a show and people yelled, "Play Youth of Today!" I think Shelter has a lot more to offer as a band. That's why with the Civ thing, we're not trying to make it like a new Gorilla Biscuits. It's a new band and all of that stuff was over five years ago.

You play Gorilla Biscuits songs on stage with Civ. Were you getting bombarded with a lot of requests?

Yeah, we were getting a lot of requests. Also, a lot of kids are young and they never got to see Gorilla Biscuits. So if we can play one or two Gorilla Biscuits songs and make their day, then we'll do it. With Civ, in the beginning it was really hard because people didn't know what it was. We played a few shows before our album came out. We did a two month tour in Europe with Sick Of It All and the kids didn't know any of the songs. We figured if we did three or four Gorilla Biscuits songs then they could get into it. But we are trying to steer away from that. It's not that we don't love those songs, it's just that we have our own material.

Do you think that it is possible for somebody to be "True Till Death?"

Never say never. You never know what will happen in life. It is nice to get into something gung ho and 100 percent and give it all you've got, but there is no telling. I've seen kids who were screaming "true till death" who are total burn outs now. I don't hold it against them but I think they kind of make fools out of themselves by being like that. I wore X's, and I was into straight edge, and I was proud of it, but I never put other people down if they weren't into it.

I've got another catch phrase for you to comment on, "If you're not now, then you never were." Have you seen those T-shirts?

I've seen a lot of T-shirts. All I can say is that is not what straight edge was about for me. Straight edge for me was about caring for yourself and caring about the world around you—that's why I became a vegetarian. It's not about putting people down for being unlike you. "If you're not now, then you never were" might be easier to say for somebody who is protected by a group of friends or somebody who is really young and not facing a lot of the things in life that happen when you get older. The reality is you do get older and things do change.

How do you feel about being so involved in the whole indie music thing, from going to the more DIY thing to being on a major label and being on MTV and in mass media?

I think that there are many different ways to go about being in a band. I think that I have explored the Indie scene a lot, putting a lot of records out on Revelation and Schism. I think that is a totally cool way to do stuff and very smart in a lot of ways. For me and for Civ right now, if we were to do another album on an independent label, we'd just be reaching the same amount of people. We want to reach new people as well as old people. We want to get new energy into this and hopefully show these kids what we are about because we're proud of it. I think it is a really special and cool thing. It is important to show other people that you can listen to aggressive music and still be really positive. It helps to have a major record label behind us. We have been on tour since last May, and it is March right now, and there is no way we would be able to do that with any independent label. We get tour support and total creative freedom. In a way it is very independent. Our A&R person is Mike Gitter, who has been involved in hardcore since way before I was and most of the people at Atlantic know about Youth of Today and Gorilla Biscuits.

"I've seen kids who were screaming "true till death" who are total burn outs now. I don't hold it against them but I think they kind of make fools out of themselves by being like that."

Do you have any connection with the straight edge scene today?

My connection is that I was in the straight edge scene for seven years. It means a lot to me still. I will always respect it, and it will always have a place in my heart. Obviously, a lot of straight edge kids are into Civ, so I still see them and do interviews for their zines. I've connected with all kinds of people. Some of my best friends while I was straight edge were smoking weed and drinking. It all depends on where your head is and where your heart is.

It is not a satisfying feeling if you are living a stagnant life. Playing to the same people, same clubs—you want to progress in life. It makes you feel good. If you're doing what feels right, it shouldn't matter. People get so involved in the politics of it all that they forget what we are - we're a band, and our message is just to live a good life and enjoy yourself and be positive. It shouldn't matter who is putting out the record. When we were on an independent label people were complaining that it's hard to find the records and this and that.

TIM OWEN

People are going to complain no matter what—no matter if you put the record out yourself or on some label making millions of dollars. People are going to constantly point their fingers.

I am so happy—I am in a great situation. I don't let it bother me—even back then people would make up rumors. Things like "Ray isn't straight" or "Porcell is a drug addict" or that I sell drugs. People are going to do that—you can't listen to that—you've got to do what you got to do. I'll always do interviews because I care about our fans and our scene, but I wish people weren't so quick to judge. The whole hardcore thing is so special to me, and I am thankful that I got to play in all those bands and am thankful that I am still able to do it.

Arthur Smilios

JOSHUA LANE STANTON

January 15, 1996—Arthur played bass in Gorilla Biscuits and Token Entry. This interview was conducted on 15 January 1996 in a cafe in Seattle while he was on tour. I'll let him finish his own introduction ...

Arthur and Civ (Gorilla Biscuits)

Hi, I am Arthur. I play bass with Civ, and I am sitting here in Seattle—one of my favorite cities in the world—doing three of my favorite things with a beautiful person. That would be conversing, drinking coffee and smoking cigarettes—three of my favorite, favorite things—things that make my life blessed. So let's talk about hardcore...

How did you first get interested in hardcore? How did it all start? When did you throw away your Led Zeppelin albums?

I never threw them away—ever. I grew up in Queens, New York—Jackson Heights. I had a cousin that was considerably older and was involved in the punk scene when it was Max's Kansas City and everything. When we used to go over for holidays, to my aunt's house, my cousin would play records—I heard the [New York] Dolls that way, the Sex Pistols that way, I heard The Clash. I remember seeing the Sex Pistols on television when they came to America—I was really young, and they looked so atrocious they couldn't possibly play music well at all. Then I went to [my cousin's] house and put it on, and I was surprised because I thought punk was the way that it was portrayed on television shows and whatever else. All of the sudden I heard the best straight ahead rock and roll. I was confused after that with a punk moniker because I thought this was just describing a fashion thing, and it is not describing the music because the music is straight ahead rock and roll. I thought it was great, and so those are the initial things. The Dolls I loved too because the Dolls were more like blues—they had a harmonica and everything. Back then—and I still like the harmonica—but my theory then was that if a song had a harmonica in it then it was a good song, and they had a harmonica, and I thought it was great.

The Clash—all I had to do was see them. I saw Paul Simonon, and I just lost it. I decided to get boots and cut my hair, and it wasn't popular in my junior high school at all because words like "fag" were used to insult people, and I got called that a million times. But in junior high it wasn't that bad. It was all in jest because we all grew up together, but it was more malicious when I moved to Astoria. I remember when I got my first pair of creepers, and I can not believe the abuse that I sustained. They were Doctor Martens. Now you can go to Wall Street, and people that work on Wall Street wear Doctor Martens, literally. But back then they were looked at as a freak show. You look at them now, and they are the most normal looking shoes. So I got into punk rock that way.

When I was thirteen, I moved out of my mother's house and into my grandparents house in Astoria. There

Arthur and Walter (Gorilla Biscuits)

were these kids that I knew from when I was a child and would spend summers there. I went back, and I ran into them. They were Ernie Token Entry and Johnny Token Entry. I just ran into Ernie one day on the street and I asked him, "Hey what's going on? Can I come down to a show with you one day?" So I was lucky in the sense that I got into it with people who knew what was going on. As anyone who has ever been involved with the scene knows, there is this whole stupid thing of earning your stripes. But everyone has been the new kid at some point. A lot of kids went through the dorky phases, and you learn. I was lucky because I was schooled by Ernie and Anthony Killing Time—who was singing for Token Entry at the time. One of the first people I met outside of them was Jimmy Gestapo. Jimmy is a sweetheart. I first met him in Astoria, and the second time I saw him was at CBGB's and he came up to me and said "Hi." I thought, "Yes! I'm in!" because people saw that. When you're sixteen that is how you think. That was it. It was over then. All of the sudden I could be in a band and could play our own music in front of people instead of all my friends that were playing cover songs in garages. It was just great.

The first time I went to a hardcore show I saw people slam dancing. Although I hate to say it, the way it is done now in many respects is kind of trite. Not with hardcore shows. There was a whole ethic because it was so underground and so tight. You didn't do it to hurt people, and ou hurt somebody you would say you were sorry, and it was circumstantial because you are banging into each other. There s a certain amount of style involved. It just wasn't going around flailing your arms trying to hit people. That came later. I was long out of the pit by then—with scars and a crooked nose. I wasn't born with a broken nose. My sister used to yell at me, "Why are you so stupid? You had a great nose and now you don't." I just fell right into it. I loved it.

e best thing in the world is ane, not in a dangerous way the sense that you live your life actly in the way that you want to live it."

JOSHUA LANE STANTON

I could do what I wanted. It was just utter freaks. What I realized over time is how insane so many of the people that I met through hardcore that I still know now—and still meet—just how insane these people are. To me, the best thing in the world is to be insane, not in a dangerous way but in the sense that you live your life exactly in the way that you want to live it. That has always been the good thing about punk rock. It has plenty of bad things though, especially in those days. Kids always ask about those days and glorify them. Yeah, they were fun and all, but there were idiots back then and stupidity and closed mindedness and whatever else, but for the most part you could do pretty much what ever you wanted to. There were some really creative people who played in bands and wrote beautiful songs—like Walter.

I first met Walter 11 years ago, and he could barely play guitar, and he started Gorilla Biscuits. He had this little Peavey guitar without a case, and it was in the summer in Astoria, and he brought it over to this kid George's garage. The way that he brought it over was in a Glad bag with the neck sticking out. As we all know, a guitar has six strings, but Walter's had five. He wrote silly songs, and he is a flower. Quicksand just broke up, and his new stuff is amazing. Just a couple of months ago, watching Quicksand, it just occurred to me that my life with Walter is like watching a flower grow. A silly kid with a five-string guitar, someone who could barely play guitar, who is now writing some of the most beautiful, poignant music there is.

So you had that strain of great song writers and great musicians, but you had great artists that did cover work for 7"s. You had people who put out the records. You had great writers who put out fanzines. The whole DIY thing—which I have been accused of selling

PHOTOS THIS PAGE: JOSHUA LANE STANTON

Arthur and Gorilla Biscuits

JOSHUA LANE STANTON

Gorilla Biscuits

out because my band just got signed to a major label—I support entirely. Essentially, nobody can ever tell my band anything because we've done it, we've done it several times. We've done it before everybody. The fact remains that the whole DIY thing started not necessarily as a grand "fuck you" to the industry because of business, but because that industry didn't have an intention, and there was no other way to get around it. People concern themselves far too much with lifestyles of people in bands that the music becomes secondary. I love playing hardcore shows. I love kids getting on stage as long as they respect my equipment. I really love my equipment, and its not the money—it's just that I love my bass and I do not want it to break. If they are going to break, I want to be the person who does it. For the most part, kids are respectful. So I love playing shows. I just always want to play music.

DAVE STEIN

Dave Stein used to book shows in Albany. He now practices law in New York City. We spoke on 30 October 1995.

How did you initially get involved in straight edge?

Just recognizing that everything about punk that was cool—the rebellion, the angst, the being fed up with status quo —lost all of its validity when people were doing all of these things that destroyed themselves and bought into everything that they claimed to be against—supporting the companies, supporting the addictions, supporting all of those things was something that I recognized really defeated what I thought were really the greatest things about the whole music scene. It was, I thought, all a big hypocrisy.

So, you were living in Albany, and you started putting on shows?

When I was in college, there was stuff going on in Albany, and there were people putting on shows, but it was few and far between. I was going out of town to see a lot of bands that I liked because they just weren't playing in Albany. I was heading down to the Anthrax in Connecticut a lot, I was heading up to Syracuse to see shows, and it very much dawned upon us that we could be in a position to do exactly the same types of things that we were seeing people in other scenes do, that we could find a place to put on shows and do it independently, away from the bars, away from restricted ages, and do something, as I always said, "Do something by, of and for the kids." That's when we started doing shows.

Where did you put on the shows?

We started out doing them in a VFW Hall, and we did them there for a couple of years, starting out with local East Coast bands, but we did stuff there in that particular hall as big as Suicidal Tendencies and Black Flag—everything from local bands—Youth of Today played there plenty of times. Everybody who was around from '84 through '88 played through Albany at some point or another.

How do you remember the straight edge shows?

There were very few shows that I would call "straight edge" shows. That was sometimes frustrating that not everybody would ever get it. There would definitely be bills that were straight edge bands, but there would still be people out behind the hall, drinking beer. But that's part of it too, this being the hardcore scene in general, anything that is so far different from the mainstream, you're going to attract all types of crowds. Unfortunately, some of it was a negative element. I think it's that way, by and large, with anything that is off the beaten path—be it music, be it sports with hooligan fans, be it politics—anytime you're off the beaten path, you're going to have people who don't quite understand what's going on, but want to be there, yelling and screaming nonetheless. That's a real problem, I think, for any sort of movement because you have a fringe element around you, and that is often what people see the most of.

Don't you think that could also be good in that it exposes people to new things that maybe they would catch on to?

To an extent, yes, but I know a very few people who were real drinkers, whatever, that got into straight edge, and it really had a life-long impact on. I think for most people, those decisions are more or less made earlier on, and the whole straight edge scene kind of led these people who were otherwise, for a large part, cast out of their schools, off to the side, whatever, let them stand up and be in the center of things. It kind of let people have a sense of community and a sense of pride for what mattered to them. But I would venture to guess, and this is just my guess, obviously, that it doesn't really have the wide range impact that people would like to think that it has had, that probably I thought that it had at one point. I've just seen so many people that I'd thought that it had made an impact on, turn around and have real drug and alcohol problems, people who wore "X"'s on their hands, people who said that they were straight edge. So I don't think that it really has the impact that people would like to think that it did or people think it does.

"If there are people who can survive doing what they enjoy doing, and nobody's toes are getting stepped on in the process, no one should be pointing a finger and proclaiming that this shouldn't be done simply for the reason that it's not the hardcore way of doing things."

So, you do think that it is possible for someone to be "true till death?"

Oh, absolutely, absolutely. I surely intend to be and expect that I will be. There's no reason to believe that I won't. There are definitely some of my friends that I could say the same of.

Any great straight edge memories or anecdotes?

I think that the most fun that we used to have was when Porcell was going to school, he used to come down to Albany for the weekends. We used to have so much fun—me, him and Ray. It could have been Ray that had three way calling, I think Jordan may have gotten involved in this at some time, too, we used to play prank phone calls all the time. We used to do corny shit, funny stuff.

What was your involvement with New Beginning Records?

Somewhat tangential. I was friends with all of the people who were involved with that when it began. For a while, Bessie Oakely, who was one of the people who started it.... When the first stuff came out, I was selling the stuff locally in Albany. I used to sell records at shows. At the time the idea was to have records that weren't in the stores. I was buying all of those records and sending them to people who were doing the same thing in other scenes. I was friends with the bands who were coming out on that at the time—Underdog and Crippled Youth. When the Underdog record came out, Bessie was living up in Albany. She was sharing my apartment with me. I was helping out, mailing things out, getting ads in fanzines, the regular stuff that anyone who helps out on a record label does.

How did you get out of being so involved with straight edge and into doing what you're doing now?

There came a point where it became a question of not having enough time to do everything that I wanted to do. I wanted to pursue my legal career seriously. At that point, I had a record label called "Combined Effort" that I put a bunch of records out on. I knew that I was not doing as much for the bands as they deserved to be done for them. Part of that was the fact that I was in law school, and I was doing a lot of animal rights stuff. I had undertaken too much to do, and something had to give. I recognized that I wasn't going to be able to continue to do the record label and be fair to the bands that were on it. So, the record label came to an end. I was in New York City, so I wasn't in a position to be booking any shows. At that time, I was out of law school and a full time lawyer with not much time to do anything like that.

What type of law do you practice?

I practice entertainment law. I spent a long time doing commercial litigation, which I found interesting, but I recently was able to find my way into the entertainment department in my firm. It's really a lot more up my alley. It's where my background is and where I hope that I can do a lot with the music I care about. The reason why I didn't try to get into music law straight out of law school was because I had such a love and admiration for the music, that I never—and I was always asked this in interviews when I was interviewing with all of the law firms, "Why aren't you going for a job at a record label?" or whatever. I just had too much of a love for it and always thought that it should remain a hobby. I got annoyed when I saw people profiteering off of it. I got very annoyed, very self-righteous.

In the last five years, since I got out of law school, I think the scene has changed significantly. I think a lot of bands have gotten screwed, a lot of smaller labels have gotten screwed as bigger labels have gotten involved in what was once our nice, small, tight, "everyone knew everyone" community. Someone's got to be there, I think, to make sure things are done the right way for the bands and the small record labels who are having large record labels try to pull bands from them. It just seemed natural to me, that as this music scene was growing, that it was time for me to do some work with bands and with record labels involved in the scene, to protect interests. I've also grown up a bit and recognized that if one can combine a profession with something that they enjoy doing, that it's not selling out. If there are people who can survive doing what they enjoy doing, and nobody's toes are getting stepped on in the process, no one should be pointing a finger and proclaiming that this shouldn't be done simply for the reason that it's not the hardcore way of doing things.

DREW THOMAS

Drew played drums in Bold and Youth of Today. While his current band, Into Another, was in town recording, we spent an afternoon at Green Lake in Seattle. It was 22 February 1995.

I guess like every other kid that gets involved with something that's not of the social norm, it's because they hated something. I particularly hated being in junior high school and high school where I lived. My companion who shared those feelings was Matt (Warnke). We both kind of had a distaste for where we lived. We got into the same music, we were into punk, Sex Pistols records and all that, as much as we could.

When we were in eighth grade, we started going to a place called the Anthrax in Stamford, Connecticut. We'd do that on the weekend rather that going to high school parties. It was reckless in a different way. High school parties with a bunch of people that we couldn't stand was meaningless to me back then. I wanted something more. At the time, my main purpose was just to rebel against that. The health thing wasn't so much a part of it.

Matt and I played music together and had been doing it for a while, so after going to the Anthrax for about five or six months, we got a show there. At the first show we played there we met Ray Cappo and John Porcell. We hit it off really well.

We would do shows together with X's on our hands and "E-D-G-E" written on our fingers. We had a certain look, pants cuffed, hooded sweatshirts and whatever. It was definitely a style, and I

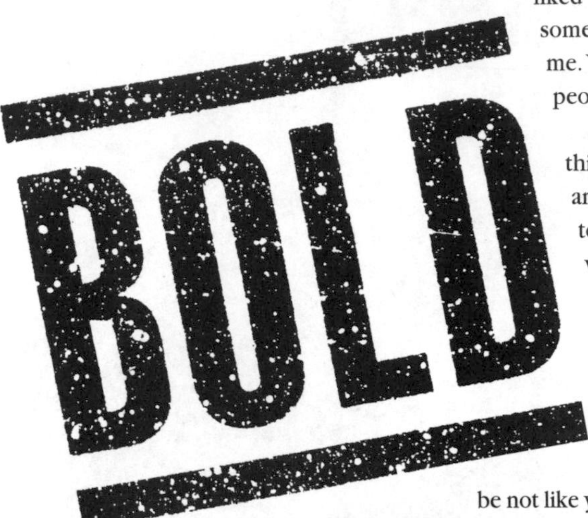

liked that. I've always loved style. It's something that's always appealed to me. You should have something that people can relate to.

That was definitely the right thing at the right time for us. It was amazing to see the way kids started to grab on to it. When I saw that, I wasn't really sure how to perceive it. On the one hand I thought, "Well, this is cool, if they are into for the reason that I got into it, then it's a valid reason." They're into it because they're saying, "Get away from me, I want to be not like you, I want to be on a different side of the tracks." Maybe they feel that a lot of people out there can start feeling like, "Let's just get more done, let's do something bigger and better" (than the shit I was exposed to at the time). Unfortunately, that really wasn't the case. Unfortunately, it was the look and the image, everything that I just mentioned—I think that took over.

A lot of kids were into it because they started having a hero worship thing going on. Looking back on it, the people that they were hero worshipping were telling them what to fucking do. I got so sick of that. I got so pissed off because I got into it because I didn't want to listen to anybody. I never was a hero worshipper and I never wanted to have anyone look up to me per se, or to anyone else, but rather to just get off on it in a more personal way. I think that kind of broke it for me. People were surprised when I said, "This is bullshit," but to me what was bullshit was the fact that these people were just a giant clique of what I tried to escape before. I couldn't take it anymore. I couldn't take going places and having people expect me to be a certain way because I've always tried to be the opposite of that.

When I joined Into Another, I went 100 percent the other way. I did not want to be in a band again where people are going to pin me down to a certain thing. I want to be in a band where I can be as expressive as I want to and do whatever I want to and still be an individual who is an artist and super creative and isn't locked into anything. I think that's the most important thing for people to realize.

I'm not knocking straight edge. I think it served its purpose and that was a great thing. It probably was a really good thing for me health-wise that I was able to grow up in those years not drinking or smoking or things like that. It was probably the best time in my life that I could have done something like that. But, it also—to quote a Bold song—really "wised me up" to the fact that later on in my life,

I was not going to make people look at me that way anymore.

It's easy to be straight edge if you have a really clean lifestyle and your parents are rich. It's not that difficult. But there are people who are really suffering out there, and they just want to get fucked up because they're really upset with the condition of their life. Some people can go beyond that. I really admire those people. Some people can say, "I don't care what my situation is, I'm going to live as healthy as I can, and I'm not going to get myself fucked up because nothing good comes of it." That's correct, yeah, nothing good does come of it really, except momentary escape. I'll tell you though, I just couldn't deal with it anymore. I was feeling too messed up to want to stay straight edge. I wanted to get out and experience more.

A lot of times, being too straight, I do damage to myself. I'm just sitting there being this ultra-pent-up person, which is probably why I play drums. I just didn't want to feel certain things anymore, so I got involved with experimenting with different drugs. I think to a certain extent, at the time, it was great because I want to try everything. I'm the kind of person that wants to try everything that comes my way. I don't want to overindulge in everything, but I'm here on this earth. I guess it's kind of like a devilish kind of thing in a way. I'm tempted, and I'll take it. I'm only going around once—everyone is. If someone is going to say to themselves, "Well, I'm going to cut myself out of this forever," What is that really? What you're looking at is abstinence from life. If you're going to hide away and not try anything, it's your prerogative. But I think a lot of people are going to miss out on things that can really further their journey in life.

For me, just trying stuff was an adventure. I really liked to play around with different drugs and kind of just see where it would take me because underneath it all there was someone who was in love enough with his craft. I felt like I could try things but still come back to my drums. That's always been my route back. When you wake up after five or six years of doing stuff though, you say, "All right, I might as well fucking be straight edge because I just feel like shit anyways when I'm not." That's kind of where I'm at right now. I'm 23 years old and I'm really digging what I'm doing right now with Into Another. I think that I don't want to continuously fuck myself up because I know what it's like waking up from every kind of feeling, from waking up after smoking too many cigarettes, to waking up after doing too many pills, or waking up after being drunk. It all comes down to the same thing—you feel like shit. I'd rather not feel like shit anymore, so I pretty much have come to the conclusion that it's best to be naturally high on what you do. What I do gets me off.

There's no other drug like playing live for me. That's why I've stuck to what I do, the feeling of going up there on stage and making everybody else feel really good. I am a drug. That's the coolest thing, for other people to get off on that, it makes me happy.

Most of all, I don't like it when people are straight edge because it's cool. I mean, everybody's guilty of posing to some extent—I sure do—but I've never been a hypocrite about shit. When I wasn't going to do something, I didn't say I was going to do it. People thought, "Oh, you stabbed us in the back!" That kind of stuff cracks me up, man, because it's my life. If someone said to me at any time, "Are you doing this?" I would say, "Yes, I am." I had a great time while it was happening. We were all so pompous. We were fucking snotty kids.

Like that song, "Walk Tall, Walk Straight"

"There's no other drug like playing live for me."

Yeah! It was so great. It was so funny writing shit like that. I remember being in my house and coming home and just being so pissed off and writing these completely pissed off lyrics about kids being screwed up, being assholes. They border on nonsensical. They're just so funny. It's just the writings of a kid who's pissed off. That's what I like about it. I never was trying to make them these holy lyrics. Some people try to make these straight edge things like the prophecy, and it's so dumb. Get real, because it's all just about rebelling. It's not about more than that.

If you're talking about it as a health issue, you get into things like "Are you vegetarian?" I'm a vegan, actually, that is in my eating habits because my shoes are made of leather. But, I won't eat any animal products. It's just horrible for you. You're harming the planet. You're killing animals. You're wasting tons of land to raise beef that you could be growing crops on to feed the whole United States where there's people starving in our urban environments. It's a waste to be worried about things like straight edge.

When you got out of straight edge, was that right after Youth of Today for you? What was the end of it for you?

The end of it for me was probably, I wouldn't say Youth of Today because I stopped doing shows with Youth of Today quite early on actually. I did *Break Down the Walls*.

Bold was still going on?

Yeah, but I was getting tired of playing the double drummer. It was getting to be a pain in the ass.The last show I did was actually the first show I ever did with Richie. He played guitar for the first time. It was in Philadelphia, and I played my last show with them. I think I was in 10th grade. I told Youth of Today,"You have to get a new drummer. I can't do this anymore." That was right before they got Sammy.

I still stayed straight edge probably for about another year, until I met a wicked woman who corrupted me, and I thought to myself,"You know what, I have to try things in my life."At that point, I was really sick of it anyways. I would go to shows and I would see

CHRIS TOLIVER

Into Another

the reaction that I would get from kids I would think,"I don't want you to look at me as an icon for straight edge, I want to shoot it down now. I want to shoot it down because I'm sick of what it's come to."All these kids with X's on their hands, it's becoming an army of bullshit. Give me a break.The reason I went into it had become totally nullified.

I went off and did my own thing. I pretty much stayed away from that scene. I had different friends.When I started to get into my later years in high school, it was never the same thing again for me. I just wanted to go out and play the shows. I loved to play music. I was more intent on worrying about the music at the time. With Bold I was worrying about the attitude first. The attitude was all that mattered, but then we got stigmatized by that and we got called a "mini-Youth of Today." I was like, "Fuck this. I don't want that anymore."

We got Tom Capone to play guitar for us, who I think is an incredible guitar player. I thought, "Finally. I can work with this guy musically." We wrote songs together which we put on the EP. I was really ecstatic about that because for me, it was the first time when the music spoke, not the look or the image. I wanted to be true to what I was doing.

When the *Bold* EP came out, everybody said that it sucked because it was a progressive hardcore rock thing. Four years later, everybody was playing those progressive hardcore things. I'm really happy about that more than anything to do with straight edge. I look at it as the last thing we did being an important move for us, or for me personally as a musician. I think I put stuff down on that recording that showed that there was more there than just an X on my hand.

How do you feel about all these straight edge bands today?
They probably have a certain motivation for it, I wonder what it is. Is it coming from what bands did like Youth of Today or Minor Threat? If that's the reason, I think it's kind of stupid. If you're talking about something because a certain band talked about it, that's stupid. If I'm into David Bowie, I'm not going to write a song about Ziggy Stardust. It just doesn't work like that.

I think some people though, straight edge really affects them. I think that if people come from families where the father is an alcoholic or they get upset about things, and they are really passionate about something from something that they have learned, then that is the right thing. The bands that fake it, and the people that fake it have got to hang it up.

When I go on tours, people come up, and they want to know if I'm straight edge. It surprises me that they would wonder that more than they would wonder about what I'm doing musically. It's the old fans that feel that way, the people who knew Bold. It upsets me partially that people talk about the straight edge thing rather than say something like, "Well I like this particular song..."

I actually am envious of Rich because I think that he didn't take a lot of those things to his music like Bold did. Therefore, people dig what went on with his band because of the music itself, more than an ideal. That's what I've learned. Now with Into Another, it's the new fans that come up, and they want to know more about the music, which is great. I'll never take an ideal to the music again. I'll take fashion to the music, and I'll take the best drumming and soul that comes from me to the music, but I'll never take an approach to it that this band stands for something. The closest we have to that is that we're all vegetarians.

Don't you have a vegan song?
"Herbivore," yeah. That's the closest I think the band comes to a stance. We are vegetarians who all happened to start a band together. If people kind of want to pin us as that, fine. I'm proud of it.

Richie has that big "VEGAN" billboard on his arm.
Yeah, Richie likes that, and that's OK. That's his prerogative. I'm sure he's got certain things he feels about that. There are people out there who are really outspoken about things to the point to where they want people to know what it's about. Some people have to see it in big bold letters to really get it. I don't really feel that way. I've always been someone who liked to remain anonymous about things than to show people the big heavy print. I'd rather let them guess at it a little more about what's going on.

Into Another is much more like that than Bold ever was, less direct, less in your face. Your music gives the mind so much space, so many places to wander around.
Yeah, I think that's just a matter of being real music. I'd rather get up on stage and be the drug for the people than be given drugs. I've had people come up and say, "I get super high on your band." You don't have to be really messed up or be out of it to get the band. Sure, it can be a sensational experience if you were high and saw us play, but some people get really off on getting the energy. We go through a lot of different places when we play. I think that it's more important than just being mono-faceted. For example when a band says, "OK this is our first straight edge song," then they get to song number five and say, "All right, this is our fifth song about the same topic!" Then they close the show with a slight variation, instead of a song being about not

smoking and drinking, "This song is about not being addicted to love," or whatever.

So what's going to happen with Into Another now?
I guess we're just going to try to make as much money as we can. My main concern is when I get straight edge kids asking me things like, "Now that you're not on Revelation anymore, do you think you sold out?" How many records did I do on that label? A lot. I'm a grown up person now, and now I need to make money for myself so I can live, so I'm not in the gutter when I'm 40 years old I have a lot of great things that I want to do with my money when I make it. At the same time, we've always been a benefit band for things like animal rights.

You have a record coming out.
Yeah, there's an EP that's going to be coming out on Revelation, It's the *Herbivore* 7". All of the money is going to donated to Earthsave and PETA.

We got something good for us—which was a good deal for this record that we're doing, or the next couple of records that we're doing—and it's good to give a little bit back. There's a karma to it that's more important than anyone's individual feelings about how they're going to treat their body or how anyone else should. What right do we really have to tell people specific things about how they're going to destroy themselves? When people ask, "What about this whole thing telling people that you don't animals and this and that, and you shouldn't either?" Well, there's a difference. The difference is that you're helping destroy my planet, too. By doing that, you're ruining a lot of other people's lives and the lives you're killing. There's a difference between killing yourself and killing off the planet and killing other living beings. That's the difference to someone who has a good set of ideals or understands or thinks about life a little bit more, it's all part of the process. I think there's a lot of kids out there that are straight edge now that will go through changes and might come back to it, but the bottom line is that hopefully all the people that are will be thinkers rather than conformists, and that's the reason they're doing it. That's probably a good way to close.

Becky Tupper

Becky was another one of the few girls in the straight edge scene. She currently lives in New Haven, Connecticut. I spoke with her on 14 December 1995.

Describe your personal involvement with straight edge.

My personal involvement with straight edge at this point in my life is quite limited. I rarely attend shows of any kind anymore, and I feel like my life is so different from my hardcore days. The part of me that I can still call "straight edge," however, is the fact that I do not drink or do drugs. I would not currently label myself as "straight edge," but I am proud of the fact that I manage to enjoy life without the interference of alcoholic or synthetic substances of any kind.

When and where did you first start going to shows?

The first shows that I attended were in the spring of 1984 at The Twilight Zone in New Haven, Connecticut. I believe the Ramones and Gang of Four were some of the first bands that I saw. Although both of these bands are not typically labeled as "hardcore," these particular shows certainly gave me a taste of a world that I was not even aware existed.

My first straight edge show was Violent Children and Crippled Youth during the summer of 1984 at The Anthrax in Stamford, Connecticut. This was when I started to experiment and try and create some sort of identity for myself. At that point, I was only 16 years old and had friends who were punks, skins and just plain different. The straight edge movement really appealed to me. It was just a bunch of kids who enjoyed music, hanging out and there was no alcohol or drugs involved. To me, this was the ideal situation. Having grown up with an alcoholic father, I was afraid of alcohol and the way it made me feel and lack of control that I had when I abused it. Having drunk a number of times in my junior high school and early in my high school career, I never enjoyed the affects of alcohol and was looking for an excuse to stay away from it. So, drawing the X's on my hands, calling myself "straight edge" and refraining from the dangers of mind-altering substances not only created a world where I could enjoy music and hang out with a group of people and places where I felt totally comfortable, but it also protected me from the physical ramifications that came with drinking and drugging.

Describe your memories of the straight edge scene.

My memories of people in the straight edge scene are nothing but warm and nostalgic. I miss those days more than I can verbalize. However, I also know that the straight edge scene and hardcore scenes have changed so much, for the worse, I believe. There was a

SUSAN MARTINEZ

Becky—
Spring 1986

point where I think it became a lot less about music and a lot more about clothes and social circles. Don't get me wrong, there was lots of socializing going on when I was hanging out, there was a point when it all became less personal and more big business.

How did you feel as a girl in the straight edge scene?

I never felt any different about being a girl at straight edge shows, and I think that point perfectly illustrates the beauty and personality of the scene when I was hanging out. There were no differences, particularly, aside from the physical, between girls and guys in the hardcore scene. We were all just there to enjoy the music, get away from our parents and have a good time. Whether you were a punk or skin, drinking or not drinking, everyone was created equal and everyone was friends. If you chose not to drink, that was your choice, and there was a lot less judgement going on about what each person's practices were. As I said above, I think there was a point at which straight edge changed and became competitive and judgmental and less about just being yourself.

How did you become less interested in hardcore?

When I graduated from New York University and moved out of New York City, there was much less of an opportunity for me to see shows in my hometown of New Haven, Connecticut. I guess I sort of grew out of it. That's not to say that I don't love my occasional dose of music, whether it be live or not. But I think somewhere along the way, I decided that I was growing older and the age range of the people at shows were either staying the same or getting younger. It started to feel like I was old enough to be a parent to some of the kids at these shows, and it felt really weird.

What do you think of the straight edge scene today?

I think that it is not what it used to be. That's not to say that it's not a good thing. For example, I have noticed that the practice of vegetarianism has become a general practice of straight edge kids and hardcore kids in general. Being a herbivore myself, I think that this is fantastic. However, I think that the straight edge scene has grown at such a rapid rate, that it feels a lot bigger and less personal. I am happy for all of the bands that I used to spend time with that have made it big in the industry, but no one can deny that it has changed the hardcore atmosphere and the approachability of a lot of the people.

Kevin Seconds mentioned something about the song "Trust" during his interview.

The "Trust" story about Ray Cappo and I is still an example of the most romantic thing that anyone has ever done for me. Maybe that was a part of my being 16 years old and being in love for the first time, but it still sticks out in my mind. Ray had written me a letter with the lyrics from "Trust" written in it. He had asked me in the letter to read the lyrics and try and understand what that song meant to him and in respect to our relationship. 7 Seconds were touring in the fall of 1984 and came to play at The Anthrax. Ray, without my knowing, asked Kevin Seconds if he could sing "Trust" to me with the band. Kevin agreed and Ray got up on stage and dedicated this song to me and sang every word as I stood on the side of the stage in total awe.

PETE VERBAL ASSAULT

JOSHUA LANE STANTON

A former member of Verbal Assault from Newport, Rhode Island, Pete also played in Rain Like the Sound of Trains. He now lives in Washington State. I interviewed him on 23 January 1996.

Verbal Assault

So how did you get interested in hardcore?

I guess I got into it by way of my sister's first Clash album when I was in sixth grade. I really thought I wanted to be a punk rocker or something. My best friend, Chris Jones, and I got into punk as much as we could in the seventh and eight grades. I got a Black Flag album, and we both got really into that. By eighth grade we decided that we'd start a band even though we didn't know how to play any music.

I hadn't really seen a show by then. I guess the first show I saw was in ninth grade which would have been 1983. I saw Black Flag a few times and then started going to shows pretty regularly. I saw Minor Threat probably in the summer of 1983.

Where were you living?

We were all living in Newport, Rhode Island. Newport is a really nice little town, but it is really isolated. That is where we all grew up.

Minor Threat was, for me, the big inspiration. As a ninth grade Rhode Island kid I did not have anyone that I could identify with. Bands that were my big influences were straight edge like Minor Threat and SSD because they were a little more applicable to my life. I definitely considered myself straight edge for a few years, al-

JOSHUA LANE STANTON

Verbal Assault

though I didn't really think about it all that much.

There wasn't really anything like it that was going on in Rhode Island. Newport wasn't exactly a major stopping point for any of the touring bands, so we either had to go to Providence or Boston. We would miss a lot of shows. We did have cool parents. When we were fourteen we could just go to Boston.

How did you start getting into playing music?

I've always played music throughout my life. I played piano when I was a really little kid and trumpet through junior high school. Then I traded in my trumpet and got a guitar. I played it the first time at a Verbal Assault practice. It just kind of felt like something that I had to do. By the time Chris and I had gotten to ninth grade, Chris was a total letter writer. He would get letters from Henry Rollins or somebody, and we'd sit around and read them over and over again. It was apparent, even then, that there was this little world starting to form that was a lot cooler than anything that we had experienced up until then.

We grasped on to this thing that was starting to happen because it was really exciting, especially at that age. We had just started high school and there was different social crap that people had to deal with in high school. By tenth grade, school was a waste of half a day. We just practiced every day.

So how would you describe Verbal Assault?

Verbal Assault was sort of a miracle in terms of how it worked out and how it went on for so long and stayed interesting to everyone involved. The band was together for eight or nine years, mainly because it started when we were so young. It started when I was fourteen, and we broke up when I was twenty-three.

I guess I would describe the music as 80s American hardcore. I never felt like we were really involved thoroughly with any particular scene. We were involved and associated with the straight edge world and also had a lot of ties with the whole DC scene.

Getting back to straight edge and Verbal Assault, there was definitely a split among the band members. When the band was still very young, maybe in '85 or '86, we may have been considered a straight edge band. I honestly can't really remember if we said we were straight edge or not. By '87 or so, I remember being pretty uptight about it because Chris started drinking and Doug, our drummer, drank a lot, so we weren't a straight edge band anymore. I held on to the concept for a little while. We did a really big tour with 7 Seconds in 1986 or 1987. People in the band were just starting to drink around that time and maybe because I was just younger or closed minded or whatever, it bummed me out.

I thought we were one kind of band, and we weren't, but that didn't last too long. People can get into a small, little world and anything that changes within that world can have a great effect on you

if all you see is that little world. Throughout high school my own little world was hardcore. I remember wanting Verbal Assault to be a straight edge band and then it quickly just didn't matter. I knew that I loved the band, and I loved Chris and Doug just as much as I always did, even though they drank.

Verbal Assault went to Europe for the first time in 1988 or 1989. For the first time in the band's life there was free beer every night. That is when things exploded out of control. Almost every night there were two people in the band who were not drunk, but pretty happily had a few beers in the van. I'd usually be driving and listening to it. At first it annoyed me that I had to drive around with slightly drunk people, but after a while it just became pretty funny. I think I may have drank once that whole trip and I remember it being a pretty big deal. By the time we went to Europe for the second time I still didn't drink, but I realized that I felt that I kind of missed out a lot of times that people in the band had during the first trip. A lot of drinking goes on in Europe. It seems to be more of an accepted social thing than it does here. I realized that I would rather stay up until six in the morning drinking with a band from Norway and talking with them than go to bed early. Forever I felt that I could hang out with people who drank and not drink and it was fun, and you can. But I drink by fairly often now, and there is a different kind of bonding that goes on. What I am saying is that by 1989, I found that I would much rather be involved with experiences around me than stick to an idea or a kind of philosophy I had in the back of my mind. For me one of the best things about straight edge was learning to be a little flexible and to enjoy my life rather than holding on too strong to something that always didn't work for me.

"... by 1989, I found that I would much rather be involved with experiences around me than stick to an idea or a kind of philosophy I had in the back of my mind."

So you look back upon straight edge positively?

Definitely. I look back on my own personal experience with the whole scene and philosophy itself very positively. If you are at that age where you are the kind of person who looks around the world and doesn't exactly like what you see, then being involved with this really creative little world that was rejecting a lot of that bullshit, apathy and confusion and really trying to take charge of it, really focuses your energy and thoughts. That is the positive experience.

What have you been doing since Verbal Assault?

I was living in DC for about five years. I was in the band Rain Like the Sound of Trains, but I just wasn't very happy in DC. I just don't like that city very much. It wore my general spirit down. About a year ago I moved to Olympia, Washington and studied farming for a year. I just finished school a few weeks ago. That was at Evergreen State College. Right now I am just kind of collecting my life. I'm working on a music project with Aaron from Seaweed. Basically, we are trying to buy this pretty big farm in Eastern Washington with money that Aaron is trying to talk his label into giving him for a five-project deal. That is the biggest thing that is going on in my life right now.

For the last year I haven't been inspired musically all that much. I've been tired of the whole situation. Music has just become, in general, pretty safe and easy and not very challenging. In the past month or so, I have definitely been inspired. The whole concept we have of trying to make this album to buy this farm has put a kind of urgency into making the music.

JOSHUA LANE STANTON

So basically, you're trying to put out this album to buy the farm?

Basically, yeah.

So it is kind of like Farm Aid then?

(laughter) Yeah, I guess it is. I realize that I definitely would not be doing what I am doing now, which is studying and pursuing organic farming, if it was not for my involvement with music. Throughout the year I was studying, I would go to a lot of farms and noticed the parallels between organic farming and hardcore. It is amazing. I was constantly astounded by all the problems that organic farming goes through by dealing with everything from large corporations to having to put little stickers on every apple. And also just how farmers on a smaller scale had to do everything on their own.

It is like Indie food.

It is like Indie food! It is definitely the same thing. The whole scene that the farmers have with each other is a very similar spirit. It is really cool. Whereas music was for a lot of people the main focus, organic farming is just as much a part of their whole lifestyle. Trying to get your life going on in every way, ways that are philosophically acceptable to you, to me they are very much the same. I see myself focusing on music for the next who knows how many years. I still want to do music, but I definitely see this as the way I want to live down the line. I will probably be on some small farm just kind of living with all the daily interactions.

Do you think that you could ever be fully self sustained?
I think I probably could, but I don't think that I would be all that happy. For a lot of years, maybe I thought about things too much. But I was definitely a little angry for the last few years of my life. I was over-analyzing what's going on in the world and what people are doing to it. I feel that in just the last year I found peace with the whole situation of what's really happening and what I can realistically do. I used to work for Greenpeace and was concerned with and involved in social change for a long time. It made me just fucking miserable. I really feel that living the life I want will be the best thing that I can do for myself. I think we are getting off the track...

We are way off the track, but this is interesting. I like to talk about this kind of stuff.
In my case, I feel that is kind of a combination of my whole physical and political life together. It is—add it all up and you'll become an organic farmer maybe.

The world will be full of organic farmers.
Yeah, that is how I feel. And even if it does not happen, that is fine. I will find a way to reconcile that because it probably won't. The world probably won't become organic farmers any time soon. Five years ago I would have been an organic farmer to save the world. Now I want to be an organic farmer because I think it will be fun to grow vegetables without chemicals and watch it happen.

What do you think about straight edge today?
I honestly don't really know what is going on with the new straight edge generation. By 1988 or 1989, I didn't really listen to it anymore. What straight edge was when I first sort of associated myself with it and what it became were two totally different things. I knew a lot of the people and sort of came up with them in the musical world. I really liked them and definitely respected them, but I definitely knew that it just wasn't my thing. Why I listened to music wasn't

just because of straight edge. That whole scene developed and Verbal Assault was playing along side of it. It was never really our world. It wasn't really the music that was pulling me at the time. What generation are we in now?

I think the third or fourth.

What would be early third generation bands?

Beyond, Wide Awake...

Third generation I would not know. At the time, I probably smirked at it a little bit. Now, that is not something I am proud of. It's like when you're growing up you just start to see new generations of things going on, you might think, "Oh, well, I already saw that." If you are not directly involved in that music it can just seem like a regurgitation of what already went on in a more intense form. I know now that I can't say that because I don't know anything about it to make that call. It has not been a part of my world for a while. For the last year I've been thinking about growing garlic or something. What is going on now, I don't know.

There are a few bands that I like, and I'll go see them. Richie from Into Another is one of my dearest friends, but a lot of people in bands that I like now are people that I grew up with. I still find inspiration from them as friends and musicians.

Do you have any stories?
I have hundreds of stories. Often the stories get condensed into a general feeling. I spent a lot of time with Ray and Porcell when Youth of Today was just beginning. I can't remember how we first got in touch, but I think our first real bonding was in 1986 when 7 Seconds came out to the East Coast and my friend Boofish drove Youth Brigade up. We were on the tour that 7 Seconds was on. At the time, it was kind of a toss up between Minor Threat, Youth Brigade and 7 Seconds as to who my favorite band in the world was. It was kind if Youth Brigade at that moment—and we took Youth Brigade to the airport and by the end of the day I lost all respect. It was just so deflated after meeting them. The first night there was a show in New York with 7 Seconds, SNFU and Youth Brigade. By the end of the night I just hated Youth Brigade, and we started hanging out with the 7 Seconds van everytime we pulled over. I remember Ray and Porcell were there a lot, and I can't remember exactly how it all happened, but that is how we all started to bond. Kevin Seconds was starting Positive Force label, and he put out the first Verbal Assault record and the first Youth of Today 7", so we sort of had this camaraderie. Everything kind of all blends together.

The general Youth of Today vibe was a collective charisma and just unbridled belief in what they were doing. You could of either laughed at it or gotten behind it. For me, because of my beliefs, I could never do anything but respect it.

Matt Warnke

DAVE SINE

Matt is the former singer for Bold, one of the most popular straight edge bands in its time. I spoke with him on 20 September 1994.

Bold at Fender's, 1989

How did it happen? Well, let's see...Tim, Drew, and I went to the same elementary school. Me and Drew had similar taste in music at sort of an early age, around fifth and sixth grade. We were into the Stones, the Who, Hendrix, and things like that.

In sixth grade he got his first drum set. One of my older sisters had taken a few guitar lessons, and she had a guitar. I would bring that guitar over to his house and we would make a lot of noise. We got the idea of having a band and needed a bass player. We asked Tim. We were 12 or 13 by that time.

The summer before seventh grade, we would go over to John Zuluaga's. He was listening to a lot of hardcore and punk and our musical taste started to change and we started playing that kind of music in seventh grade. So we just got together and played, started to write some of our own songs.

What songs did you play at first?

When me and Drew first got together, we'd play "Sympathy for the Devil." I started taking guitar lessons at this time, so I would learn Beatles songs, Stones songs, Hendrix, Van Halen. I would get together with Drew and work with him, and we started to write our own songs.

Were you called "Crippled Youth" back then?
No, we were called "The Rodents," and then we were called "The Future Presidents." Our first show as "Crippled Youth" was the summer after seventh grade.

Where was your first show?
Our first show as Crippled Youth was during the summer of 1985 at the old Anthrax. We had already had a few performances. We played a show at our junior high school Latin banquet. Tim and Drew were both taking Latin, and they were in good with the teacher, so they said, "We have a band, we'll provide the musical portion of the program." It was just me, Tim and Drew. I played guitar and sang.

Who else played at that Anthrax show?
The bill was us, CIA, another band and the Descendents.

I remember seeing you play with 7 Seconds as Crippled Youth.
Where was it?

It was at the old Anthrax.
I remember that, yeah.

The best thing about that show was that you played 7 Seconds songs. You played the same songs that then they played and I thought that was great.
(Laughter) Yeah, I remember us playing that show. That was the early formation, around seventh grade.

How did you explain to your parents when you were that young that you had to go play shows in Connecticut?
That was a touchy thing. They didn't know where we were playing, the type of rough atmosphere. It wasn't the easiest thing in the world to get out of the house. Older friends would take us to the early shows. The first Anthrax show, we met Ray and Porcell and they totally adopted us as their own, took us under their wing. So after that Porcell would drive us to all the shows. One of the best things to happen to us was to meet those guys. They had excellent record collections. They treated us like we were brothers, looked out for us. We met them at the first show. We went on right before the Descendents, I think sort of as a novelty act. We used CIA's equipment. They had loud amps and let us borrow them. So right before we were going to go on, Ray and Porcell struck up a conversation with us. The rest is history. I would really not want to hear a tape of that first show.

How did you get hooked up with the Anthrax?

Me and Drew went to a show, probably in the winter of 1984. I knew about it from people in high school, my sister's grade. Porcell was one of them. They'd always be going, so I said, "Let's go to that place, the Anthrax." My sisters went once, and then took me and Drew, and we totally got into it. We thought it was the coolest thing in the world. We were only 12-year-old kids at the time.

After that it sort of took right off. After that first show, we played one of those 7 Seconds shows at the Anthrax. We played right after that at a Geek Attack party. A lot of the people from the New York scene were there. We went over pretty well. We were pretty young to be in that situation. It was fun. That was the show Tim couldn't play, so it was me, John played bass and Drew played drums.

Who wrote the songs and the lyrics?

In the beginning, me and Drew. I would write the guitar and then get together with Drew and we'd put it to a beat. We both wrote the lyrics.

We recorded the Crippled Youth EP in the winter of 1985, eighth grade. We somehow scraped up the money and went to an eight track place in Bridgeport, Connecticut. When we went to mix it, the engineer, Sam Eckhardt, was probably laughing behind our backs the whole time. We brought SSD *Get it Away* and told him that this was what we want it to sound like. He said, "In other words, you don't want to be able to hear any of the instruments." So we did the tape, hoping that someone would want to put it out as a 7".

Ray and Porcell were helping to get our name out, to get a following. In the spring of 1986, Youth of Today went on tour. They brought the tape with them and played it for a bunch of people, which helped get our name out West. In the meantime, we played shows. The tape got passed around quite a bit, so by the time we played our first show at CB's in June of 1986, quite a few people had heard it.

Our first show at CB's was us, Rest in Pieces, WarZone and Youth of Today. We were all under sixteen. We were worried about playing, but my biggest fear was that they wouldn't let us play if they found out we were all under 16.

Were you still called "Crippled Youth" at that point?

Yeah, definitely. We were called "Crippled Youth" until the fall of 1986. We decided to change that name just because there were so many band's names with the word "youth" in it. We started to pick out names, and we came up with "Bold" one day coming back from Manhattan on the Metro North (commuter railroad). It was me, Tim, Drew and Porcell. It might have even been Porcell, I don't remember. When the 7" came out, probably around that time, winter of 1987, but it came out as *Crippled Youth*. When the second pressing of the 7" came out, we had a stamp on the back cover that said "Bold."

The only time I ever talked to Ian (MacKaye) was at the Anthrax with Mark Ryan. We went to see Marginal Man. This was after the Anthrax moved to Norwalk, Connecticut. Mark introduced me to him and said that I was in "Bold." Ian knew that we used to be called "Crippled Youth," and he said that he liked the old name better.

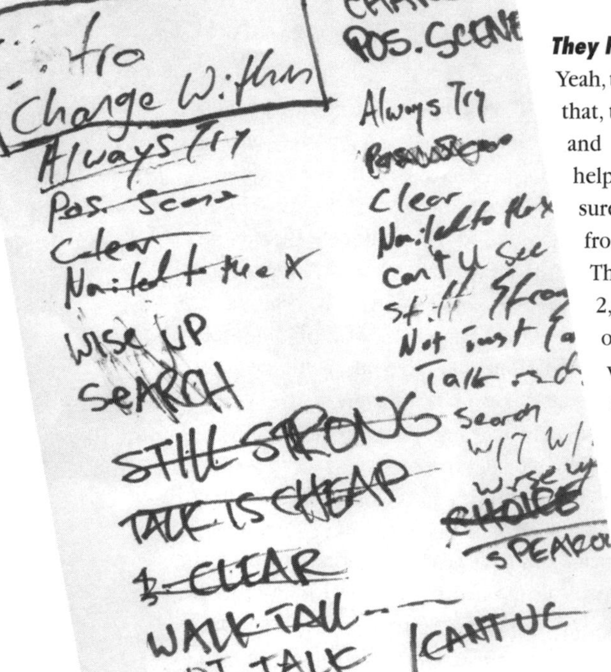

Bold set list

Yeah, right (Laughter).

The 7" came out on New Beginning Records, which Ray called "Fetus Records."

They had a great logo.

Yeah, they had that logo. After that, they put out Underdog and Negazione. The 7" helped a lot, as far as exposure. I got a ton of mail from all over the world. The first pressing was 2,000 copies and the second pressing—the one with the stamp—had messed-up covers originally, so there's two different covers for that. The first cover is black and white with two hockey players. On the second pressing there's a line from under the name *Crippled Youth* to the *r* in *Crippled* to the *t* in *Youth*. On the back cover, is a picture of me and Tim from Lupo's in Rhode Island, which was our first out of state show in the spring of '86, shortly after we recorded. The show was us, 76% Uncertain, Murphy's Law, Dagnasty, Scream and maybe Verbal Assault. It was an all star crowd. Jon Anastas and Dave Smalley from DYS were there.

How did you get into straight edge?
From those Youth of Today characters.

Were you basically straight edge before you met them?
No. We were pretty young, so it wasn't like we were not straight edge, but we drank a little bit, stuff like that.

Then you just said, "No!"
Then we curtailed that altogether. Straight edge became something to believe in, to form an identity around. After a while, probably around the time that we changed the name to Bold, us and Youth of Today had a bad reputation for being militant straight edge, being very closed minded. In those days, my natural feelings were that I didn't feel right judging anybody after a while. I thought it was pretty stupid to get up on a high horse and say that I'm better. People in my family and also some of my friends drank and smoked cigarettes and other things.

What did they think of the band?
I remember getting a lot of shit. I went on a family vacation right after we recorded. I remember really trying to defend my position that it was better to be clean of all toxins. They were giving me a hard time about it, saying that being straight edge doesn't give you the right to convince someone who isn't. I don't remember the exact argument that they used on me back then, but they were basically refuting every reason I had for being straight edge. They said it was unhealthy to be so extreme about anything.

School was where there were also a few incidents, not so much with me. People had never heard of it, and we had to explain it. Drew told me that one time that he went to a party around the corner from his house, and there were kids drinking. They must have known that he was straight edge, because they said, "Come on, man, have a beer!" They tried to hold him down and force the beer down his throat. He wasn't having it! Our peers were having high school keg parties while we were off playing shows.

We kept writing new stuff, and then we recorded the album where Youth of Today did *Break Down the Walls*, a place called Electric Reels. It's about an hour-and-fifteen-minutes north of Katonah, and we'd go up there for marathon 12-15 hour sessions. It was a really nice studio, but the other stuff that they had done there were

Bio for Looking Back

BOLDS "LOOKING BACK" REPRESENTS
THE FINAL MATURATION OF A BAND
FORMED IN 1985 BY FOUR 13-YEAR
OLDS. ALONG WITH YOUTH OF TODAY, GORILLA
BISCUITS, SIDE BY SIDE AND WARZONE
HELPED TO DEFINE THE SOUND
OF NEW YORK CITY HARDCORE CIRCA
1986-88. THE BAND RELEASED A 7"
ENTITLED "JOIN THE FIGHT" (RELEASED
AS CRIPPLED YOUTH) IN 1986.
WHICH CAUGHT THE ATTENTION OF THE
HARDCORE COMMUNITY FOR ITS
STAUNCH STRAIGHT EDGE MESSAGE. THE 1989
RELEASE OF THE 11 SONG "SPEAK OUT"
HELPED TO SHED THE BANDS' MILITANT
STRAIGHT EDGE LABEL
WITH A PROGRESSION TOWARDS
LESS EXTREME VIEWS.
"LOOKING BACK", THE BAND'S FINAL
RELEASE, WAS RECORDED FIVE MONTHS
BEFORE THE BREAK-UP OF THE BAND
IN AUGUST 1989. THE ADDITION OF

TOM CAPONE ON GUITAR, THE BAND
WAS ABLE TO CREATE THE DISTINCTIVE
SOUND OF THEIR FINAL RELEASE.

folk records, and they had done a few rap records there. It wasn't like going to Don Fury's or Inner Ear, so that was something of a handicap.

The record took a long time, and the recording didn't end up being as good as the time and money invested in it. When we finally finished it, Wishing Well wanted to put it out. They had heard a tape through correspondence beforehand and they said they wanted to do it. We finished the recording in March of 1987 and sent it and the art work to Wishing Well.

Months and months and months passed. I would talk to Longrie, and he would give me the song and dance, but nothing was moving on the album. Ray told me that Jordan was starting Revelation and that we would be much better off putting it out on that, but we had already committed to Wishing Well. They had done Blast! I wanted to be on Wishing Well because I wanted to be associated with those bands. Ray told me that in the long run, I wouldn't regret it, so I discussed it with Drew. On the last day of the 11th grade, we decided to switch to Revelation.

I had to call up Longrie and break it to him that they were taking too long and since Jordan was in New Haven and Ray was around here, we could have a more hands-on approach with the production of the record. He wasn't exactly thrilled, but he mailed all the stuff back to me, and we gave it to Jordan.

From the time we recorded the album until it came out was a year-and-a-half, and all the songs were old. If the record had come out a year earlier it would have been better. We had moved on and become much better musically. I thought the production was bad. If we could have rerecorded, it would have been better.

Was the song from the* Together *7" from the same recording?

No, we did a different version. We recorded the 7" version at Music Box. Bold and Supertouch got time together and recorded at the same place.

During the summer between 11th and 12th grade, me, Tim and Drew got plane tickets to San Francisco and met the guys from Unit Pride. Porcell and Alex Brown were out there already. We played a bunch of shows with Alex on guitar in a two-or-three-week period. I wish I could remember how many shows we played. People out there knew all the Crippled Youth stuff. The Bold record wasn't out by then.

The first week we were up in northern California with those guys from Unit Pride. They were nice kids. We played basketball and hung out with all their friends. When we went down to southern California and met up with Porcell and we hung out with the Sloth Crew. They were a lot of fun, big troublemakers, but in a good way. We'd go out with a fire extinguisher in the back of one of their vans and drive around and spray people.

The record came out right around the end of December. It was the winter of our senior year, and we were starting to think about the future. We played as many shows as we could, all up and down, DC, Boston, Rhode Island, Philly, trying to support the record, but in the back of all our minds was the end of high school. We didn't know what was going to happen with the band.

How did Tom Capone join the band?

I heard the Beyond tape on the flight out to California. I remember talking to Drew and saying, "This guy's really good. I was thinking that we could use a second guitar player, and maybe this guy would go for it." At this point what we wanted to do with Bold was to get our own sound, less generic, breaking away from the typical thrash sound. I called him up and asked him. I told him that I didn't want him to quit Beyond, but if there was any way he could balance it, would he like to be in Bold, too? That's how he joined our band. We played a few shows with him, the Anthrax show after the record came out. I was really liking the direction that the band was going in. I thought our sound was maturing and that we were standing up on our own. We weren't the little kids in the scene anymore. We were trying to stand on our own two feet.

In the spring of 1989, our senior year in high school, we knew that with college approaching the following fall, a break up was imminent. So we decided to write some songs for what was to be our final recording. We ended up writing all of the songs that are on the 7" and also *Looking Back* in four or five days at my house. They came out really well, and we booked time at Baby Monster. I think Agnostic Front mixed their live record there.

Did any of you get accepted to college?

We were all getting our school plans together when we were starting to book the tour. This tour was our last hurrah. John was going to USC in the fall of '89, Tim ended up going to Colby in Maine, Drew went to Hunter, and I went to Fordham.

The last tour was just me, Drew, Tim, Tom, Porcell and Howie, from Alone in a Crowd, was our roadie. Unfortunately, John Zulu couldn't make the tour, but he was able to play with us at the Anthrax, which was the best show of the tour, I'm sure due in no small part to his presence.

We left from Katonah on June 27 and drove straight to Florida, 26 hours straight. We played West Palm Beach, Miami, and then drove back north to play City Gardens, Boston, the Anthrax, Pittsburgh and Memphis. Then we drove to L.A. and spent a month out there. A lot of our shows got canceled, about half the tour for whatever reason, but we played out in L.A., San Diego, Frisco. The last

show with Drew and Tim was at Fenders. It was with Judge, Supertouch, Youth of Today—their last show ever—Insted, and Chain of Strength. It was a really emotional day, you know, it was pretty weird.

After that Fenders show, those guys flew home. They left right from the show and went to the airport and so I was really, really down thinking that the rest of the tour was going to suck. Howie was going to play bass. Judge played the rest of the tour with us. We drove to Gilman Street the next day, and that was one of the best shows of the whole tour, surprisingly. Sammy played drums—Sammy, Howie, Tom and me.

That's not Bold.

It was weird because the one thing that I always liked about our band was that we weren't one of those bands that had revolving members. We didn't have that, but then on the last tour, I looked around, and it was none of the original people. But anyway, we played Gilman Street, Salt Lake City, Chicago, Cleveland, and Buffalo was our last show ever. The last song we ever played was "Wise Up." Tom did a stage dive with his guitar into the crowd, and I jumped on top of him, and that was the end. We drove back to Westchester, and two weeks later I went to college.

So you saw the* Bold *EP for the first time out there?

It hadn't come out yet, that was just the advance. The record itself came out around October of '89, posthumous. To this day, that's the record of ours that I like, that I'll listen to and play for other people.

I think it's a shame that it came out after we broke up. Even *Speak Out* came out less than a year before we broke up. We had the 7", but circumstances, we maybe could have gotten a little bit better.

How do you feel about* Looking Back *coming out not too long ago?

Glad. I'm really glad it came out. Me and Drew got together the summer after our sophomore year of college, 1991, to remix that. The 7" was good, but "You're the Friend I Don't Need" wasn't in the mix at all at the time. We didn't get the chance to mix it when we put it out, the rough mix was good enough at the time. When we went back and remixed all that stuff it came out, "Always Try" and "Looking Back" were never released. They were recorded during the same sessions, we hadn't had the chance to mix them. I'm glad that it's all out, it's all mixed. If you get that record, *Speak Out* and the *Crippled Youth* 7", it's a good representation of the evolution of the band. Plus, there's a lot of good pictures in *Looking Back*.

When you look back at Bold, how do you feel about it today?

I think it was good in its time period. It sort of all came together and happened. When Youth of Today first started coming up in New York, straight edge wasn't the most popular thing. It was looked down upon. There wasn't any sort of straight edge scene until Youth of Today came along, and then it really blew up from there.

There were obviously straight edge bands before Youth of Today. They were in DC, Boston and California. Youth of Today and Bold were sort of the New York contingent. But that's neither here nor there, because the great thing about the New York scene is the diversity of the music. Everyone was very supportive of Youth of Today because their music was hard. It was New York hardcore at the same time as being straight edge—rough and hard—so it was accepted and liked. It was definitely unique to its time and place. It was weird how big it really became.

Going on tour sort of showed me, it was sort of a phenomenon. It still is, from what I understand. I wonder if it has the same energy and fervor that we had back then, or if it's trying to ape what we had, try to almost reenact what we did. Side by Side, Gorilla Biscuits, Youth of Today, Bold—the beauty of it was that we were all friends, so the scene was good. We would totally get along and mix with people who weren't straight edge. Plus, we were all roughly the same age. The bottom line was that it was a lot of fun. I'll never forget it, the greatest times. Nothing like getting up there, the rush you get getting up there, kids going buck wild.

Yeah, you were mobbed. What did that feel like when you looked out and there were tons of kids in sweatshirts jumping on top of each other?

It was really unbelievable. The more people would mosh and stage dive, I've always noticed that the more we'd get into it, the more the crowd would get into it, but vice versa also. We were lucky enough to usually play in front of a pretty good crowd and that was good, but if people wouldn't be killing each other and going off, I'd be like, "Shit, maybe we don't sound good." There's a relationship between the band and the audience.

During some of those shows, we were getting kicked in the face by stage divers and getting landed on by people. I was lucky because I didn't have an instrument to get untuned by people. At the Anthrax and CB's, people would always be getting up on stage to sing along. In remembering after the show talking about it, Tim and John would say, "Yeah, you know, I kept getting untuned" or, "My cord would get unplugged." But that's hardcore for you. The beauty of it and charm of it is that you're not separated from the crowd by a huge stage and tons of security. The kids that are in the crowd get up and play next. There are no rock stars.

Didn't you all get wireless guitars for Christmas one year?

(laughter) Those guys did, Tim and John did.

That just changed Bold forever. They could jump higher.

That was the greatest thing, jump out into the crowd.

You're not straight edge anymore.

Right.

Do you ever get hassled for your straight edge past?

At Fordham I was sort of anonymous. I kept a low profile. I never really told anybody about the band until my roommate saw a Bold poster hanging up in Second Coming Records. Sophomore year, I met my friends that I still keep in touch with. When we first started hanging out, I never told them about the band. Then, this kid who lived across the hall had the poster from the 7" up on the wall. They were totally dying of laughter when they found out I was in a hardcore band. They said, "You're really quiet, but then I hear you screaming, and it doesn't fit."

I feel like our having existed has definitely influenced some people in bands. I don't look at being straight edge as being just a phase. I think for the most part, it's a good way to be, definitely. Where you run into problems is when you start thinking that you're better than anyone else. It's just a personal choice. It's good, but it's not something that you can force people to do. It was good for me. It was good for the band. If we hadn't been straight edge, I don't think we would have had our shit together as much as we did.

It was unique for its time and place. A bunch of things all came together, a bunch of people all met at the right time. Jordan was definitely a big contributor by getting all that music out. He may not have always agreed with the lyrics or the ideology, but he was instrumental.

How do you feel when you look around to those people who were a part of it then, what they're doing today?

I'm happy for everybody who's still into music, making a name for themselves, being successful, being happier, getting shows and putting out records, especially now that with the current music scene.

Do you think that people are bound to constantly grow out straight edge, or do you think that anybody can actually say "true till death" and mean it?

I think people can say "true till death" and mean it, but I think the reason would probably change. In a way, it was a way of being unique, especially in the hardcore scene, a way of standing apart and distinguishing oneself. I think the people who are able to stay with that, their motives change. As an adult, I doubt if they still have that attitude of rebelling. I don't know anybody who's still straight edge, but I'm sure they're out there.

Do you ever talk to Drew anymore?

We hung out last May in Katonah. I was sitting right by the train station, and I saw someone who I knew must have been Drew walking off the train. I caught up to him, and we went up by the elementary school by his house and had a little chat about the past four or five years. I told him that I was psyched about his success with Into Another.

STERLING WILSON

JOSHUA LANE STANTON

Sterling is a former member of No For An Answer, Inside Out and Reason to Believe. He currently lives in Southern California. I interviewed him on 10 May 1995.

No For An Anwer

I was in eighth grade. This guy who was my best friend in grade school invited me over to his house, and he was getting into punk. The record that he turned me on to was Youth Brigade's *Sound & Fury*. He sat me down and gave me the lyrics and said, "You gotta read the lyrics. Every time you see stuff about punk on TV, they always say how bad it is, but look what they're saying, it's cool." So it just kind of caught on from there.

I don't know how it was on the East Coast, but out here there was kind of a big rebirth of punk. We were kind of caught up in that.

A couple of months later, we went to our first show. It was Social Distortion.

Sometime in late spring, May or so, my sister took my friend David and I up to Hollywood to this store called "Poseurs" that had all kinds of punk stuff. We found Minor Threat *Out of Step* and he said, "Oh Sterling, I've been looking for this."

I said, "OK, buy it and I'll tape it from you." At the time, I was taping everything. When he gave me the tape, I just remember the bass on it, the way he played with a pick, and I just remember hearing that. Not knowing where Minor Threat were from, I thought, "Wow this is the *real* stuff, this is rad." Anyone on the street could listen to the Sex Pistols or The Clash, but Minor Threat, just the sound. I pictured guys with short hair and dress shirts untucked running around in the pit or something, and I just remember being captivated by it, and their lyrics were really cool. In 1983, it was all about American punk. And then summer rolls around.

Then I went to a different high school, Mater Dei High School, which was a private Catholic school. There were a lot of punk guys there. We had to wear uniforms, but we wore them as punk as could be. The year I came was the year before Pat Dubar. Dan O'Mahony was a junior when I was a freshman.

Mater Dei, from '83-'86, was the straight edge school. Where

Costa Mesa High or Huntington High had punk, Mater Dei had straight edge. If you went there, that's what you got into. So I just kind of subconsciously got into straight edge there. That's what my idols, or the guys I looked up to, were into.

There were guys putting out zines, always skater guys who just loved American punk. English punk was cool, but American punk was better; Black Flag, The Misfits, Government Issue. Then the Blast! record came out, so that was all going on. I started putting X's on my hand. The straight edge that I was into at the time was totally Dischord stuff. When I thought about bands out here in L.A. on the West Coast—bands like Black Flag, Social Distortion, Youth Brigade—they were punk bands. When I thought about bands out East, I thought about straight edge and DC. I did get into some New York bands. I got into Kraut.

Now that I think about it, I never made a decision like, "Now I'm going to be straight edge." I was at a high school where the majority of the guys who were punk were straight edge guys. What was I, 13, 14? I had never drank. I had never smoked. I didn't even know what masturbating was. So when I heard Minor Threat saying, "I don't drink, I don't smoke, I don't fuck." I thought, "Yeah, OK cool, I'll do it."

This gets into another thing. For me, when I was in high school, I had a lot of anger. I was always a real friendly guy, but I think everyone in high school has a lot of anger. You know, you're young, you're going through puberty, you're pissed off. The way I got my anger out was through straight edge. During my freshmen and sophomore years, I was into straight edge. I hated guys who partied, who smoked and who talked about getting laid. I hated that. I wasn't into that.

"My whole motive was, 'I'm in this for the ride, I'm having fun'"

My junior year I switched to Costa Mesa High School. In public school, I was the only guy who even knew about straight edge. I kind of went through a change the Summer before that. I really started getting into SST, Black Flag.

Tom Trocolis's Dog?

No. I got into SWA, Chuck Dukowski's band. Chuck Dukowski was my big, big hero. I also started playing bass my sophomore year, and I got into Blast! I was totally into straight edge, but there was so much more out there. You know, Chuck Dukowski is a great bass player.

At about that time, I remember Youth of Today came out. Up until Youth of Today, it was always American punk, and there were a few bands like 7 Seconds and Youth Brigade that straight edge guys listened to, but they weren't necessarily straight edge. Youth of Today was the first group that I came across that came out and just said, "Hey, we're straight edge!" I remember their first show, and they were doing "Me You, Youth Crew" and they were jumping around, and they were so into it. They were a New York straight edge band. I was into it.

I joined the band Reason to Believe. I was really into that band Second Wind. At the time, Reason to Believe sounded like Second Wind. I started playing with them. After a couple of months—they were up in Torrance, and I was down here in Costa Mesa—things just weren't happening. We only played one show, but we did have a 7" coming out.

No For An Answer had been playing. I had known Gavin (Ogelsby), and I was like, "Oh you guys are straight edge, I'm straight edge, too, but you guys are claiming that whole straight edge thing, that's not that cool." But, I also knew that Dan and Gavin were—to use a lame phrase—"old school." Gavin saw The Germs, they knew what was up. Their 7" had been out for a while, and, I remember after their first show telling Dan that I didn't like them. I said, "Dan, you know, I don't see what the big hype is—you guys are all right, but what's the big deal?" It turns out, John Mastrapaolo quit No For An Answer to play in Uniform Choice, and Dan needed a new bass player. He called me up and played me some stuff from the 12". I remember thinking that it wasn't really my style, but they were playing shows, I could go on tour to New York, and that's where I wanted to hang out. When I was in Reason to Believe, I was really serious. I had been in a million bands before that, but it was my first notable band. After No For An Answer, every band that I played in except Inside Out, I was just along for the ride. I was just going to have a good time, going to New York, playing shows. I was just along for the ride. I was into it, too, but I was having a great time. So I told Dan I'd do it.

In '88 and '89, I was hanging out with Hollywood bands, Orange County bands, but none of the bands really did anything for me, the way bands like Ill Repute and Stalag 13 did, except for Hard Stance. They were cool.

All of that started coming out, like being hard, listening to the Cro Mags. I like the Cro Mags record as much as the next guy, but come on, there I was, a white, pudgy, going-through-puberty Orange County kid. I didn't know what it was to be "hard." Hard Stance, they could pull off that hard thing because they were all kind of jocks. Take a look at the Hard Stance 7". They were all good looking, muscular guys. No For An Answer were just kind of fleshy, white, pudgy kids. So there was another boat I missed, that whole being hard thing. What was that?

I didn't drink until I was 22. I'm 24 now. One day, this guy left the AC/DC tape *Back in Black* in my car. I remember taking it in my room late at night and thinking, "Look, I listened to *Damaged* 20 times, I've listened to *My War*, now I'm going to check out this

SATURDAY, JULY 23RD 1988 6:30

WALK PROUD - REASON TO BELIEVE
FREEWILL - SCREAM SO FREE

V.F.W. HALL (714) 887-0511
1541 W. 24th ST.
SAN BERNADINO
$5.00

AC/DC tape." I remember listening to it once and thinking, "Oh this is metal, this is so silly, this is corny, but god I think I'm going to listen to it again." I tell you, Beth, it's all been down hill from there.

So AC/DC came into my life. You know those straight edge bands are good, but they just don't drive me the way AC/DC does. So I got a guitar for the sole reason to learn AC/DC songs on guitar. If I never did anything with music, I could just learn every AC/DC song and play guitar in my room. I would come home from school at three. From three to five, Sterling was in his room listening to AC/DC. I had magazines out with pictures of Angus, reading up on him, doing all this stuff.

You were doing a lot of studying.

Yeah, yeah, going through a lot of changes. I started wearing pants cut off at the knees, which was kind of punk—but it also kind of

looked like Angus—shorts and sneakers. I totally perfected the Angus dance, duck walk around. I bought "Let There Be Rock" so I could watch it and check out Angus' moves. In the hallway at school, I had people calling me "Angus." I bought a hat with an "S" on it. Angus had an "A", I had and "S" for Sterling. This stage went on for a long time. Ever see any No For An Answer footage from when I was in the band? I would do Angus moves. You know how Dan has a "Poison Free" tattooed on his arm? I would write "AC/DC Let There Be Rock" right where he had that on his arm.

Are you also the guy who wrote "Frozen Pea" on your arm?

Yeah, that was in San Francisco. In No For An Answer, Dan was always serious because he wanted to do something, move people, or make money, pick up girls or I don't know what. My whole motive was, "I'm in this for the ride, I'm having fun," and on stage I was screwing around.

I remember one time we were up in San Francisco, up at Gilman, and I came up to Dan—I was always coming up to Dan with new ideas—and I said, "Dan you know what we should do? We should dress you up like King Henry XIII, in a big robe and everything, and we could stick the microphone in a turkey leg," and you could sing into that. Picture Dan yelling, "NOOOOOO!" into a turkey leg. It would be totally funny.

Do you know what Dan said? "Oh no, I would never do that, I'm a vegetarian."

Dan and Gavin wanted to get us all dressed in black. There were shows where Chris, Dan and Gavin would be wearing black, and I would be wearing shorts and sneakers, banging my head like Angus.

Why did they want to do that?

Because Dan wanted an image, a powerful image. Dan's always been into uniforms, kind of fascism style. But it's kind of cool. I can see where Dan's coming from. It was kind of plugged into the straight edge scene, a bunch of guys, all with short hair, all looking the same, into some kind of knowledge. I was kind of looking at it and thinking, "I'm not into that." But still, I was married to the same values.

I graduated high school and started up at Orange Coast College. One day Zack (de la Rocha) comes up to me and says, "Let's start a band!" He used to come over my house all of the time, and we'd go for walks, hang out. The whole thing was that he wanted to start a band that was like Minor Threat—American punk straight edge. It wasn't going to be any of this Youth of Today, Side By Side "Jocks on Stage" stuff.

I always played bass with my fingers. I never used a pick, and I was thinking back to the days when I was in my room in eighth grade hearing that Minor Threat, listening to that bass sound. I said, "You know what Zack? In this band, I'm going to use a pick." The first practice I tried it, I couldn't pull it off, and I just went back to using my fingers, but Zack and I started up Inside Out.

Inside Out was the first band since Reason to Believe that I took seriously, that I wasn't just along for the ride. The whole thing with Inside Out was that we were going to do everything ourselves. Zack came up with all the music. We went through a couple of lineup changes. Finally it all came together. We got Vic, he moved out here. I remember Chris Bratton watching us and saying, "He's serious."

Zack was getting into spirituality, and that was another thing, the whole Hare Krishna thing. I was raised Catholic. I had this really solid Catholic upbringing. My sister is a nun. So spiritually, when somebody came up to me with some new idea, I said, "I don't need that." Whenever I have spiritual problems, I just fall back on Catholicism, that's where I feel the most comfortable. I went to a Krishna temple twice, and I felt really uncomfortable, just because I grew up here in the West. That was another thing with straight edge. When people started talking about Hare Krishna, I said, "Nope, don't fit in that boat." Inside Out got swept into the Hare Krishna movement. The second I quit the band, they were on Revelation.

Then I started up at Cal State Long Beach, and I started to really get into school. My major was history, I started really getting into it. I remember talking to my history professor and he would always ask me, "Sterling, why don't you drink?"

I would say, "Well you know, partying, I don't want to be like that." His whole thing was taking me and opening me up to a world. The way I look at it, up to that point, there I was, a kid from Orange County, who had been to Arizona, New York, Connecticut, but was just in this shell.

The University opened me up to a whole new world. I took a step away from punk rock hardcore straight edge Sterling Wilson. It is a bit sad, the way things change when one grows up. I mean, everything was so 100 percent forever when I was 15, 16, 17. The Faith said it best with their second record, *Subject to Change*.

...about the author

Beth Lahickey is a veteran of the East Coast hardcore scene. Upon graduating from Sarah Lawrence College, she worked at Revelation Records. Previously she has published poetry in literary journals. This is her first book. Beth currently resides in Seattle, Washington.

DIONA MAVIS